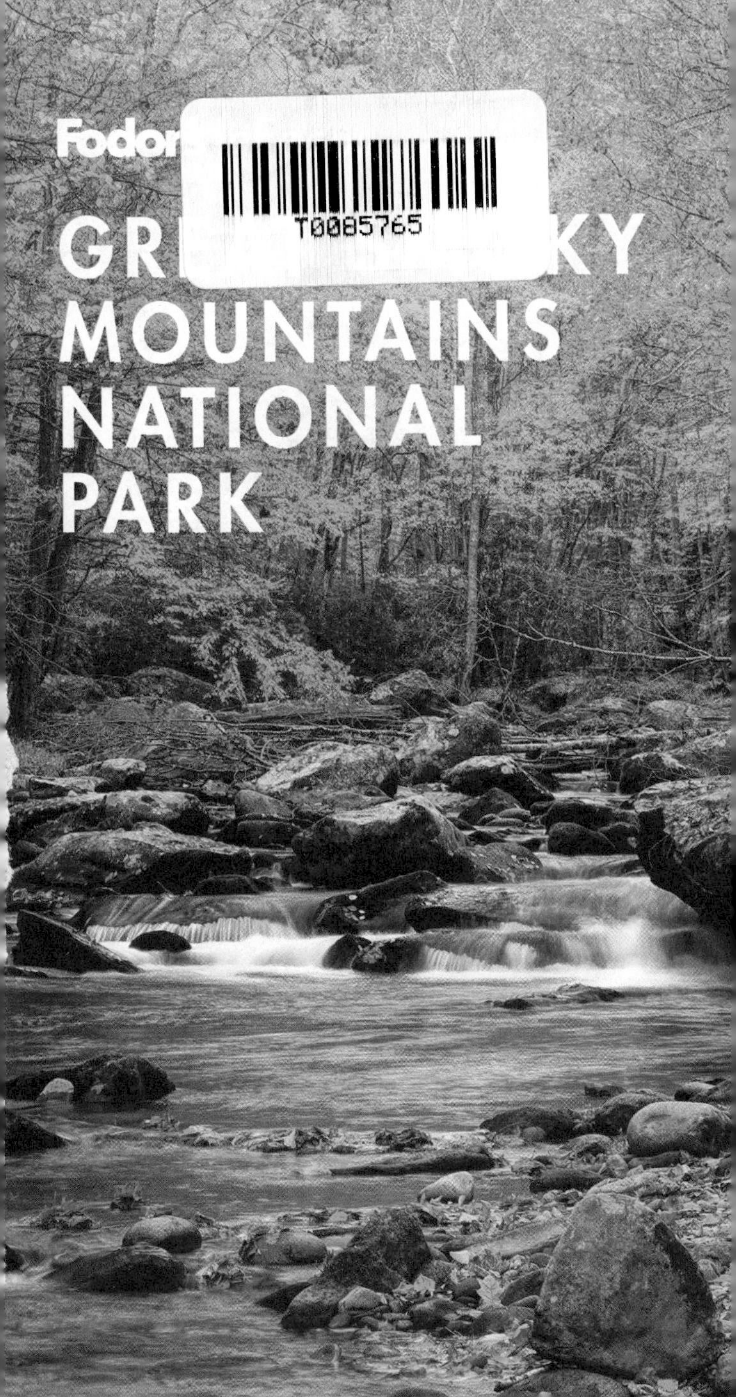
Fodor
T0085765
GR
KY
MOUNTAINS
NATIONAL
PARK

Welcome to the Great Smokies

The most-visited national park in the country offers extensive hiking, camping, rafting, wildlife, Native American culture, and regional history, all easily accessible through Tennessee and North Carolina. As you plan your upcoming travels, please confirm that places are still open and let us know when we need to make updates by writing to us at editors@fodors.com.

TOP REASONS TO GO

★ **Top of the World:** Clingmans Dome is most famous, but the Great Smokies have many impressive peaks.

★ **Backcountry Adventures:** It's not hard to get away from the crowds when you explore the park's less-traveled trails.

★ **Hitting the Road:** Without leaving your car you'll see amazing scenery from Cades Cove Loop and Newfound Gap Road.

★ **Urban Adventures:** Head to Asheville or Knoxville for some of the region's intriguing eateries and adorable B&Bs.

★ **Family Fun:** Tennessee gateways like Gatlinburg and Pigeon Forge are filled with kid-friendly attractions.

Contents

MAPS

Chapter 1

EXPERIENCE GREAT SMOKY MOUNTAINS NATIONAL PARK

12 ULTIMATE EXPERIENCES

Great Smoky Mountains National Park offers terrific experiences that should be on every traveler's list. Here are Fodor's top picks for a memorable trip.

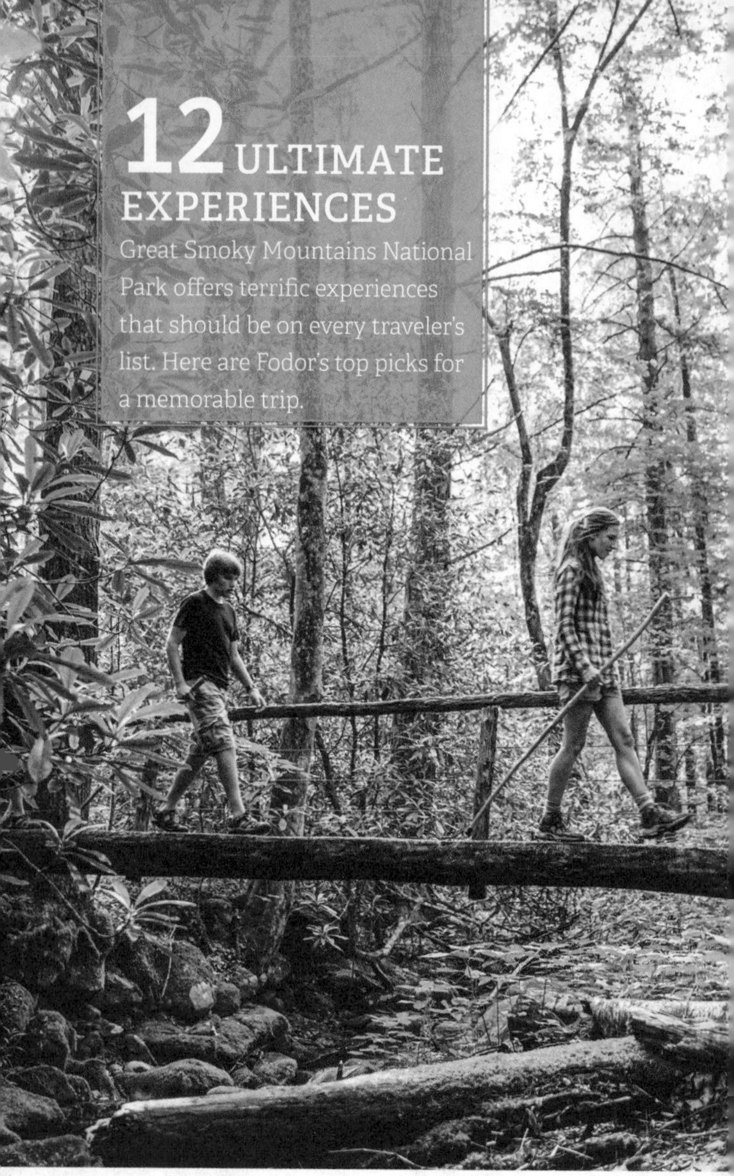

1 Hitting the Trail

More than 800 miles of hiking and biking trails run through the national park, including 72 miles of the famed Appalachian Trail. *(Ch. 3, 4)*

2 Exploring the Backcountry

Requiring a hike of several miles and a robust sense of adventure, backcountry camping is the best way to get off the beaten path. *(Ch. 3, 4)*

3 Dollywood's Thrills

Dolly Parton's amusement park in the touristy town of Pigeon Forge—with live music, carnival games, and roller coasters—is a country-style Disneyland. *(Ch. 5)*

4 Bears Are Just the Beginning

Home to more than 400 species of mammals, birds, reptiles, and amphibians, the park offers nearly limitless opportunities for wildlife viewing. *(Ch. 3, 4)*

5 Driving the Blue Ridge Parkway

This winding route through the protected forests of the Appalachian Highlands is known for its breathtaking vistas and endless outdoor adventures. *(Ch. 6)*

6 Uncovering History

The abandoned cabins and churches of Cades Cove and Cataloochee are a glimpse of what life in this region was like more than a century ago. *(Ch. 3, 4)*

7 Climbing Clingmans Dome

The spaceship-like observation tower at the crest of Clingmans Dome offers panoramic views of the park from the highest point in Tennessee. *(Ch. 3)*

8 Riding the Rapids

Several rivers in the region offer guided rafting trips over challenging Class III and IV rapids, an adventurous way to experience the breathtaking scenery. *(Ch. 6)*

9 Cherokee Nation

North Carolina's fascinating Museum of the Cherokee Indian and Oconaluftee Indian Village tell the story of the region's first inhabitants. *(Ch. 6)*

10 Biking Cades Cove

The 11-mile Cades Cove Loop is an easy scenic ride where sharp-eyed cyclists can spot wild turkeys, deer, or even the occasional bear. (Ch. 3)

11 Gatlinburg Kitsch

A main gateway to the Smokies, the Tennessee town of Gatlinburg entertains the whole family with a lively downtown full of cheesy oddball attractions. (Ch. 5)

12 Fishing the Waterways

With more than 2,100 miles of trout-stocked rivers, streams, and creeks, the Great Smoky Mountains are a superb destination for anglers. (Ch. 3, 4, 6)

WHAT'S WHERE

1 Great Smoky Mountains, TN. If you're looking for a family-friendly vacation, the Tennessee side is your best bet. Just inside the main entrances at Gatlinburg and Townsend are easy-to-reach attractions like Cades Cove, where you might catch a glimpse of black bears and other wildlife. Nearby towns are brimming with amusement parks, go-kart tracks, and mini-golf courses.

2 Great Smoky Mountains, NC. A little quieter than the Tennessee side, the North Carolina side is home to Fontana Lake and historical sites like Cataloochee, a ghostly reminder of the past. Its main gateway is at the bustling town of Cherokee, where numerous attractions tell the story of the Cherokee Nation.

3 The Tennessee Gateways. If the packed-to-the-brim tourist towns of Gatlinburg, Pigeon Forge, and Sevierville aren't for you, consider using slower-paced Townsend or the college town of Knoxville as your base for exploring the region.

4 The North Carolina Gateways. About 40 miles east of the Cataloochee park entrance, the artsy city of Asheville makes a good base for exploring. Along the Blue Ridge Parkway are a string of picturesque mountain towns.

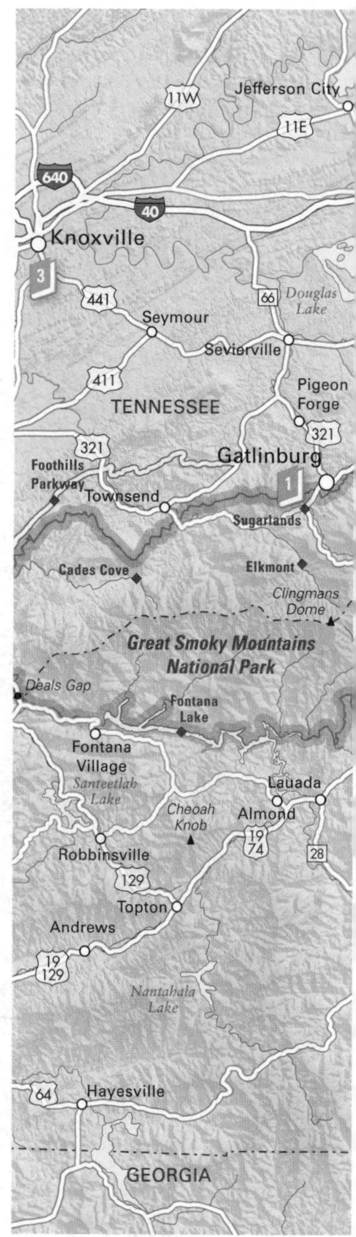

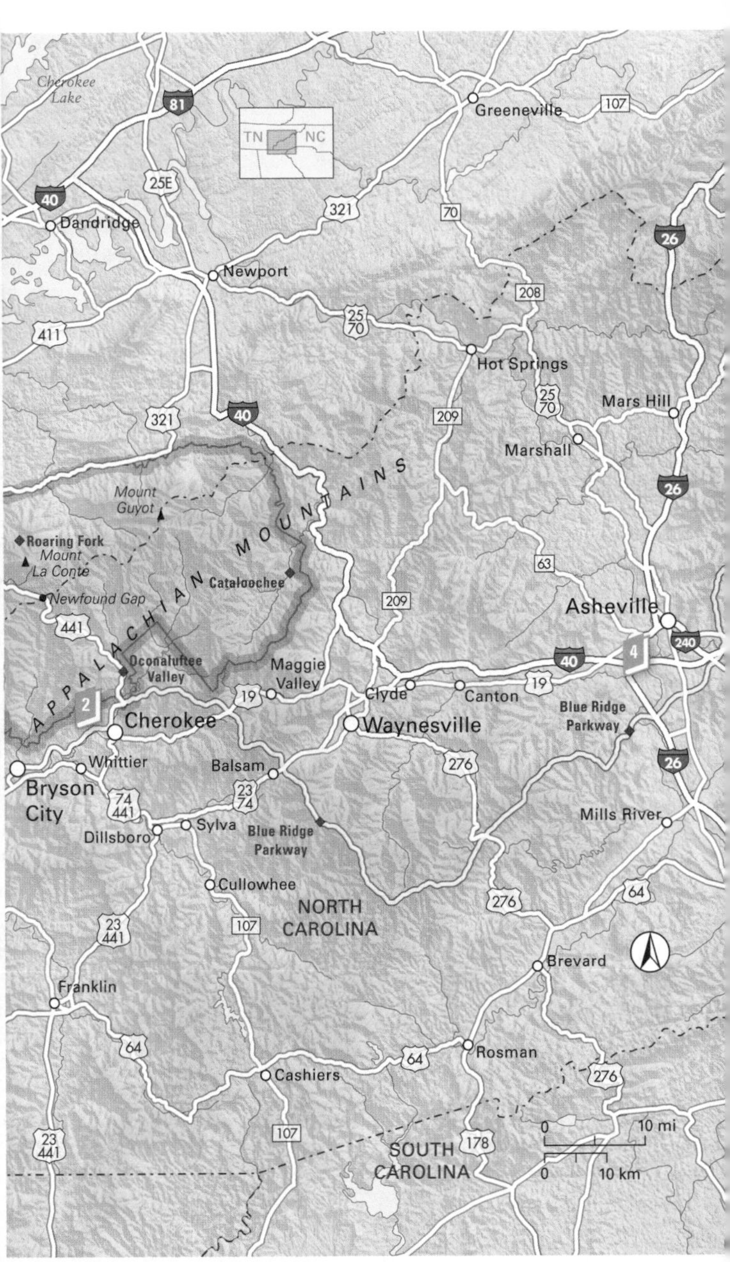

Cherokee Lake
TN
NC
Greeneville
Dandridge
Newport
Hot Springs
Mars Hill
Marshall
Mount Guyot
Roaring Fork
Mount La Conte
Newfound Gap
Cataloochee
APPALACHIAN MOUNTAINS
Oconaluftee Valley
Maggie Valley
Clyde
Canton
Asheville
Blue Ridge Parkway
Cherokee
Waynesville
Whittier
Bryson City
Balsam
Dillsboro
Sylva
Blue Ridge Parkway
Cullowhee
NORTH CAROLINA
Mills River
Brevard
Franklin
Rosman
Cashiers
SOUTH CAROLINA
0
10 mi
0
10 km

Animals of the Smoky Mountains

NORTH AMERICAN BLACK BEAR
Black bears usually range in length from 5 to 6 feet, standing about 3 to 4 feet at the shoulder, and weigh 250 to 500 pounds when fully mature.

BOBCAT
About twice the size of a domestic cat, bobcats have grayish-brown coats, black tufted ears, and a short black-tipped tail. They primarily prey on rabbits and are occasionally spotted in the park at dawn or twilight.

SOUTHERN GRAY-CHEEKED SALAMANDER
Great Smoky Mountains National Park is known to biologists as the "salamander capital of the world." You'll find this species in creeks, streams, and other damp areas all around the park.

GREAT HORNED OWL
The largest owl in North America, the great horned owl's disk-shape face acts like a radar dish, catching faint sounds of prey in a wide range of frequencies. This nocturnal predator can see well in dim light and can swivel its head 270 degrees.

NORTHERN COPPERHEAD
One of only two venomous snake species in the park, the copperhead is pale-to-pinkish tan in color, overlaid with a series of tan or light brown cross-bands. It's unlikely you'll come across one in the park.

TIMBER RATTLESNAKE
This venomous snake varies in color but has unmistakable W-shape lateral markings across its back. The rattles at the end of its tail are used as a warning for predators, though some snakes lose their rattles.

ELK
The male elk's bugling mating call is one of the most distinctive sounds of autumn. The best place to see these majestic animals is in the open fields of the Cataloochee Valley in the southeastern part of the park.

RED SQUIRREL
Red squirrels may only be about half the size of their more common gray cousins, but hikers will be delighted by the outsize personality of these deep-forest denizens, chattering and barking from nearby fir trees.

WILD TURKEYS
Wild turkeys are plentiful in the park, especially in the Cades Cove area on the Tennessee side and the Cataloochee Valley on the North Carolina side. They travel in flocks of up to 60 and roost in the trees at night.

SYNCHRONOUS FIREFLY
For a few short weeks every summer, these fireflies put on an amazing light show. During their illuminated mating dance, entire hillsides seem to blink in rhythm, as if they are covered with Christmas tree lights.

Plants of the Smoky Mountains

CATAWBA RHODODENDRON
With its waxy green leaves and brilliant purple flowers, this is one of the showiest flowering shrubs in the park. It thrives on mountain slopes at elevations above 3,500 feet and blooms in June and early July.

FRASER FIR
Named for 18th-century Scottish botanist John Fraser, this fragrant evergreen makes an ideal Christmas tree. In the Smokies, it is found only at the highest elevations, typically above 4,000 feet.

GINSENG
"Sang," as it's locally known, is valued in traditional Chinese medicine as an aphrodisiac, a stimulant, and a treatment for diabetes. This slow-growing perennial is native to well-drained hardwood forests.

TULIP POPLAR
The tulip poplar, also known as the yellow poplar, is one of the tallest trees in the Smokies, reaching heights of almost 200 feet. The largest are in the virgin stands of the Joyce Kilmer Memorial Forest, just outside the park.

EASTERN HEMLOCK
Also known as the Canadian hemlock, this towering tree frequently reaches as tall as a 10-story building. It can live for hundreds of years, with the oldest known specimen estimated to be more than 550 years old.

TRILLIUM
Species of Great Smokies Trillium are easy for even an amateur to identify, since everything about the plant comes in threes—they have three bracts (similar to leaves), flowers with three petals, and three-lobed fruit.

FLAME AZALEA
When in bloom, this shrub's bright orange flowers make it unmistakable. This native azalea prefers shadier locations and lower elevations in the national park. It is also common along the Blue Ridge Parkway.

MOUNTAIN LAUREL
This evergreen shrub, which can grow up to 40 feet tall, is common on mountain slopes in the Smokies. It has waxy, star-shape pink or white flowers that make an appearance in May and June.

ROSEBAY RHODODENDRON
The most common rhododendron in the Smokies, the rosebay variety is usually found in wet areas along creeks or streams. Its clumps of white flowers usually bloom in early June through August.

CHESTNUT
In the mid-20th century, an invasive fungus devastated the tree that once dominated the Smokies. Sprouts from wild American Chestnut roots still spring up now, but they typically don't make it past 10 or 20 feet tall.

The Best Hikes in Smoky Mountains

ELKMONT NATURE TRAIL
Grab a brochure from the visitor center, or just follow the markers along the way as you explore this easy and accessible trail that's fun for the whole family.

ALUM CAVE TRAIL
On a path lined with blooming rhododendron in the summer, this moderate-to-difficult 4.6-mile round trip takes you to Alum Cave. If you're feeling energetic you can continue to the summit of Mt. LeConte.

THE APPALACHIAN TRAIL
It's a claim to fame to say you've hiked the Appalachian Trail (even a small part of it). At the moderately difficult 3.4-mile section located near Newfound Gap, you'll pass some of the park's most impressive landmarks.

CHIMNEY TOPS TRAIL
This steep trail will take a lot out of you, but the sweeping views of Mt. LeConte from the observation point make it worth the uphill climb. There and back you'll cover a distance of about four miles.

CLINGMANS DOME
This dome-shape mountain is the highest point in Tennessee. It's an easy but steep half-mile walk up the spiraling ramp to the observation tower, where you can see for more than 100 miles on a clear day.

ANDREWS BALD
A fairly difficult 2.8-mile round-trip hike on the Forney Ridge Trail takes you to Andrews Bald, one of just two balds maintained in the park. The tree-free space at the top has great views of Fontana Lake.

GREGORY BALD
This is a busy trail for how remote it is, but the uphill climb is rewarded with some of the best views in the park. The 11.6-mile out-and-back journey requires you to be in good physical shape.

LAKESHORE TRAIL
For an adventurous but fairly easy day of hiking, take the ferry across Fontana Lake to the Lakeshore Trail at Hazel Creek. Along

The Appalachian Trail at Newfound Gap

the way, you'll spy the remnants of the abandoned town of Proctor.

LAUREL FALLS TRAIL

While it's by no means off the beaten track (it gets quite busy during high season), this 2.3-mile round trip is an easy hike to the falls. There's slightly less traffic if you continue on the Cove Mountain Trail.

LITTLE CATALOOCHEE TRAIL

Take a moderately difficult 6-mile hike along the Pretty Hollow Gap Trail to the Little Cataloochee Trail, which takes you to an abandoned village whose houses and churches can still be spotted among the trees. In the spring it's known for its beautiful wildflowers.

Welcome to Great Smokies

With more visitors than Yosemite or Yellowstone, Great Smoky Mountains is the most popular national park in the entire country. From its roadside overlooks, hilltop trails, and lakeside campgrounds, you can see the mountains marching toward the vast horizon. The park has more than 800 miles of trails ranging from easy half-hour nature walks to weeklong backpacking treks. While backcountry hiking has its wonders, some of the most interesting sights in the park are viewable from the comfort of your car.

GEOLOGIC WONDERS, BIOLOGICAL RICHNESS

Geologists say the formation of the Smokies began about a billion years ago. Here you'll find some of the tallest peaks in the eastern half of North America, but they used to be much higher—at least as high as those in the Rockies. Tens of millions of years of ice, wind, rain, and erosion have worn down the mountains; scientists estimate that peaks in the Smokies lose two inches every 1,000 years.

The highest peak in the park, Clingmans Dome, was reputedly the original inspiration for the folk song "On Top of Old Smoky." It rises 6,643 feet above sea level and 4,503 feet above the valley floor. These are also some of the oldest mountains in the world, far older than those in the Rockies, the Alps, or the Andes.

Due to a fortuitous combination of moderate climate and diverse geography, Great Smoky Mountains National Park is one of the most biologically rich spots on earth. Bears are the most famous animal in the park, but reintroduced elk are also making this region their home for the first time in 150 years. The Smokies have been called the "salamander capital of the world," with at least 30 different species. This is also one of the few places on earth where, for a few evenings in June, you can see synchronous fireflies flashing in perfect unison.

THE MOST VISITED PARK IN THE COUNTRY

In his classic 1913 book, *Our Southern Highlanders,* Horace Kephart wrote about his experience living in the area that he later helped to establish as a national park: "For a long time my chief interest was not in human neighbors, but in the mountains themselves—in that mysterious beckoning hinterland which rose right back of my chimney and spread outward ... mile after mile, hour upon hour of lusty climbing—an Eden still unpeopled and unspoiled."

The most popular park in the country has been receiving a steadily increasing number of visitors each year. In 2021, it had a record-breaking 14.1 million visitors—more than twice as many as the second-most visited national park, the Grand Canyon. Despite the occasional country-road traffic jam or crowded trail, there are more than 814 square miles of protected land here, and it's still easy to immerse yourself in Kephart's "unpeopled and unspoiled" wilderness.

WILDERNESS RECLAIMED

Many visitors don't realize that the Smokies were not always wilderness. Before the park's creation in 1940, thousands of people lived in communities nestled into every valley and waterway. These families were given a difficult choice: sell their land and buildings to the government or stay put and lose the ability to live off the land, harvest firewood, pasture cattle on mountaintops, and in some cases, bury their dead in family cemeteries. Within a decade, most people left and the majority of their homes were burned or torn down by the Park Service. The few that remain have been restored to offer a window into life before the park. Likewise, the forest has made a remarkable comeback in the century since these mountains' old-growth trees were last logged.

UNTOLD STORIES OF THE SMOKIES

African Americans are an integral, but often overlooked, part of Great Smoky Mountains' history: as inventors of the banjo (an instrument iconic to Appalachia), railway builders, foresters, Union soldiers, and so much more. While slavery was not as widely practiced here as in other parts of the South, some landowners did own slaves: an 1860 census report lists 650 enslaved people in North Carolina's Jackson and Haywood counties.

The Great Smoky African American Experience hopes to highlight the stories of African Americans in the park and region. Historians, academics, and park employees are partnering with locals to learn about their African American ancestors, with the goal of sharing these stories with park visitors—and the wider world—through a variety of future ventures. Another collaborative project works with archaeologists and aims to identify African American gravesites within the park—starting at the Kerr African American Cemetery in the Cataloochee section.

The Smoky Mountains with Kids

With so much to do in and around the area, Great Smoky Mountains National Park is an ideal destination for families. Aside from the obvious outdoor fun, families can hop on horses, ride the rapids, or even take nature-based classes together.

FUN AND GAMES

For a day of amusement parks, go-kart tracks, or miniature golf courses, head to the towns of Gatlinburg, Sevierville, and Pigeon Forge on the Tennessee side. Yes, they are incredibly touristy, but kids do love them. Among the most popular attractions are the inimitable Dollywood in Pigeon Forge, with 150 acres of carnival games, sideshow thrills, and roller coasters. Ober Mountain, an amusement park near Gatlinburg, is also a perennial draw. There are an ever-growing array of Ripley's Believe-It-or-Not operations in Gatlinburg and carnival rides at The Island in Pigeon Forge to round out your vacation.

HAYRIDES

Guided hayrides in a trailer pulled by a heavy-duty truck (some led by a park ranger) leave from the Cades Cove Riding Stables every evening in the summer and fall. The cost for a two-hour trip is $20 per person.

HIKING

Many of the trails through the national park are challenging, even for those in top physical condition with years of experience in the backcountry, but some of the best were designed with kids in mind. One good choice is the easy Elkmont Nature Trail, a mostly level path that has a series of markers about the area's plant and animal life. There's a good chance you'll spot deer, elk, and other forest creatures.

HISTORY LESSONS

Although you may have some familiarity with how the Cherokee were forced to leave this area during the Trail of Tears, the epic outdoor drama *Unto These Hills* brings this tragedy to life. The musical extravaganza has been running for decades and shows no signs of slowing down. The Museum of the Cherokee Indian and the Oconaluftee Indian Village also tell the story of the area's original inhabitants through interactive exhibits and hands-on demonstrations. Kids can learn how the Cherokee used specific plants for medicinal and artistic purposes.

HORSEBACK RIDING

About 550 miles of the national park's trails are open to horses, making this a perfect place for family-friendly rides. You can rent a horse along with the proper riding gear for around $45 an hour from commercial stables in the area, including the Cades Cove Riding Stables. These facilities are open mid-March through late November. If you want to bring your own horse, five horse camps are open April to early November.

JUNIOR RANGER PROGRAMS

During summer months, the park presents a busy schedule of classes, programs, and nature walks led by park rangers. Kids ages 5 to 12 can fulfill the requirements to become a Junior Ranger, complete with a cool merit badge and a swearing-in ceremony with an actual ranger. Pick up an activities booklet at one of the national park visitor centers, or download instructions before your trip if your kids can't wait to get started.

SMOKY MOUNTAIN FIELD SCHOOL

The Smoky Mountain Field School is a partnership between the Great Smoky Mountains National Park and the University of Tennessee at Knoxville. The school offers workshops, classes, and other activities. Take a full-day class on orienteering (using a map and compass to find your way) or a half-day class, ideal for kids, called "Totally Buggy", where you catch spiders and insects.

What to Watch and Read

BEAR IN THE BACK SEAT: ADVENTURES OF A WILDLIFE RANGER IN THE GREAT SMOKY MOUNTAINS NATIONAL PARK BY CAROLYN JOURDAN AND KIM DELOZIER

Fun and informative, this book offers a firsthand glimpse into the life of a park ranger through a series of entertaining encounters and unexpected adventures with tourists, skunks, and black bears. These behind-the-scenes tales are entertaining and sometimes somber, leaving readers with a great respect for the park's wildlife (especially the bears).

CATALOOCHEE: A NOVEL BY WAYNE CALDWELL

Asheville writer Wayne Caldwell penned this multigenerational saga about a family in the Cataloochee Valley and a way of life that is at times in harmony, and at times at odds, with the mountain terrain and spirit. The novel begins after the Civil War and stretches into the 1940s, when the government annexed Cataloochee to create the Great Smoky Mountain National Park. A second novel, *Requiem by Fire*, continues the story of these families as they depart Cataloochee.

THE CHEROKEE NATION: A HISTORY BY ROBERT J. CONLEY

Cherokee writer Conley's comprehensive history of the Cherokee people includes the Eastern band of Cherokees, who now live on the Qualla Boundary at the southeast entrance of the national park.

COLD MOUNTAIN BY CHARLES FRAZIER

Frazier's debut novel is an *Odyssey*-like love story about a Confederate deserter trying to get home to his wife. Running a farm alone near Cold Mountain, North Carolina (in the Pisgah National Forest, to the east of the park), she learns some tough lessons about rural life. If you can get past the very mediocre Southern accents, the movie starring Renée Zellweger is well worth seeing.

STRANGERS IN HIGH PLACES: THE STORY OF THE GREAT SMOKY MOUNTAINS BY MICHAEL FROME

Before you visit the Smokies, Michael Frome's well-written nonfiction account will instill in you a proper sense of wonder and awe for the beautiful region. Frome, a well-known environmentalist and conservationist, offers a comprehensive understanding of the park's past and present.

Chapter 2

TRAVEL SMART

Updated by
Stratton Lawrence

★ **CAPITAL:**
Raleigh (NC);
Nashville (TN)

POPULATION:
10,488,084 (NC);
6,829,174 (TN)

LANGUAGE:
English

$ CURRENCY:
U.S. Dollar

AREA CODES:
828 (NC); 865 (TN)

EMERGENCIES:
911

DRIVING:
On the right

ELECTRICITY:
110 volts

TIME:
Eastern Standard
Time (NC);
Central Time (TN)

WEBSITES:
www.nps.gov/grsm

AIRPORTS:
AVL, TYS

KENTUCKY
VIRGINIA
TENNESSEE
Knoxville
Gatlinburg
NORTH
CAROLINA
Asheville
Cherokee
*Great
Smoky Mountains
National Park*
GEORGIA
SOUTH
CAROLINA

Know Before You Go

Covering more than 800 square miles of forest-covered hills, wide valleys filled with wildflowers, and mile-high mountains, Great Smoky Mountains National Park is best approached with a free spirit and a sense of adventure. Here are a few rules and recommendations to ensure that you—and future park visitors—can enjoy all that the Smokies have to offer for many years to come.

KEEP YOUR DISTANCE

Many of the animals of the Smoky Mountains seem unfazed by humans, but don't be tempted to get close for the perfect picture. Elk, for example, can charge when they feel threatened, so stay at least 150 feet away. And never approach a bear or allow it to approach you. Interactions are rare but potentially dangerous. Maintain at least 150 feet of distance between yourself and the bear. If it comes too close to you, act aggressively to scare it away and stay away from any food that might be around. Breaking wildlife rules can come with a hefty fine, and may even lead to arrest.

LEAVE NO TRACE

It's illegal to pick any wildflower or disturb any plant or tree within the park. In general, adopt a "leave no trace" policy within the park. When exiting an area of the park, take anything you brought with you and nothing more. Likewise, follow signs for closures and other regulations within the park; these are often for your safety and for the preservation of the wild and beautiful terrain.

ELEVATION IS NO JOKE

Clingmans Dome, the highest point in the park, is more than 6,600 feet. It's just one of many high-altitude hikes you can enjoy in the Smokies. Keep elevation in mind when planning a hike. A trek listed as being just two miles round-trip might seem like a breeze, but if you're starting at a high altitude, traversing steep inclines—gaining hundreds of feet in elevation along the way—can take a lot of exertion. In general, it's best to give yourself an hour per mile when hiking at an incline in the park.

NO LIFEGUARD ON DUTY

Water-related injuries—even drowning—are much more common dangers in the Great Smokies than, say, a bear attack. When you're swimming in the park, keep in mind that more remote areas could be hours away from medical help. Don't dive into water in the park, and be mindful of swollen rivers and canals after big rainstorms—sudden flooding can be very dangerous.

IT'S UP TO THE ELEMENTS

Hazardous conditions (fallen trees, rockslides, and flooded rivers) can temporarily close roads and areas of the park at any time—though rangers try their best to keep delays short. Each visitor center will have the most recent information about closures. The Twitter account Smokies Road Info (@SmokiesRoadsNPS) shares real-time road closure info.

IT'S MOSTLY A STATE OF MIND

Aside from a few markers, you are unlikely to notice whether you're in North Carolina or Tennessee while you're in the Smoky Mountains. In fact, while exploring the region, a scenic drive or challenging hike might cross the official border several times without you knowing it. Within the park, fishing permits are valid from either state, no matter which one you are in at the time.

YOU'RE ON CHEROKEE LAND

The Qualla Boundary, at the southeastern entrance to the park, belongs to the Eastern Band of Cherokees and is part of their ancestral home. When you're in the Cherokee area, and the Smokies in general, respect the fact that this is sacred land. Take the time to learn about its fascinating history from places like the Museum of the Cherokee Indian, and consider buying your souvenirs at shops like the Qualla Arts and Crafts Mutual. Some things are also a little different on Cherokee land: you'll see that signs posted in the Qualla Boundary include translations in the Cherokee language, and you'll need a special permit to fish here.

BRING YOUR OWN SUPPLIES

Aside from firewood (which you must purchase inside the park or from approved sources to avoid invasive species of insects), you should plan to buy any supplies you'll need for a day hike or overnight trip (food and water, bug spray, sunscreen) before you arrive at the park. There's a camp store at Cades Cove where you can find snacks and supplies in a pinch.

LOOK BEYOND THE BIG ATTRACTIONS

From your first glimpse of the Smokies, you'll be overwhelmed by the natural beauty of this area. Allow time for surprises; small wonders like unmarked vistas, sudden streams, backroad drives, roadside stands, and adorable small towns make the Smokies even more magical.

WATCH YOUR STEP

Rocky footpaths are made easier by using trekking poles, which also help you keep your balance if you stumble. Copperheads and rattlesnakes are not uncommon during summer—and they're masters of camouflage—so keep your eyes peeled, especially near water and fallen limbs. The most common peril isn't dangerous at all—because many of the park's trails are open to horses, keep your eye out for "landmines" that will leave a nasty mess on your shoes.

Getting Here and Around

Although there are small regional airports for private planes in towns near the national park, including the Gatlinburg–Pigeon Forge Airport (GKT) in Sevierville, most visitors who arrive by air fly into one of the major airports and make the last leg of the trip by car. The closest airport on the North Carolina side is Asheville Regional Airport (AVL), about 60 miles east of the Cherokee entrance. On the Tennessee side, the closest major airport is McGhee Tyson Airport (TYS), about 45 miles west of the Sugarlands entrance in Knoxville.

There's no public bus transportation to Great Smoky Mountains National Park. Greyhound provides bus service to Asheville on the North Carolina side and to Knoxville on the Tennessee side. Schedules change frequently, so check ahead for the latest information.

Driving in the Tennessee gateway town of Gatlinburg and the surrounding area usually means bumper-to-bumper traffic, especially in the summer. When you can, leave your car in a parking lot and take advantage of the handicap-accessible local transportation. Gatlinburg Trolley has more than 100 stops in Gatlinburg and the surrounding area. Five different color-coded routes whisk riders to destinations within the city. Additional seasonal routes run to Dollywood and several locations in Great Smoky Mountains National Park.

Also in Tennessee, the Pigeon Forge Trolley runs frequently to Dollywood, Dollywood Splash County, and other popular destinations. All-day access is $3.

On the North Carolina side, Cherokee Transit has two routes running through downtown. Shuttle buses stop at many hotels, tourist attractions, and the casino. One-way fares are $1.

Coming either from the east or west, Interstate 40 is the main interstate access route to the Great Smokies; from the north and south, Interstates 75, 81, and 26 are primary arteries. U.S. Route 441, also called Newfound Gap Road, is the main road through the park, and the only paved road that goes all the way through. It travels 31 miles between

Cherokee and Gatlinburg, crossing Newfound Gap at nearly a mile high.

The nearest sizable city to the park in North Carolina is Asheville. This hip happening city is about 50 miles east of Cherokee and the Oconaluftee Visitor Center. It takes a little more than an hour to get from Asheville to the Cherokee entrance of the park via Interstate 40 and U.S. Routes 19 and 441. If you aren't pressed for time, however, we advise traveling via the Blue Ridge Parkway—it takes longer, but the scenery is worth it.

The closest Tennessee city is Knoxville, about 40 miles west of the Sugarlands entrance via U.S. Route 441. Avoid driving through the center of Gatlinburg even in the off-season (take the bypass instead), as intense traffic means you can spend an hour crawling through this small and very touristy town.

GASOLINE

There are no gas stations or other automotive services in the park. There are numerous service stations in Bryson City, Cherokee, Gatlinburg, Pigeon Forge, Townsend, and other towns around the park.

RENTAL CARS

If you're flying into Tennessee or North Carolina, you will almost certainly need a rental car to visit the Great Smokies. National car rental companies are located at the major airports in Asheville, Knoxville, and Charlotte.

ROAD CONDITIONS

As the old saying goes, you can go down a mountain road too slowly a thousand times, but you can go down too fast only once. Driving in the mountains can pose difficulties you may not face back home: steep grades of 6%, 8%, or even 10% or more are not uncommon. While these are probably not a problem for most modern cars, heavy RVs and vehicles towing trailers run a risk of overheating when going up and burning out brakes when coming down. Even in a car, you should shift to a lower gear when going downhill to save your brakes. Blind curves and switchbacks can be scary even for experienced drivers, especially at night when your visibility may be limited and you run the risk of hitting a deer or other animal.

Nor will sticking to the interstates always necessarily mean smooth sailing. For example, Interstate 40 between Canton, North

Getting Here and Around

Carolina, and the Tennessee line is notorious for severe accidents. This section is heavily used by big tractor-trailer trucks, has some unexpected curves, doesn't have breakdown lanes in some stretches, and is often shrouded in fog. It has twice the fatality rate of any other interstate in North Carolina. This highway is also known for rockslides. One particularly bad slide in 1997 closed Interstate 40 for six months.

But most roads in the Smokies and elsewhere in the region are well maintained, and warning signs alert you to dangerous curves and steep grades. With all these factors in play, you need to allow more time for driving in the mountains. The Blue Ridge Parkway, for example, has a 45-mph speed limit, and on many curvy sections you will average much less than that. In the Smokies, the main road through the park, Newfound Gap Road, also has a 45-mph speed limit (lower in some places). Some secondary roads in the park have speed limits of only 10 or 15 mph.

Newfound Gap Road and higher elevation sections of the Blue Ridge Parkway are often closed in winter due to snow and ice. Some secondary roads—including Balsam Mountain Road, Roaring Fork Motor Nature Trail, and Parson Branch Road—are closed all winter.

ROADSIDE EMERGENCIES

In the event of a roadside emergency, call 911. Depending on the location, either the state police, local police in Cherokee or Gatlinburg, or a county sheriff's department will respond. To reach park rangers, call ☎ 865/436–9171. You can call rangers to report problem bears, animals hit by cars, injured or lost hikers, a car breakdown or accident in the park, and other emergencies.

RVS AND TRAVEL TRAILERS

RVs and travel trailers are, up to a point, welcomed in the Smokies. The National Park Service prohibits RVs, trailers, and buses on some secondary roads in the park, including Balsam Mountain Road, Greenbrier Road, Heintooga Ridge Road, Roaring Fork Motor Nature Trail, Rich Mountain Road, and the road exiting the park at Metcalf Bottoms Picnic Area. Some other roads, such as the unpaved road leading into Cataloochee Valley, permit RVs, trailers, and buses, but because these roads are narrow (one lane in places) and have many blind curves, extreme caution is advised.

About half the campsites (Abrams Creek, Balsam Mountain, Big Creek, and Cataloochee) don't allow RVs of any size. Three large campgrounds, Elkmont and Cades Cove on the Tennessee side and Smokemont on the North Carolina side, are the most RV-friendly, with easy access and a sizable percentage of RV sites. Most of the larger campgrounds have dump stations, but none have electrical, water, or sewer hookups. You'll be boondocking it here. Note that several of the campgrounds restrict the use of generators from May through October, prohibiting them in certain sections of the campground.

Many private campgrounds are located near entrances to the park. On the North Carolina side, there are numerous campgrounds in Cherokee, Bryson City, and elsewhere. On the Tennessee side, there are at least 50 campgrounds around Pigeon Forge, Gatlinburg, Sevierville, and Townsend. Nearly all commercial campgrounds have electric, sewer, and water hookups, along with restrooms, showers, and dump stations. Many have cable TV and Internet connections. Some have swimming pools.

If you don't own an RV or trailer but want to try out traveling in one, you can rent one. Typically, you'll pay around $75 to $150 a night, plus a mileage fee of around 30¢ to 35¢ a mile, which doesn't include your gas. (Many RVs get just 6 to 10 miles per gallon, so fuel can be a major expense.) Off-season and longer-term rental specials may offer some bargains. One of the largest and best-known rental outfits is Cruise America, with about 125 locations nationwide, including three in North Carolina and three in Tennessee.

Train

The Amtrak train stations closest to the Great Smokies are in Greenville and Spartanburg, South Carolina.

Essentials

Admission Fees

Admission to the park is free. Parking requires a $5 daily (or $15/week) pass, which you can purchase and print at home, or buy at national park visitor centers. Admission to all historical and natural sites within the park is free. Frontcountry campgrounds are $30/night and backcountry camping requires an $8 permit.

Dining

Dining options in the park are almost non-existent; the best idea is a picnic at one of the park's attractive picnic areas.

Outside the park you'll find many dining options, from fast food to fine dining—the latter especially in Asheville, which is known for its farm-to-table food culture. Gatlinburg and Pigeon Forge have myriad fast-food and family-dining choices.

⇨ *Dining reviews have been shortened. For full information, visit Fodors.com.*

What It Costs in U.S. Dollars

	$	$$	$$$	$$$$
AT DINNER				
	under $15	$15–$25	$26–$35	over $35

Lodging

Aside from campgrounds, the only accommodations inside the park are at the hike-in LeConte Lodge. Outside the park, you have a gargantuan selection of hotels of every shape, size, and price point. On the Tennessee side in touristy Gatlinburg, you'll see a street sign that reads "2,000 Hotel Rooms" (and that's just referring to downtown). On the North Carolina side, lodging is more low-key. You can choose from old mountain inns, bed-and-breakfasts, and motels in the small towns of Bryson City, Waynesville, and Robbinsville. A seemingly ever-expanding number of hotel towers are connected to the giant Harrah's Casino in Cherokee, the largest lodging in North Carolina. About 50 miles away, Asheville has one of the largest collections of B&Bs in the Southeast, along with hip urban hotels and classic mountain resorts.

Camping is abundant and reasonably priced. The park has nearly 1,000 camping spaces at 10 developed campgrounds. Two of them, Cades Cove and Smokemont, are open year-round. In addition, there are more than 100 backcountry campsites, shelters, and horse camps. Immediately outside the park are many commercial campgrounds and RV parks.

Permits are required for all backcountry camping. You can get a backcountry permit online at smokiespermits.nps.gov or at the backcountry office at Sugarlands Visitor Center. Sites at developed campgrounds must be reserved in advance at www.recreation.gov.

⇨ *Hotel reviews have been shortened. For full information, visit Fodors.com.*

What It Costs in U.S. Dollars

$	$$	$$$	$$$$
LODGING FOR TWO			
under $150	$150–$225	$226–$300	over $300

Health and Safety

Hiking or camping in the backcountry requires you to exercise good judgment. Don't hike alone, let a responsible person know your plans, and get a backcountry permit if staying overnight. Bring a trail map, flashlights, compass, and adequate water. Check the weather in advance; dress appropriately for the weather and wear hiking boots or shoes that offer good ankle support. Follow park guidelines for avoiding problems with bears, snakes, and insects such as yellow jackets.

Crime is generally not a problem in the park, and the towns around the edge of the park have moderate to low crime rates. However, serious crimes including rapes and murders have occurred in and around the park, so use the same common sense that you would use anywhere else.

Be especially vigilant when you leave your vehicle in more remote areas of the park, as potential thieves know that you'll be away from your vehicle for an extended period. Although trailheads are regularly patrolled by rangers, there are things you can do to protect your vehicle: look around the parking lot for signs of break-ins, avoid leaving any valuables, and don't leave blankets or towels in the vehicle that may look like you're concealing valuables.

Packing

While you don't want to overpack, you need to be prepared for a variety of weather conditions. Elevations in the Smokies vary widely, and temperatures and precipitation with them. For example, temperatures at Clingmans Dome may be 10 to 20 degrees lower than in Gatlinburg or Cherokee. It could be raining atop Mt. LeConte and be completely

Essentials

dry below. Remember to pack rain gear, especially in spring and summer. Believe it or not, the Great Smokies get more rain each year than Florida's Everglades.

It can be cool in the mountains, even in the summer, so bring a light jacket. In spring and fall bring several layers of shirts and fleeces in different weights rather than just one bulky sweater or coat. Wear fast-drying synthetics instead of cotton. In winter you'll need to be prepared for temperatures below freezing and even below zero at high elevations.

Bring sturdy footwear for hiking or walking. If you're hiking in the backcountry, you'll want boots with good ankle support. Wicking socks, in wool rather than cotton, will keep your feet warm and dry.

If you'll be tubing, rafting, or swimming, bring a backpack or large fanny pack for carrying food, water, snacks, insect repellent, sunscreen, a first aid kit, and other items you may want on hand.

For backcountry trips, bring plenty of drinking water and a purification system suitable for killing bacteria. Flashlights or headlamps are a must.

When not hiking or camping, casual outdoor wear is appropriate almost everywhere. The exceptions are a few upscale restaurants in Asheville and Knoxville, where shorts and T-shirts will look out of place at dinner.

Permits

Camping and overnight hiking in the backcountry require a permit ($8 per night). To camp in the backcountry, you must preselect an official campsite and complete a permit at a visitors center or online at smokiespermits.nps.gov. All campsites have raised wire systems to elevate packs and food from bears and rodents.

Pets

Pets are permitted in some areas of the park but are strictly prohibited in others. Pets are allowed in most campgrounds, picnic areas, and along roads, but they must be kept on a leash measuring no more than six feet at all times. Pets are not allowed on park trails except the Gatlinburg and the Oconaluftee River trails, and they are not permitted anywhere in the backcountry. Pet excrement must be immediately collected and disposed of in a trash can.

Restrooms

All visitor centers, campgrounds, and picnic areas have restrooms. Most have flush toilets and running water. There are no showers at the campgrounds or anywhere else in the park. Showers are available at most commercial campgrounds outside the park.

Visitor Information

There are three main visitor centers in the park: Oconaluftee Visitor Center near Cherokee, Sugarlands Visitor Center near Gatlinburg, and Cades Cove Visitor Center on the Cades Cove Loop. Some of the best hiking trails fan out from these facilities, making them hard to pass up despite the crowds. In addition, there is a compact visitor contact station at Clingmans Dome.

There are five information centers just outside the park (one in Bryson City on the North Carolina side and one in Sevierville, one in Townsend, and two in Gatlinburg on the Tennessee side). All the gateway towns around the park entrances have their own visitor information centers.

When to Go

High Season: The biggest crowds arrive June to August, as well as in October for fall foliage viewing. Beat the crowds by coming on weekdays and also early in the day. By mid-June, haze, heat, and high humidity have arrived. In July, highs at the lower elevations average 88°F, but at Clingmans Dome (elevation 6,643 feet) the average high is just 65°F. In September, expect warm sunny days and cool nights.

Low Season: Winter in the park can be beautiful, especially when there's snow on the ground or frost on the tree limbs. The air is usually clearer, and with leaves off the trees the visibility is excellent. Winters can bring significant snow, especially at higher elevations. Many visitor centers, roads, campgrounds, and other services close for the winter season. On the other hand, January has just a sixth of the visitors you'd encounter in July.

Value Season: Late spring is a wonderful time to visit the park, as wildflowers are in bloom and it's before the heat, humidity, and crowds of summer. Weather varies a lot; one day it may be a balmy 70°F, and the next may be bitterly cold and snowy.

Great Itineraries

The fun and lively city of Asheville is an hour from the national park but makes an excellent base before and after your time in the Smokies. If you're coming from the Tennessee side, Knoxville is a fine option. Whichever gateway city you choose, remember that traffic jams are often a problem at the most popular park entrances near Gatlinburg, Tennessee, and Cherokee, North Carolina. Unless you're planning a stop at one of the visitor centers, choose one of the less traveled entrances.

DAY 1

Arriving in Asheville, head downtown for some shopping. Stores range from bohemian-chic boutiques to specialty shops offering one-of-a-kind treasures. Have lunch in the River Arts District, where you can stroll along the French Broad River and visit artist studios and watch them work at **Asheville Cotton Mill Studios**. Take in the permanent collection at the beautifully restored Italian Renaissance–style **Asheville Art Museum**, or step back into history at the **Thomas Wolfe Memorial**. There's much to do at night in downtown Asheville, with farm-to-table restaurants, local microbreweries, and creative cocktail lounges around every corner.

DAY 2

From Asheville, take the relatively slow (but definitely worthwhile) **Blue Ridge Parkway** past unforgettable sights like majestic **Mt. Pisgah** as you make your way to the historic community of **Cherokee**. Here, learn about the Cherokee people at the **Oconaluftee Indian Village** and the **Museum of the Cherokee Indian** before checking out locally made crafts at the **Qualla Arts and Crafts Mutual**. Take an afternoon for fishing at the **Qualla Boundary** or visiting one of the charming nearby towns like **Sylva** or **Bryson City**.

DAY 3

Stop for picnic supplies before heading past the Oconaluftee entrance and into Great Smoky Mountains National Park. **Newfound Gap Road,** the park's main throughway, takes you to the **Oconaluftee Visitor Center** to get oriented and plan your next few days. Spend an hour or so exploring the nearby **Mountain Farm Museum**, then drive the half mile to **Mingus Mill** and see corn being ground in an authentic working gristmill. Continue on to **Clingmans Dome**, where you can hike the winding path to the park's highest point via the beautifully designed observation tower. Stop for a leisurely lunch at **Collins Creek Picnic Area**, then walk off all those calories on the **Kephart Prong Trail**. Spend the rest of the day exploring the park from Newfound Gap Road, which leads to other hikes. Catch the sunset at a scenic overlook.

DAY 4

Get your endorphins going today. If it's summer, consider cooling off by tubing or whitewater rafting. Or you can break a sweat by hitting the trails on foot, on a bike, or on a horse. In winter there's snowshoeing or cross-country skiing. Consider spending a night or two camping at one of the rustic campgrounds or stay overnight at **LeConte Lodge**, the only lodging inside the park. Either way, it can be a magical experience to wake up early inside the park to explore popular areas like **Cades Cove** and the century-old community of **Elkmont**.

DAY 5

Explore the Tennessee side of the park today, starting out early to beat the crowds to the 11-mile **Cades Cove Loop Road**. Although it's the most popular area of the national park, **Cades Cove** is well worth your time because of its valley views, gorgeous fauna, and well-preserved settlers' homes. Spend some time in the Cable Mill area, visiting the water-powered gristmill and other historic buildings. Keep an eye out for the plentiful wildlife, including black bears, white-tailed deer, and wild turkeys. Many trails and nature walks beckon along the way. You can hike the **Trillium Gap Trail** to Grotto Falls or explore the **Roaring Fork Nature Trail** before heading out of the park for dinner in **Gatlinburg**.

DAY 6

Take a break from nature with some old-fashioned fun at **Dollywood**, Dolly Parton's Appalachian-themed amusement park. If you don't want to commit the time and money at Dollywood (or equally family-friendly attractions like **The Island in Pigeon Forge**), take a tram up the mountain for eye-popping views. Pigeon Forge has a wide range of hotels, plenty of restaurants, one-of-a-kind country music spots, and other lively evening entertainment spots like the **Comedy Barn Theater** and **Dolly Parton's Stampede**.

DAY 7

Squeeze in one more morning activity in the national park today, perhaps taking in the carefully restored cabins at the **Elkmont Historic District** or hiking the **Alum Cave Trail**. Take your time heading back to Asheville, stopping along the way in the charming towns of **Waynesville** and **Brevard**.

On the Calendar

March

Big Ears Festival. This free-spirited music and film festival is held over two weekends in downtown Knoxville. 🌐 *bigears-festival.org*

April

Junior Ranger Day. Usually held in April, children complete a variety of activities around the national park to earn a Junior Ranger badge. 🌐 *www.nps.gov/grsm/planyourvisit*

Spring Wildflower Pilgrimage. Wildflower enthusiasts come for five days of natural history walks, seminars, photography tours, and other events in late April. 🌐 *www.wildflowerpilgrimage.org*

May

Flower & Food Festival. Dollywood's celebration of spring features topiary art crafted from the blooms of Appalachia. 🌐 *www.dollywood.com*

June

Firefly Watching. Get tickets early for the national park's yearly wonder, the synchronous firefly show. Space is limited and determined by a lottery. 🌐 *www.nps.gov/grsm/learn/nature/fireflies.htm*

July

Folkmoot Legacy Festival. Held in Waynesville, this music and culture festival showcases local and international artists. 🌐 *www.folkmoot.org*

Gatlinburg's River Raft Regatta. Hand-crafted, brightly colored floats (some the size of a dinner plate) race their way down the Little Pigeon River as part of Gatlinburg's all-day July 4 celebration. 🌐 *www.gatlinburg.com/event/gatlinburgs-river-raft-regatta/21*

August

Smoky Mountain Folk Festival. At Lake Junaluska, traditional Appalachian dancing and culture take center stage over Labor Day weekend. 🌐 *lakejunaluska.com*

September

Dumplin Valley Bluegrass Festival. This popular event featuring regional performers has been drawing crowds to the Tennessee town of Kodak for more than two decades. 🌐 *www.dumplinvalley-bluegrass.com*

North Carolina Apple Festival. In Hendersonville, local growers sow off the fruits of their labors in late August or early September. 🌐 *www.ncapplefestival.org*

October

Monarch Migration. Volunteers at Cades Cove help the Great Smoky Mountains Institute tag monarch butterflies before their annual journey south. It's held on multiple dates. 🌐 *gsmit.org*

Smoky Mountain Trout Tournament. Held each year in Gatlinburg, this fishy festival gives out prizes for the angler catching the biggest trout. 🌐 *www.rockytopoutfitter.com/cv*

Smokies Harvest Celebration. At the Mountain Farm Museum in Oconaluftee Valley, discover traditional processes of apple cider pressing, sorghum processing, broom-making, and blacksmithing. 🌐 *www.nps.gov/grsm/planyourvisit/special-events.htm*

November

Candlelight Christmas Evenings. At the Biltmore Estate in Asheville, candlelight tours, live seasonal music, dramatic decorations, and other festivities take place beginning in November. 🌐 *www.biltmore.com*

Gatlinburg Chili Cookoff. For $10 you can grab a spoon and help decide which Gatlinburg-area chef deserves the chili crown. 🌐 *www.gatlinburg.com*

December

Fantasy of Lights. On the calendar for almost 50 years, this holiday parade includes marching bands, huge balloons, and lots of twinkling lights. 🌐 *www.gatlinburg.com/event/fantasy-of-lights-christmas-parade*

Festival of Christmas Past. Celebrate an old-timey mountain holiday in the national park with storytelling, traditional music, and children's games. 🌐 *www.nps.gov/grsm/planyourvisit/special-events.htm*

Contacts

 Air

Asheville Regional Airport (AVL). ✉ *61 Terminal Dr., Fletcher* ✣ *Off I–26* 🌐 *flyavl.com.* **Charlotte Douglas International Airport.** ✉ *5501 Josh Birmingham Pkwy., Charlotte* 🌐 *www.cltairport.com.* **McGhee Tyson Airport (TYS).** ✉ *2055 Alcoa Hwy., Alcoa* ☎ *865/342–3000* 🌐 *flyknoxville.com.*

 Bus

Cherokee Transit. ✉ *Cherokee* ☎ *828/359–6300* 🌐 *www.cherokeetransit.com/downtown.html.* **Gatlinburg Trolley.** ☎ *865/436–3897* 🌐 *www.gatlinburgtrolley.org.* **Pigeon Forge Trolley.** 🌐 *www.pigeonforge.com/trolley.*

 Car

RV RENTALS Cruise America. ☎ *800/671–8042* 🌐 *www.cruiseamerica.com.*

Camping

BACKCOUNTRY PERMITS Great Smoky Mountains National Park Backcountry Information Office. ☎ *865/436–1297* 🌐 *www.nps.gov/grsm/planyourvisit/backcountry-camping.htm.*

CAMPGROUND RESERVATIONS Great Smoky Mountains National Park Campgrounds. ☎ *877/444–6777* 🌐 *www.recreation.gov.*

Emergencies

Great Smoky Mountains National Park Rangers. ☎ *865/436–9171 for non-life-threatening emergencies* 🌐 *www.nps.gov/grsm/planyourvisit/emergency.htm.*

 Train

Amtrak. ☎ *800/872–7245* 🌐 *www.amtrak.com.*

Visitor Information

Great Smoky Mountains National Park. ☎ *865/436–1200* 🌐 *www.nps.gov/grsm/planyourvisit/index.htm.* **Cades Cove Visitor Center.** ✉ *Cades Cove Loop Rd., Great Smoky Mountains National Park* ☎ *865/436–1200* 🌐 *www.nps.gov/grsm/planyourvisit/visitorcenters.htm.* **Oconaluftee Visitor Center.** ✉ *Newfound Gap Rd., MM 30.3, Great Smoky Mountains National Park* ☎ *865/436–1200.* **Sugarlands Visitor Center.** ✉ *1420 Fighting Creek Gap Rd.* ☎ *865/436–1200.*

Chapter 3

3

GREAT SMOKY MOUNTAINS, TN

Updated by Stratton Lawrence

Camping	Hotels	Activities	Scenery	Crowds
★★★★★	★★★☆☆	★★★★☆	★★★★★	★★★☆☆

WELCOME TO GREAT SMOKY MOUNTAINS, TN

TOP REASONS TO GO

★ **Hit the Trail.** Take an easy hike on the Alum Cave Trail, or challenge yourself on the path to lofty Gregory Bald.

★ **Sleep in the Park.** It's a long but rewarding hike to the park's only lodging, the rustic LeConte Lodge.

★ **Pedal Power.** Cycle miles of paved roads at Foothills Parkway or the winding Parsons Branch Road.

★ **Scenic Drives.** Roads like Roaring Fork and Rich Mountain Road pass through spectacular scenery.

★ **Learning Opportunities.** Find out all about the area's flora and fauna at the Great Smoky Mountains Institute.

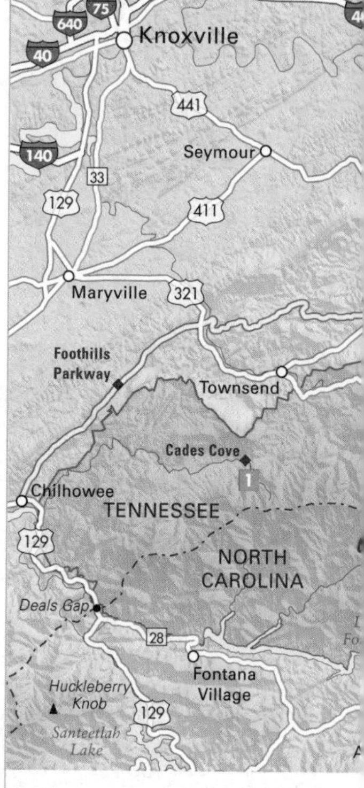

1 Cades Cove. More than two million people visit this verdant valley every year, enjoying gorgeous views while navigating the 11-mile loop road.

2 Clingmans Dome. Clingmans is the highest point in the park, in the state of Tennessee, and on the entire Appalachian Trail.

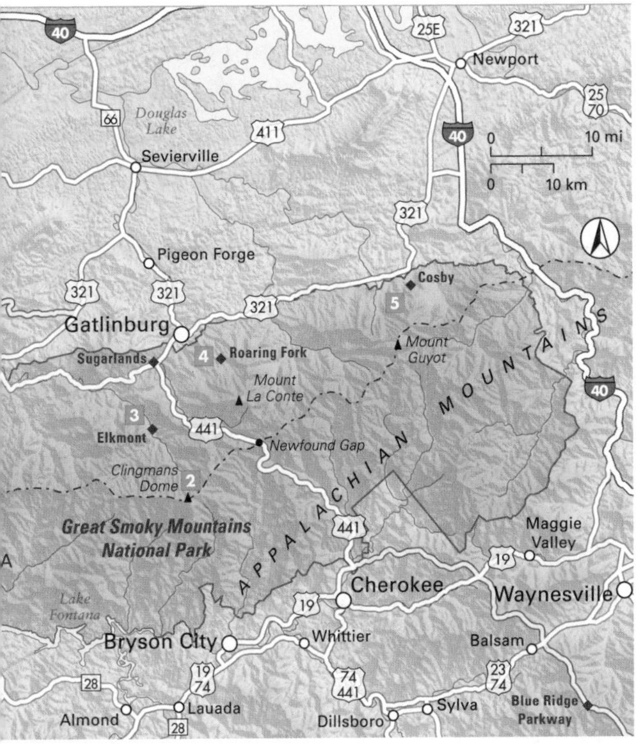

3 Elkmont. Explore the remaining cottages and clubhouse of an early-20th-century summer colony for wealthy families.

4 Roaring Fork. Walk through an authentic mountain farmstead and the surrounding hardwood forest.

5 Cosby. Away from crowds on the park's northern border, Cosby offers a solitary place to explore the backcountry.

The Tennessee side is the family-fun half of the Great Smokies. From a base on this side of the park, you can tour historical sites, treat the family to mini golf or go-karts, tire the kids out at nearby theme parks, try a different restaurant for every meal, or enjoy some grown-up time at a bar or music theater.

The nearby gateway of Gatlinburg has an almost carnival-like atmosphere, with nearly every business—souvenir stores, fudge shops, oddities museums—focused entirely on the tourist market. On some days, more than 35,000 visitors stay in its chain hotels, pack its casual eateries, and crowd the main street that's less than a mile long. Rivaling its popularity are the adjacent communities of Pigeon Forge and Sevierville. If you're here for quiet time in nature or your primary destination is Cades Cove, the nearby Townsend entrance may be more appealing.

Even inside the national park, the Tennessee side gets heavy action. Some two million people per year tour Cades Cove. On a busy fall weekend, the traffic on the Cades Cove Loop may remind you of midtown Manhattan. The Tennessee side also has the largest and busiest campgrounds and picnic areas.

If you prefer peace, quiet, and natural beauty, all is not lost. With just a little bit of effort, you can find your way to lovely and little-visited parts of the park. Greenbrier, for example, is a picnicking paradise that's often virtually deserted. The Roaring Fork Motor Trail, a five-mile winding road that passes historic buildings, old-growth forests, and waterfalls, is a delight. The Foothills Parkway, a scenic, unfinished road along the western and southern edges of the park, is an undiscovered gem. Even Cades Cove can be explored without congestion on Wednesdays, when only bicyclists and pedestrians are allowed on the loop road.

Great Itineraries

ONE DAY ON THE TENNESSEE SIDE

If you have one day and are entering the park from the Tennessee side, start early, pack a picnic lunch, and drive to the **Sugarlands Visitor Center** to get oriented. Beat the crowds to **Cades Cove Loop** and drive the 11-mile round-trip route, stopping to explore the preserved farmsteads and churches. Spend some time in the **Cable Mill** area, visiting the **Gregg-Cable House** and other historic buildings. Depending on your timing, you can picnic at one of the stops in Cades Cove or at Metcalf Bottoms. Take **Newfound Gap Road** up to **Newfound Gap**. Just over the state line is **Clingmans Dome Road**. Stretch your legs and walk to the observation tower at **Clingmans Dome**. Return down Newfound Gap Road and then proceed to **Roaring Fork Motor Nature Trail**. Stop to explore the preserved cabins and other sites along the trail. Park in the lot at the Trillium Gap trailhead and—if you have the time and are up for a moderate 2.6-mile hike—walk to **Grotto Falls**.

THREE DAYS ON THE TENNESSEE SIDE

Begin your first day touring Cades Cove. Then, drive Parson Branch Road near Cable Mill and picnic in the woods. Turn right on U.S. 129 and drive part of the "Tail of the Dragon," beloved by motorcyclists and sports car buffs for its many curves. At Chilhowee, turn right on Foothills Parkway and drive the 17.5-mile scenic parkway. Stop at Look Rock and take the short hike to the lookout tower. Have dinner in Townsend.

On Day 2, follow the one-day itinerary to Newfound Gap and Clingmans Dome. Have lunch at Chimneys Picnic Area and walk the easy 0.75-mile trail. Keep following the itinerary to Noah "Bud" Ogle Farm, Roaring Fork Motor Nature Trail, and Grotto Falls and have dinner in Gatlinburg.

On Day 3, depending on your interests, spend the day horseback riding at Cades Cove, river tubing in Townsend, biking Cades Cove Loop, fishing the Little River, or hiking Alum Cave Bluffs. Alternatively, drive to Pigeon Forge and take in Dollywood, the go-kart tracks, mini golf, and other family-friendly attractions. Have dinner in Pigeon Forge.

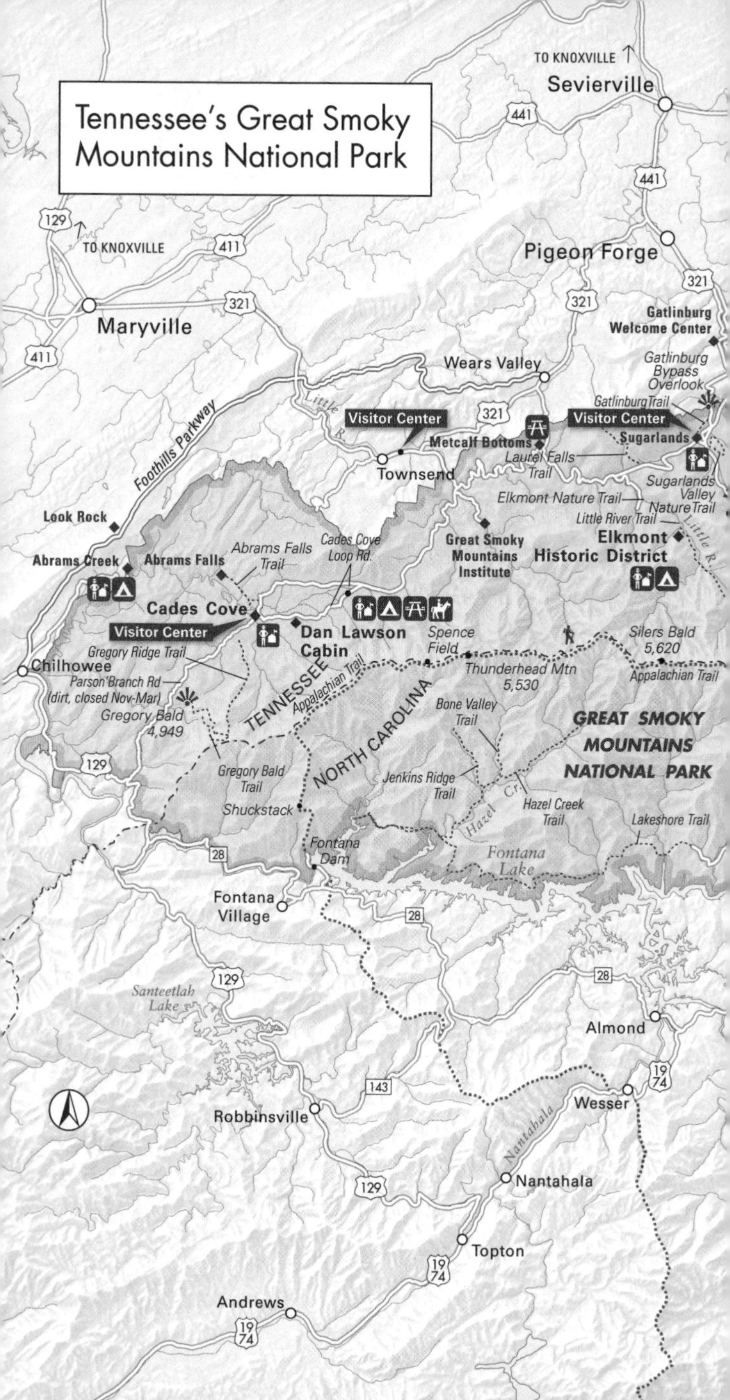

Tennessee's Great Smoky Mountains National Park
TO KNOXVILLE
Sevierville
441
129
TO KNOXVILLE
411
Pigeon Forge
321
Maryville
Gatlinburg Welcome Center
Gatlinburg Bypass Overlook
Wears Valley
Gatlinburg Trail
Foothills Parkway
Little R.
Visitor Center
Metcalf Bottoms
Sugarlands
Laurel Falls Trail
Townsend
Sugarlands Valley Nature Trail
Elkmont Nature Trail
Little River Trail
Look Rock
Great Smoky Mountains Institute
Elkmont Historic District
Abrams Falls Trail
Cades Cove Loop Rd.
Abrams Creek
Abrams Falls
Cades Cove
Dan Lawson Cabin
Spence Field
Silers Bald 5,620
Gregory Ridge Trail
Chilhowee
Parson Branch Rd (dirt, closed Nov-Mar)
Gregory Bald 4,949
TENNESSEE
Appalachian Trail
Thunderhead Mtn 5,530
NORTH CAROLINA
Bone Valley Trail
GREAT SMOKY MOUNTAINS NATIONAL PARK
Gregory Bald Trail
Jenkins Ridge Trail
Hazel Cr.
Hazel Creek Trail
Shuckstack
Lakeshore Trail
Fontana Dam
Fontana Lake
28
Fontana Village
Santeetlah Lake
Almond
19 74
Wesser
143
Robbinsville
Nantahala
Topton
Andrews

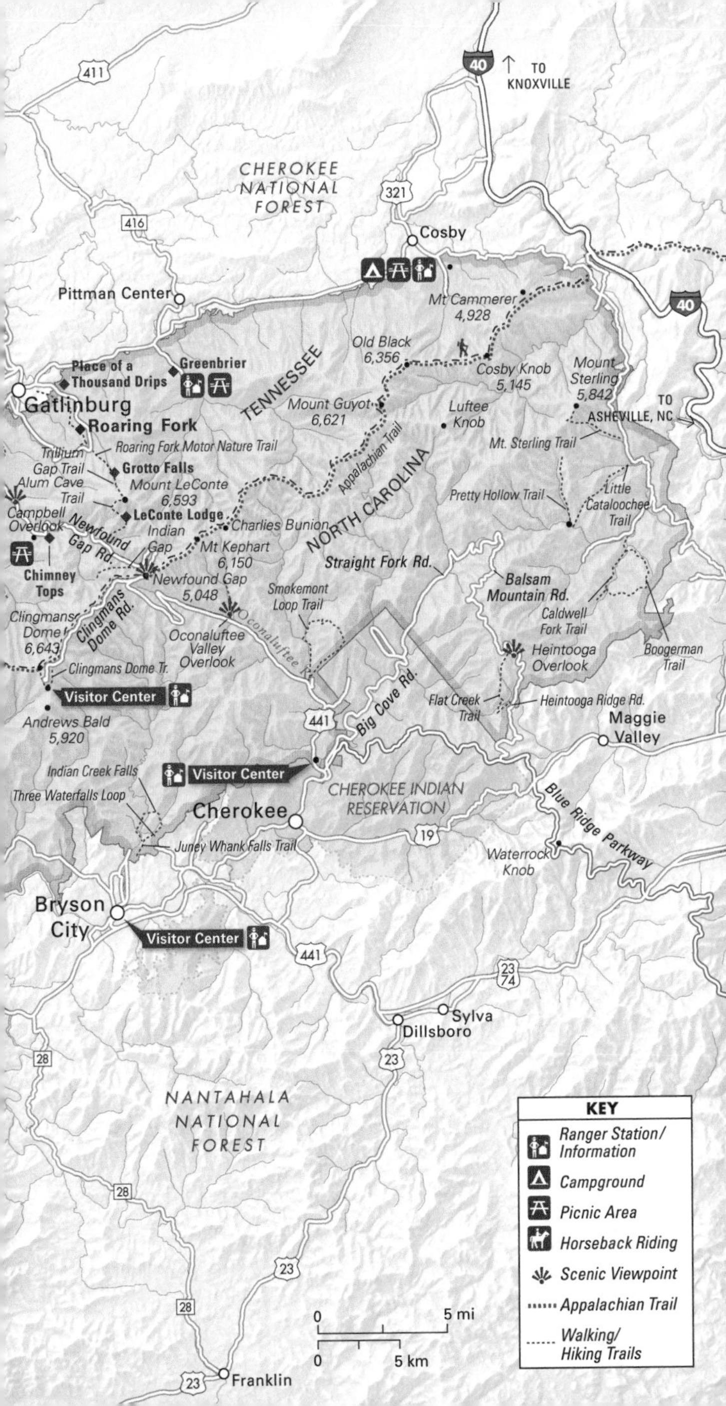

411
40
TO KNOXVILLE
CHEROKEE NATIONAL FOREST
321
416
Cosby
Pittman Center
Mt Cammerer 4,928
40
Old Black 6,356
Place of a Thousand Drips
Greenbrier
TENNESSEE
Cosby Knob 5,145
Mount Sterling 5,842
Gatlinburg
Mount Guyot 6,621
Luftee Knob
TO ASHEVILLE, NC
Roaring Fork
Roaring Fork Motor Nature Trail
Appalachian Trail
Mt. Sterling Trail
Trillium Gap Trail
Grotto Falls
Alum Cave Trail
Mount LeConte 6,593
NORTH CAROLINA
Pretty Hollow Trail
Little Cataloochee Trail
Campbell Overlook
LeConte Lodge
Charlies Bunion
Newfound Gap Rd.
Indian Gap
Mt Kephart 6,150
Chimney Tops
Newfound Gap 5,048
Straight Fork Rd.
Balsam Mountain Rd.
Smokemont Loop Trail
Caldwell Fork Trail
Clingmans Dome 6,643
Clingmans Dome Rd.
Oconaluftee Valley Overlook
Oconaluftee R.
Heintooga Overlook
Boogerman Trail
Clingmans Dome Tr.
Visitor Center
Big Cove Rd.
Flat Creek Trail
Heintooga Ridge Rd.
Andrews Bald 5,920
441
Maggie Valley
Indian Creek Falls
Visitor Center
Three Waterfalls Loop
CHEROKEE INDIAN RESERVATION
Blue Ridge Parkway
Cherokee
19
Juney Whank Falls Trail
Waterrock Knob
Bryson City
Visitor Center
441
23 74
Sylva
Dillsboro
28
23
NANTAHALA NATIONAL FOREST
KEY
Ranger Station/ Information
Campground
Picnic Area
Horseback Riding
Scenic Viewpoint
Appalachian Trail
Walking/ Hiking Trails
28
23
0 5 mi
0 5 km
28
23
Franklin

Planning

Getting Here and Around

Of all entrances to the national park, the Sugarlands entrance near Gatlinburg is the most popular. This means that you'll doubtless encounter stop-and-go traffic along the way, especially during the summer. A good alternative is the less crowded gate near the community of Townsend, about 26 miles west of Gatlinburg. There is no entrance fee, but the Park Service implemented a $5/day (or $15/week) parking fee in 2023. You can purchase a pass in advance at 🌐 www.nps.gov/grsm/planyourvisit/fees.htm or print one at a visitor center.

Hotels

The only accommodations actually in the park, besides camping, are at LeConte Lodge. Outside the park, you have a gargantuan selection of hotels of every ilk. On the Tennessee side in Gatlinburg, you'll see a street sign that says "2,000 Hotel Rooms" and points up the hill—and that's just in one section of town. From overlooks near the park, you can look down on Gatlinburg and see high-rise hotels that rise up like modern megaliths on the mountainsides. In nearby Pigeon Forge you'll find nearly every chain motel you can think of. More hotels and RV parks await in Sevierville, Townsend, and 40 miles away in Knoxville.

Restaurants

The only sit-down dining in the park is at the dining room of LeConte Lodge (breakfast and dinner are included in the rates and sack lunches are available), but the various communities have all manner of dining options. The Cades Cove Visitor Center has a small deli, and the park's picnic areas are open 24 hours. Do-it-yourself picnicking is permitted anywhere in the park, but keep an eye out for bears and pack out any trash or leftovers.

⇨ *Hotel prices in the reviews are the lowest cost of a standard double room in high season. Restaurant prices in the reviews are the average cost of a main course at dinner, or if dinner is not served, at lunch.*

What It Costs

	$	$$	$$$	$$$$
RESTAURANTS				
	under $15	$15–$25	$26–$35	over $35
HOTELS				
	under $150	$150–$225	$226–$300	over $300

Shopping

The Sugarlands and Cades Cove visitor centers have attractive gift shops and bookstores, with first-rate selections of books and maps on the Smokies and nearby mountain areas, as well as some souvenirs. Cades Cove Campground has a trading post with a deli and bicycle rentals. There is a small convenience store with picnic and camping items (including firewood) at Elkmont.

For groceries outside the national park, your closest options are the Food City grocery store in Gatlinburg and the IGA grocery in Townsend. Gatlinburg has the Nantahala Outdoor Center for camping supplies, and Townsend has the Smoky Mountain Outdoor Center.

Sights

Cades Cove should be your first stop on the Tennessee side of the national park. This broad valley with its preserved old buildings—pioneer homesteads and churches and an old mill—is the park's most popular destination. It's also one of the best places to spot wildlife, including black bears.Clingmans Dome, the highest point in the state at 6,643 feet, is reachable via a 7-mile spur road from Newfound Gap and a steep, paved half-mile trail to the summit.

Roaring Fork Motor Nature Trail (closed in winter) is a drivable tour that delivers both nature and history. The unfinished Foothills Parkway provides great views into the Smokies from its two sections, one on the western end of the park and the other on the northeast edge.

HISTORIC SIGHTS

★ Cades Cove

HISTORIC DISTRICT | FAMILY | A 6,800-acre valley surrounded by high mountains, Cades Cove has more historic buildings than any other area in the park. It's also stunningly beautiful, punctuated by verdant meadows and dirt paths, all surrounded by a ring of peaks. The Park Service keeps hayfields and pastures cleared, so

Did You Know?

Several log cabins dating back more than a century are among the sights at Roaring Forks.

you can see how the valley may have looked in the 19th century. There's a campground and multiple options for day hikes to peaks and along quiet rivers. The Cherokee name for this valley is *Tsiyahi*, "place of otters," but today you're more likely to see bears, deer, coyotes, and wild turkeys. For hundreds of years the Cherokee people hunted in Cades Cove, but there is no evidence of major settlements. Under the terms of the Calhoun Treaty of 1819, the Cherokee lost their rights to Cades Cove, and the first white settlers came in the early 1820s. By the middle of the 19th century, well over 100 settler families were growing corn, wheat, oats, and vegetables. For a while, when government-licensed distilleries were allowed in Tennessee, corn whiskey was the major product of the valley. After the establishment of the park in the 1930s, many of the nearly 200 buildings were torn down to allow the land to revert to its natural state. More recently, the remaining farmsteads and other structures have been restored to depict life in Cades Cove as it was from around 1825 to the 1940s. ■ TIP→ **Cades Cove's beauty is also its curse. To experience it in the best possible setting, without traffic, rent bicycles at the Cades Cove Campground Store and ride the loop road on a car-free Wednesday or at sunrise or sunset.** ✉ *Cades Cove Loop Rd., Great Smoky Mountains National Park* ☎ *865/436–1200* 🌐 *www.nps.gov/grsm/planyourvisit/cadescove.htm* 🕑 *No cars on the loop road on Wed.*

★ **Elkmont Historic District**

HISTORIC DISTRICT | FAMILY | What began as a logging town in the early years of the 20th century evolved into a summer colony for wealthy families from Knoxville. Many prominent east Tennessee families built vacation homes here or visited the Wonderland Hotel via train service from Knoxville to Elkmont. After the national park was established, parts of the community were placed on the National Registry of Historic Places. Today, Elkmont is primarily a campground, and most of the 74 cottages have been removed. The last families lost their leases to their cabins in the 1990s. You can see the ruins of the biggest homes along Millionaires Row, where stone chimneys stand like ghostly sentinels in the wood. In recent years, the Park Service has restored several homes along Jakes Creek that are now open to the public. The Appalachian Clubhouse, built for a hunting and fishing club, is restored to its 1930s appearance, complete with rocking chairs on the porch. There's a short loop nature trail here, or you can take an easy flat walk along the Little River Trail. ✉ *Little River Rd.* ✥ *4½ miles west of Sugarlands Entrance* ☎ *865/436–1200* 🌐 *www.nps.gov/grsm/planyourvisit/elkmont.htm.*

Watch corn being ground into flour and meal at the working gristmill in Cades Cove.

Roaring Fork

HISTORIC DISTRICT | **FAMILY** | Roaring Fork was settled by Europeans beginning in the 1830s. At its height, around the turn of the 20th century, there were about two dozen families in the area. Most lived a hardscrabble existence, trying to scrape out a living from the rough mountain land. The Noah "Bud" Ogle Self-Guided Nature Trail, on Orchard Road just before entering the one-way Roaring Fork Motor Nature Trail, offers a walking tour of a farmstead and the surrounding forest. Highlights include a log cabin, barn, streamside mill, and a wooden flume system designed to bring water to the farm. Among the historic structures on the Motor Nature Trail are the Jim Bales Cabin, the Ephraim Bales Cabin, and the Alfred Reagan House, one of the more "upscale" residences at Roaring Fork. ✉ *Orchard Rd., Great Smoky Mountains National Park* ☎ *865/436–1200* 🌐 *www.nps.gov/grsm/planyourvisit/roaringfork.htm* 🕓 *Closed late Nov.–Mar.*

PICNIC AREAS

Look Rock Picnic Area

VIEWPOINT | **FAMILY** | Accessed via the western section of the beautiful Foothills Parkway, Look Rock Picnic Area is almost never crowded. A ½-mile hike takes you to the observation tower, which offers panoramic views of the Smokies. There are 51 picnic tables, restrooms, and a ranger station. ✉ *Look Rock Picnic Area Rd., off Foothills Pkwy., Great Smoky Mountains National Park* ☎ *865/436–1200* 🌐 *www.nps.gov/grsm/planyourvisit/picnic.htm* 🕓 *Closed Nov.–April.*

The Civilian Conservation Corps

The Civilian Conservation Corps was established in 1933 by President Franklin Delano Roosevelt during the Great Depression. It gave young men a job, a roof over their heads, and something to eat. The law stipulated that the CCC was for men ages 18 to 26 who were unmarried and out of work. Enrollment was for a minimum of six months, but most CCC participants reenlisted. They were paid about $1 per day and were required to send $25 of their monthly paycheck home to their family. In the Smokies, as many as 4,000 enrollees were assigned to 22 CCC camps from 1933 to 1942, planting trees and building roads, bridges, trails, and fire towers. The legacy of the CCC—especially hiking trails and back roads—can still be seen in the park. Remains of camps can be found on several trails, including Forney Creek (building foundations) and Kephart Prong (foundations and part of a cistern used as a CCC fish hatchery).

Metcalf Bottoms Picnic Area

OTHER ATTRACTION | FAMILY | Midway between the Sugarlands Visitor Center and Cades Cove, Metcalf Bottoms makes an excellent waypoint. The Little River is nearby, where you can fish or take a cooling dip. There are 122 picnic tables with grills, restrooms with flush toilets, potable water, and a 70-seat pavilion (open early April to late October) that can be reserved in advance. Two easy hiking trails, Metcalf Bottoms and Little Brier, begin at the picnic area. ✉ *Metcalf Bottoms Picnic Area Rd., off Little River Rd., Gatlinburg* ☎ *865/436–1200* 🌐 *www.nps.gov/grsm/planyourvisit/picnic.htm.*

SCENIC DRIVES

Cades Cove Loop Road

SCENIC DRIVE | FAMILY | This 11-mile loop through Cades Cove is the most popular route in the park and arguably the most scenic part of the Smoky Mountains. The one-way, one-lane paved road starts 7.3 miles from the national park's Townsend entrance. The drive begins with views over wide pastures to the mountains at the crest of the Smokies. Few other places in the Appalachians offer such vistas across wide valleys with hayfields and wildflower meadows framed by split-rail fences and surrounded by tall mountains. Along the way, you'll pass three 19th-century churches and many restored houses and barns that are open for exploration. A highlight is the Cable Mill area, with a visitor center, working water-powered gristmill, and a restored farmstead. The Cades Cove Loop Road is also an excellent place to see wildlife, including black bears, white-tailed deer, and wild turkeys.

Whenever you visit, even in winter, you can expect traffic delays, as passing points on the one-way road are few and far between. Allow at least two to three hours to drive the loop—longer if you want to stop and explore the historic buildings. If you get frustrated with delays, there are two points where you can cut across the loop on improved gravel roads, exiting sooner. A campground and picnic area are open year-round. The road is closed from sunset to sunrise. ✉ *Cades Loop Rd., off Laurel Creek Rd., Townsend* ☎ *865/436–1200* 🌐 *www.nps.gov/grsm/planyourvisit/cadescove.htm.*

Foothills Parkway

SCENIC DRIVE | FAMILY | A 72-mile scenic roadway, Foothills Parkway has long been planned to parallel the northern, western, and southwestern edges of Great Smoky Mountains National Park, providing dramatic views of the Smokies. Construction began in the 1960s, but due to funding problems it still hasn't been completed. About 17 miles from Chilhowee Lake to Walland were completed in 1966. In late 2018, another 16-mile section of the parkway was opened, connecting with this original section and running to Wears Valley. A 5.6-mile section runs from Interstate 40 south to U.S. Route 321. In between these sections are more than 33 miles where construction has not even begun; rights-of-way have been purchased, but there is no state or federal money to build it. Known as the "Tail of the Dragon," a serpentine section of U.S. Route 129 is popular with motorcycle and sports car enthusiasts; it connects with the end of the Foothills Parkway at Chilhowee. ✉ *Gatlinburg* ☎ *865/436–1200* 🌐 *www.nps.gov/places/foothills-parkway.htm.*

★ Newfound Gap Road

SCENIC DRIVE | FAMILY | In a little more than 14 miles, Newfound Gap Road (U.S. 441) climbs more than 3,500 feet, from Gatlinburg to the gap through the crest of the Smokies at 5,046 feet. It takes you through Southern cove hardwood, pine oak, and Northern hardwood forests to the spruce fir forest at Newfound Gap. This is the primary route through the park. There are mile markers starting at the park entrance near Gatlinburg. The Sugarlands Visitor Center is at mile marker 1.7. At Newfound Gap (mile marker 14.7), you can straddle the Tennessee–North Carolina state line and also hike some of the Appalachian Trail. ✉ *U.S. Rte. 441, MM 14.7, Great Smoky Mountains National Park* ☎ *865/436–1200* 🌐 *www.nps.gov/grsm/planyourvisit/nfg.htm.*

Parson Branch Road

SCENIC DRIVE | FAMILY | Following a wagon track, this eight-mile unpaved road has been used for more than 150 years. Some believe that Parson Branch Road was named for ministers who held religious retreats nearby, but others believe it was named for Joshua Parson, an early settler in the area. The road begins at the southwestern edge of Cades Cove Loop Road just beyond the visitor center at the Cable Mill. The road was improved and re-graveled in 2022, but high-clearance vehicles are recommended. It offers no scenic vistas, but it runs through old-growth forests, with huge poplars and hemlocks along the roadway. RVs are prohibited. **■ TIP→ Parson Branch is a one-way drive leaving Cades Cove, so plan your day accordingly. Its terminus is the "Tail of the Dragon" (US-129) scenic drive, where it's accessible to bicyclists for a pleasant pedal along the namesake creek.** ✉ *Parson Branch Rd., off Cades Cove Loop Rd., Townsend* ☎ *865/436–1200* 🌐 *www.nps.gov/grsm/planyourvisit/seasonalroads.htm* ⊗ *Closed Nov.–Mar.*

Roaring Fork Motor Nature Trail

SCENIC DRIVE | FAMILY | The six-mile Roaring Fork offers a dramatic counterpoint to Cades Cove Loop Road, which meanders through a wide-open valley. Roaring Fork closes in, with the forest sometimes literally just inches from your fender. This one-way paved road is so narrow in places that RVs, trailers, and buses are not permitted. The trail starts just beyond the Noah "Bud" Ogle Farmstead and the Rainbow Falls trailhead. Pick up a Roaring Fork Auto Tour booklet at the information shelter. Numbered markers along the route are keyed to 16 stops highlighted in the booklet. A favorite sight is the old Alfred Reagan House, which is painted in the original blue, yellow, and cream, "all three colors that Sears and Roebuck had," according to a story attributed to Mr. Reagan. There are several good hiking trails starting along the road, including the Trillium Gap Trail to Mt. LeConte. The road follows Roaring Fork Creek a good part of the way, and the finale is a small waterfall called "The Place of a Thousand Drips," right beside the road. ✉ *Roaring Fork Motor Nature Tr., Gatlinburg* ✣ *From Gatlinburg, from the parkway (U.S. 441), turn onto Historic Nature Trail at stoplight No. 8 in Gatlinburg and follow it to the Cherokee Orchard entrance to the park* ☎ *865/436–1200* 🌐 *www.nps.gov/grsm/planyourvisit/roaringfork.htm* ⊗ *Closed Dec.–Mar.*

SCENIC STOPS

Campbell Overlook

VIEWPOINT | FAMILY | Named for Carlos Campbell, a conservationist who was instrumental in helping to establish the park, this overlook provides a beautiful view up a valley to Bull Head Peak and, farther up, to Balsam Point. An exhibit at the overlook explains the different types of forests within the park. ✉ *Newfound Gap Rd., MM 3.9, Great Smoky Mountains National Park* ☎ *865/436–1200* 🌐 *www.nps.gov/grsm.*

Did You Know?

Among the most popular hikes in the national park, the Alum Cave Bluffs Trail leads past some stunning geological formations.

Chimney Tops Overlook

VIEWPOINT | FAMILY | From any of the three overlooks grouped together on Newfound Gap Road, you'll have a good view of the Chimney Tops—twin peaks that cap 2,000-foot-high cliffs. Sadly, you'll also see dozens of dead fir and spruce trees, victims of the invasive woolly adelgids. ✉ *Newfound Gap Rd., MM 7.1, Gatlinburg* ☎ *865/436–1200* 🌐 *www.nps.gov/grsm.*

Gatlinburg Bypass Overlook

VIEWPOINT | This four-mile roadway runs just north of Gatlinburg toward Pigeon Forge. It tracks around the side of Mt. Harrison. Take this route to avoid the stop-and-go traffic of downtown Gatlinburg when leaving or entering the park. The second overlook when headed out of the park toward Pigeon Forge has the best views of Gatlinburg and Mt. LeConte. ✉ *Gatlinburg Bypass* ☎ *865/436–1200* 🌐 *www.nps.gov/grsm.*

Look Rock

VIEWPOINT | FAMILY | The viewpoints looking east on the western section of Foothills Parkway around Look Rock have remarkable vistas. This is also a great spot to enjoy the sunrise over the Smokies. Stargazers gather at the five overlooks south of the Look Rock exit because light pollution is especially low. ✉ *Foothills Pkwy., Great Smoky Mountains National Park* ☎ *865/436–1200* 🌐 *www.nps.gov/grsm.*

Roaring Fork Motor Nature Trail Site Number 3

VIEWPOINT | FAMILY | While most of the Roaring Fork Motor Nature Trail takes you on a narrow and winding one-way road through forested areas where the views are limited, at the beginning of the drive the first and second overlooks present good views of the distant mountain ridges. The best scenery is from the second overlook, marked as the number 3 site on the Roaring Fork Auto Tour. ✉ *Roaring Fork Motor Tr.* ☎ *865/436–1200* 🌐 *www.nps.gov/grsm* 🕑 *Closed Dec.–Mar.*

TRAILS

Abrams Falls Trail

TRAIL | This five-mile round-trip trail is one of the most popular in the Smokies, thanks to its trailhead location on Cades Cove Loop Road. Beginning at the wooden bridge over Abrams Creek, the trail first follows a pleasant course through rhododendron, then becomes steeper at a couple of points, especially near Arbutus Ridge. The path then leads above Abrams Falls and down to Wilson Creek. Though only about 20 feet high, the falls are beautiful, with a large volume of water and a broad pool below. *Moderate.* ⚠ **It is dangerous to climb, jump from, or swim near the falls.** ✉ *Cades Cove Loop Rd., between signposts 10 and 11, Townsend*

Throughout the summer, the trails to Gregory Bald are lined with the brilliant orange blossoms of flame azaleas.

☎ 865/436–1200 🌐 www.nps.gov/grsm/planyourvisit/abrams-falls.htm.

★ Alum Cave Trail

TRAIL | One of the best and most popular hikes in the national park, the fairly short 2.3-mile one-way hike to Alum Cave Bluffs contains some of the most interesting geological formations in the Smokies. Arch Rock, a natural arch created by millions of years of freezing and thawing, and Alum Bluffs, a large overhanging rock ledge, are the highlights. This very well-known trail does not offer much solitude, especially on weekends. From the bluffs you can continue on another 2.8 miles to reach Mt. LeConte, passing awe-inspiring mountain vistas. Alum Cave Bluffs is the shortest of five trail routes to LeConte Lodge, but it is also the steepest, with an elevation gain of over 2,700 feet. *Moderate. ✉ Newfound Gap Rd., MM 10.4, Great Smoky Mountains National Park ☎ 865/436–1200 🌐 www.nps.gov/grsm/planyourvisit/chimneys-alternative-alum-cave-bluffs.htm.*

★ Appalachian Trail at Newfound Gap

TRAIL | The Appalachian Trail's 72 miles through the Great Smokies are among its most scenic. The trail follows ridges, offering vistas throughout the traverse. Park in the Newfound Gap Overlook parking lot and cross the road to the trail. From Newfound Gap to Indian Gap, the trail travels 1.7 miles through spruce and fir forests, and in late spring and summer there are quite a few wildflowers. The total round-trip distance is 3.4 miles. *Easy.* **■ TIP→ Walking in the other direction (north on the AT), it's 4.4 miles**

(each way) to Charlie's Bunion, with scenic views most of the way. ✉ *Newfound Gap Overlook, Newfound Gap Rd., Great Smoky Mountains National Park* ☎ *865/436–1200* 🌐 *www.nps.gov/grsm/planyourvisit/nfg.htm.*

The Appalachian Trail

Each spring nearly 3,000 hikers set out to conquer the 2,190-mile Appalachian Trail. Most hike north from Springer Mountain, Georgia, toward Mt. Katahdin, Maine. By the time they get to the Great Smokies, 160 miles from the trailhead in Georgia, many of those hikers will already have dropped out. Typically, fewer than 800 hikers per year complete the entire AT, which takes an average of 165 days. At Newfound Gap Overlook, you can get on it for a short hike on the North Carolina–Tennessee line.

★ Chimney Tops Trail

TRAIL | Pant, wheeze, and gasp. This is a fairly short yet steep trail that will take a lot out of you, but it gives back a lot, too. The payoff for the difficult climb is one of the best views in the Smokies. In places the trail has loose rock (hiking poles are recommended), and the elevation gain is 1,350 feet. Some sections have steep stairs. A new observation deck was built roughly ¼ mile from the summit, with views of Mt. LeConte and the pinnacles. The total distance round-trip is 3.6 miles. *Difficult.* ✉ *Newfound Gap Rd., 6.9 miles from Sugarlands Visitor Center, Great Smoky Mountains National Park* ☎ *865/436–1200* 🌐 *www.nps.gov/grsm/planyourvisit/chimney-tops.htm.*

Clingmans Dome

TRAIL | FAMILY | If you've been driving too long and want a place to stretch your legs, unbeatable views of the Smokies, and an ecological lesson, take the ½-mile (1-mile round-trip) trail from the Clingmans Dome Visitor Center parking lot to the observation tower at the top of Clingmans Dome, the highest peak in the Smokies. The tower itself is a spiraling, concrete architectural marvel. While paved, the trail is fairly steep, and at 6,643 feet of elevation, you'll probably be gasping for air. Many of the fir trees here are dead, killed by an alien invader—the balsam woolly adelgid. There's a small visitor information station on the trail. In the parking lot, often full in season, there are restrooms. *Moderate.* **■ TIP→ If the paved trail isn't appealing, you can use the Clingmans Bypass Trail and the Appalachian Trail as an alternative, or make it a loop.** ✉ *Clingmans Dome Rd., Great Smoky Mountains National Park* ☎ *865/436–1200* 🌐 *www.nps.gov/grsm/planyourvisit/clingmansdome.htm* ⏲ *Clingmans Dome Rd. is closed Dec.–Mar.*

Elkmont Nature Trail

TRAIL | **FAMILY** | This one-mile loop is good for families, especially if you're camping at Elkmont. It passes by many of the remaining buildings in the Elkmont Historic District. Pick up a self-guided brochure at the start of the trail. *Easy.* ✉ *Little River Rd., Great Smoky Mountains National Park* ⊕ *Near Elkmont Campground* ☎ *865/436–1200* ⊕ *www.nps.gov/grsm/planyourvisit/elkmont.htm.*

Gatlinburg Trail

TRAIL | **FAMILY** | This is one of only two trails in the park where dogs and bicycles are permitted (the other one is Oconaluftee River Trail on the North Carolina side). Dogs must be on leashes. The 1.9-mile trail starts at Sugarlands Visitor Center and follows the Little Pigeon River. *Easy.* ✉ *Sugarlands Visitor Center, Newfound Gap Rd., Gatlinburg* ☎ *865/436–1200* ⊕ *www.nps.gov/grsm/planyourvisit/gatlinburg-trail.htm.*

Laurel Falls Trail

TRAIL | **FAMILY** | This paved trail takes you past a series of cascades to a 60-foot waterfall and a stand of old-growth forest. The trail is extremely popular in summer and on weekends (trolleys from Gatlinburg stop here), so don't expect solitude. The 1.3-mile paved trail to the falls is wheelchair accessible. The total round-trip hike is 2.6 miles. *Easy.* ✉ *Little River Rd., between Sugarlands Visitor Center and Elkmont Campground, Great Smoky Mountains National Park* ☎ *865/436–1200* ⊕ *www.nps.gov/grsm.*

Little River Trail

TRAIL | This 5.1-mile loop (if Cucumber Gap and Jakes Creek trails are included) offers a little of everything—historical buildings, a waterfall, and wildflowers. The first part of the trail wanders up the Little River, past remnants of old logging operations and cottages that were once the summer homes of wealthy Tennesseans. You'll see several inviting swimming holes, beautiful cascades, and perhaps a person or two fly fishing. Huskey Branch Falls appears at about 2 miles. The Little River Trail passes a junction with three other trails, offering the possibility for even longer hikes—Cucumber Gap at 2.3 miles, Huskey Gap at 2.7 miles, and Goshen Prong Trail at 3.7 miles. The trail is normally open even in winter. This is the habitat of the synchronous fireflies, which put on their light show on late May and June evenings. *Moderate.* ✉ *Little River Rd., near Elkmont Campground, Great Smoky Mountains National Park* ☎ *865/436–1200* ⊕ *www.nps.gov/grsm.*

Mt. Cammerer

TRAIL | Spend enough time around the Smokies and you'll see pictures of an octagonal stone building atop a mountain. This is the fire lookout atop Mt. Cammerer, and it's open to the public if you're willing to walk the 11.1-mile round trip (and 3,000 feet of elevation gain) up the Low Gap Trail from Cosby Campground. The effort is worth it for panoramic 360-degree views of the eastern half of the park. Adding to the wonder, the summit is on a windblown ridge, creating an otherworldly habitat of trees that only grow head high. For the truly adventurous, the Lower Mt. Cammerer Trail lets you turn the hike into a 16.2-mile loop. *Difficult* ✉ *Great Smoky Mountains National Park* 🌐 *www.nps.gov/grsm.*

Sugarlands Valley Nature Trail

TRAIL | FAMILY | The easiest trail in the park, it's only a quarter mile, virtually level, and paved, so it's suitable for young children, strollers, and wheelchairs. A brochure available at the start explains the numbered exhibits and features of the trail. *Easy.* ✉ *Newfound Gap Rd., south of Sugarlands Visitor Center, Great Smoky Mountains National Park* ☎ *865/436–1200* 🌐 *www.nps.gov/grsm.*

Trillium Gap Trail

TRAIL | FAMILY | Grotto Falls is the only waterfall in the park that you can walk behind. The Trillium Gap Trail, off the Roaring Fork Motor Nature Trail, takes you there through a hemlock forest. Only 1.3 miles long with an easy slope, this trail is suitable for novice hikers and is one of the most popular in the park. The total round-trip distance to Grotto Falls is 2.6 miles. Trillium Gap Trail continues on to LeConte Lodge. It is a horse trail, and llamas resupplying the lodge also use it. *Easy.* ✉ *Roaring Fork Motor Nature Tr., Great Smoky Mountains National Park* ☎ *865/436–1200* 🌐 *www.nps.gov/grsm* ⏲ *Road access closed Dec.–Mar.*

VISITOR CENTERS

Cades Cove Visitor Center

VISITOR CENTER | FAMILY | Located near the midway point on the highly popular 11-mile Cades Cove Loop, the Cades Cove Visitor Center is especially worth visiting to see the Cable Mill, which operates spring through fall, and the Becky Cable House, a pioneer home with farm outbuildings. ✉ *Cades Cove Loop Rd., Great Smoky Mountains National Park* ☎ *865/436–1200* 🌐 *www.nps.gov/grsm/planyourvisit/visitorcenters.htm.*

Clingmans Dome Visitor Contact Station

VISITOR CENTER | While not a full-fledged visitor information center, Clingmans Dome has a staffed information kiosk, along with a small park store and bookshop. There are restrooms in the Clingsmans Dome parking lot. ✉ *Clingmans Dome Rd.* ☎ *865/436–1200* 🌐 *www.nps.gov/grsm/planyourvisit/visitorcenters.htm* ⏲ *Closed Dec.–Mar.*

The Smokies by the Numbers

12,500,000: Visitors annually to Great Smoky Mountains National Park

2,000,000: Visitors to Cades Cove annually

1,700,000: Visitors in July (the busiest month)

500,000: Visitors in February (the least busy month)

90,000: Acres covered by hemlocks infested by woolly adelgid

225,000: Backcountry camping nights annually

6,643: Elevation of the highest peak, Clingmans Dome

6,000: White-tailed deer in the park

2,115: Miles of rivers, creeks, and streams in the park

1,660: Kinds of wildflowers in the park

1,500: Black bears in the park

1,000: Individual campsites

660: Picnic tables

240: Species of birds in the park

200: Elk in the park

150: Hiking trails in the park

85: Average inches of annual precipitation at Clingmans Dome

69: Average inches of snow annually at Newfound Gap

1: Hotels in the park

0: Average number of serious bear attacks annually

Sugarlands Visitor Center

VISITOR CENTER | FAMILY | The main visitor center on the Tennessee side, Sugarlands features a nature museum with extensive exhibits about park flora and fauna, as well as a 20-minute film about the park. Ranger-led programs are held from spring to fall. There are hiking trails nearby. ✉ *1420 Fighting Creek Gap Rd.* ☎ *865/436–1200.*

Restaurants

Cades Cove Trading Company Deli

$ | FAST FOOD | FAMILY | The only eatery in the park, other than the restaurant at LeConte Lodge, is a little snack bar and deli inside the Cades Cove Campground Store. Here, you can buy hot dogs, burgers, chili, and other snacks. **Known for:** convenience-store atmosphere; campground favorites; ice cream shop next door. *$ Average main: $7* ✉ *Cades Cove Loop Rd., Great Smoky Mountains National Park* ☎ *865/448–9034* 🌐 *cadescovetrading.com* ⏲ *Closed early to mid-Dec., Jan., and Feb.*

Hotels

★ LeConte Lodge

$$$$ | B&B/INN | FAMILY | Set at 6,360 feet near the summit of Mt. LeConte, this hike-in lodge is remote, rustic, and remarkable. **Pros:** unique setting high on Mt. LeConte; a true escape from civilization; breakfast and dinner included in rates. **Cons:** books up many months in advance; few modern conveniences; hike-in access only. *Rooms from: $325* *End of Trillium Gap Trail, Great Smoky Mountains National Park* *865/429–5704* *www.lecontelodge.com* *Closed mid-Nov.– late Mar.* *10 cabins* *Free Breakfast.*

Activities

BICYCLING

Tennessee requires that youth age 16 and under wear a helmet, though it's strongly recommended that all riders do so, regardless of age.

Cades Cove Loop Road. Arguably the best place to bike in the national park, this 11-mile loop is mostly level and takes you through some lovely scenery. Vehicle traffic can be heavy, especially on weekends in summer and fall. Serious cyclists come here from early May to late September, when the loop is closed to motor vehicles on Wednesdays. Bicycles and helmets can be rented in summer and fall at Cades Cove Campground.

Foothills Parkway West. Parts of this scenic 72-mile road have light vehicular traffic, making it a fairly safe place for bicycling.

Gatlinburg Trail. This is the only hiking trail on the Tennessee side where bikes are permitted. The trail takes you 1.9 miles from the Sugarlands Visitor Center to the outskirts of Gatlinburg. Pets on leashes are also allowed on this trail.

Parsons Branch Road. This narrow, unpaved back road twists and dips from near Cable Mill on the Cades Cove Loop Road to U.S. Route 129.

CAMPING

No matter your style of camping, there are plenty of campgrounds in the national park. The campgrounds at Abrams Creek, Cades Cove, Cosby, and Elkmont require reservations that can be made online up to six months in advance. The cost for a site is $30/night.

Backcountry permits are required for overnight camping, hiking, or backpacking and generally cost $8 per night. Advance reservations are required for all backcountry campsites.

Abrams Creek Campground. Beside a meandering creek, this 16-site campground sits on the extreme western edge of the park, way off the beaten path. Although it sits at an elevation of 1,125 feet, summers can be hot and humid. Several excellent hiking trails, including Gold Mine, Cane Creek, Rabbit Creek, and Little Bottoms begin at or near the campground. It's closed Nov. through April. ✉ *Abrams Creek Campground Rd., off Happy Valley Rd.* ☎ *865/436–1200* 🌐 *www.nps.gov/grsm/planyourvisit/abrams-creek-campground.htm.*

Cades Cove Campground. One of the largest campgrounds in the Smokies, the 159-site Cades Cove Campground also has the most on-site services. It has a small general store with a snack bar, bike rentals, horse stables, and an amphitheater. In spring it's covered with wildflowers, while in the fall the maples turn vivid reds and yellows. It's one of just two campgrounds in the national park that are open year-round (the other is Smokemont on the North Carolina side). This is a popular campground and often fills up in summer and fall. ✉ *10042 Campground Dr., at entrance to Cades Cove Loop Rd.* ☎ *865/448–2472* 🌐 *www.nps.gov/grsm/planyourvisit/cades-cove-campground.htm.*

Cosby Campground. Set among poplars, hemlocks, and rhododendrons, Cosby Campground sits near Cosby and Rock Creeks. Most of the campsites are reserved for tents, and RVs and trailers are limited to 25 feet. Bears are fairly common in the area, and several campsites may be temporarily closed due to bear activity. Nearby are the trailheads for Snake Den Ridge and Gabes Mountain Trails. This rarely busy campground nearly always has sites available. It's closed from November through early April. ✉ *127 Cosby Park Rd., off TN 32* ☎ *423/487–2683* 🌐 *www.nps.gov/grsm/planyourvisit/cosby-campground-information.htm.*

Elkmont Campground. Easy access to hiking trails and swimming in the Little River make Elkmont ideal for families with kids. Nearby is the Elkmont Historic District, which has old vacation cabins to explore. Even though Elkmont is the largest campground in the park, with 220 tent and RV sites available, it is often fully booked. It's closed from December through early March. ✉ *434 Elkmont Rd.* ☎ *877/444–6777* 🌐 *www.nps.gov/grsm/planyourvisit/elkmont-campground.htm.*

Look Rock Campground. At the western edge of the park, off Foothills Parkway, this first-come, first-served (no reservations) campground is the only camping area in the park with no length limit for RVs and trailers. Set in oak and pine woods, there's not much to do here except hike. Several trails can be accessed from the campground, including Cane Creek, Little Bottoms, and Rabbit Creek. ✉ *7040 Flats Road* ☎ *865/436–1200* 🌐 *www.nps.gov/grsm.*

EDUCATIONAL PROGRAMS

Great Smoky Mountains Institute at Tremont

HIKING & WALKING | **FAMILY** | Located within the national park at Tremont, this residential environmental education center offers a variety of programs year-round for student groups, teachers, and families. Offerings include photography, crafts, and backpacking trips. Accommodations are in Caylor Lodge, a climate-controlled dormitory that sleeps up to 125 people. Some 5,000 students and adults attend programs each year. There's a visitor center and gift shop open to the public. ✉ *9275 Tremont Rd., Townsend* ☎ *865/448–6709* 🌐 *gsmit.org.*

Smoky Mountain Field School

HIKING & WALKING | **FAMILY** | The University of Tennessee's Smoky Mountain Field School offers noncredit workshops, hikes, and outdoor adventures for adults and families. Participants choose from among more than 30 programs held at various locations within the park. Typical fees are $69 for courses such as wildflower identification and wild food foraging. Sign up in advance at their website. ✉ *Knoxville* ☎ *865/974–0150* 🌐 *smfs.utk.edu* ⏲ *No classes mid-Nov.–Feb.*

FISHING

There are more than 200 miles of wild trout streams on the Tennessee side of the park. Trout streams are open to fishing year-round. Among the best trout streams on the Tennessee side are Little River, Abrams Creek, and Little Pigeon River.

Everyone over 13 must possess a valid fishing license or permit from Tennessee or North Carolina. Either state license is valid throughout the park, and no trout stamp is required. Fishing licenses are not available in the park but may be purchased in nearby towns and online from the Tennessee Wildlife Resource Agency (🌐 *www.tn.gov/twra*).

For backcountry trips, you may want to hire a guide. Full-day fishing trips cost about $250 to $300 for one angler, $250 to $350 for two. Only guides approved by the National Park Service are permitted to take anglers into the backcountry.

OUTFITTERS

Little River Outfitters

FISHING | This large fly-fishing shop and school has been in business since 1994. It specializes in fly tying and other skills. Although it does not offer guide services, they manage a directory of individual guides that they recommend. ✉ *106 Town Square Dr., Townsend* ☎ *865/448–9459* 🌐 *www.littleriveroutfitters.com.*

Smoky Mountain Angler

FISHING | This well-equipped fly-fishing shop offers equipment rentals, fishing licenses, and half-day and full-day fly- and spin-fishing trips with one of its local guides. Full-day guided trout fishing trips in the park are $416 for one person and $520 for two. ✉ *469 Brookside Village Way, Gatlinburg* ☎ *865/436–8746* 🌐 *www.smokymountainangler.com.*

Tennessee Wildlife Resources Agency

FISHING | A Tennessee fishing license, required of anyone 13 and over, is valid throughout the park and also for fishing in other areas of Tennessee. A 10-day package including trout is $61 for nonresidents. Licenses for Tennessee residents vary but cost less. A special trout-fishing license for the Gatlinburg area (outside the park) costs an additional $3 for one day. **TIP→ North Carolina fishing licenses are cheaper, and since either a North Carolina or Tennessee license is good anywhere in the park, you'll save by buying a North Carolina license, even if you just want to fish on the Tennessee side.** ✉ *3030 Wildlife Way, Morristown* ☎ *615/781–6585* 🌐 *www.tn.gov/twra.*

HIKING

The national park has more than 800 miles of hiking trails, about half of which are on the Tennessee side. The trails range from short nature walks to long strenuous hikes that gain several thousand feet in elevation. Park trails are well maintained most of the year, but be prepared for erosion and washouts December through May. Weather in the park is subject to rapid change. A day in spring or fall might start out warm and sunny, but by the time you reach a mile-high elevation, the temperature may be near freezing. The higher elevations of the park can get up to 85 inches of rain and snow annually.

Although permits are not required for day hikes, you must have a backcountry permit for overnight trips.

HORSEBACK RIDING

Several hundred miles of backcountry trails on the Tennessee side are open to horseback riders.

Temperate Rainforests

When you think about rainforests, you may picture the lush tropical Amazon, but parts of the Great Smokies are considered temperate rainforests. These coniferous or broadleaf forests occur in the temperate zone and receive high rainfall. Most of the temperate rainforests in North America are in oceanic-moist climates on west-facing mountains near the Pacific coast, from southeastern Alaska south to California. However, the highest elevations of the Smokies qualify, as these areas get as much as 85 inches of rain each year. The Smokies are hundreds of miles from an ocean, but the vast changes in elevation—from less than 2,000 feet at its lowest points to more than 6,600 feet at Clingmans Dome—create clouds and locally heavy precipitation. Some parts of the nearby Pisgah, Nantahala, and Chattahoochee National Forests are also considered temperate rainforests.

OUTFITTERS

Cades Cove Riding Stables

HORSEBACK RIDING | FAMILY | Along with horseback riding, this park concessionaire offers hayrides, carriage rides, and guided trail rides. It's first-come, first-served, with no reservations except for large groups. Call the stables to find out times and dates for ranger-led hayrides. Horseback riders must be at least six years old and can weigh no more than 250 pounds. ✉ *Cades Cove Campground, 10018 Campground Dr., at entrance to Cades Cove Loop Rd., Townsend* ☎ *865/448–9009* 🌐 *www.cadescovestables.com* 🎟 *From $20* 🕒 *Closed Dec.–early Mar.*

TUBING

Little River is the most popular tubing river on the west side of the Smokies. It's mostly flat water, with a few mild rapids. Several outfitters in Townsend rent tubes and life jackets and provide shuttle buses or vans that drop you off upstream. Expect to pay from $10 to $18 per person. Outfitters are generally open May through September or October.

OUTFITTERS

Smoky Mountain River Rat

WATER SPORTS | FAMILY | This outfitter, the best of the bunch in the Townsend area, offers tubing on the Little River during warmer months. Tube rental, life jacket, and shuttle service are $20 if purchased in advance. ✉ *205 Wears Valley Rd., Townsend* ☎ *865/448–8888* 🌐 *smokymtnriverrat.com* 🕒 *Closed Nov.–Apr.*

Chapter 4

4

GREAT SMOKY MOUNTAINS, NC

Updated by
Stratton Lawrence

Camping	Hotels	Activities	Scenery	Crowds
★★★★★	★★★★☆	★★★★☆	★★★★☆	★★★★★

WELCOME TO GREAT SMOKY MOUNTAINS, NC

TOP REASONS TO GO

★ **Scenery and Solitude.** Scenic drives like Heintooga Ridge Road stay relatively off the radar.

★ **Exploring History.** A trip to Mingus Mill or the Mountain Farm Museum bring Appalachian history to life.

★ **Wildlife Sightings.** Oconaluftee and Cataloochee are the best places to view herds of elk and other wildlife.

★ **Bountiful Boating.** One of the park's most stunning sights, Fontana Lake is popular with boaters and anglers.

★ **High-Altitude Hikes.** Three Waterfalls Loop and dozens of other trails offer plenty of scenic views.

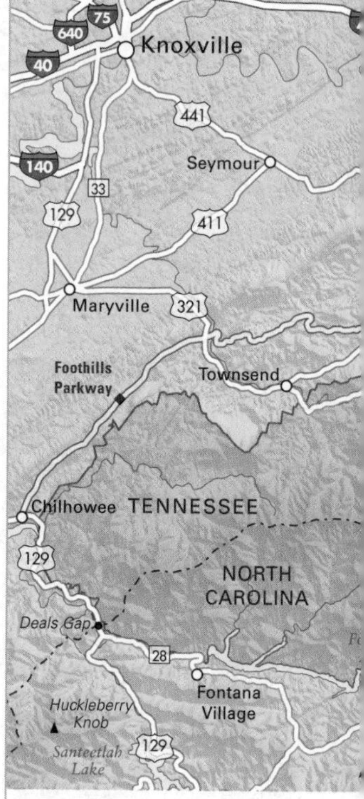

1 Newfound Gap Road. Bisecting both halves of the park, this high-altitude drive offers amazing scenery.

2 Oconaluftee Valley. Near the North Carolina side's main visitor center are many of the park's most historic sites.

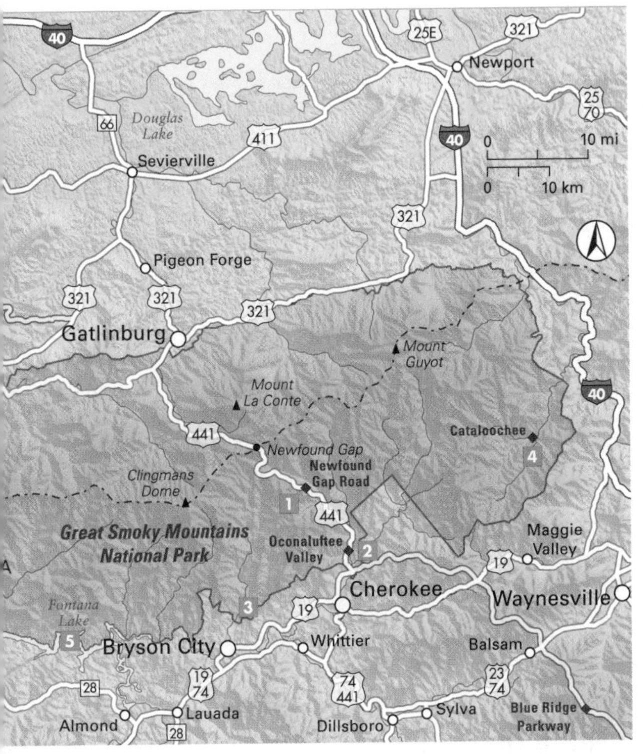

3 Deep Creek. This tucked-away park entrance has a quiet campground and adventurous tubing.

4 Cataloochee Valley. The remnants of an early-20th-century settlement are among the park's eeriest sights.

5 Fontana Lake. At the park's southwestern border, this massive reservoir is great for boating and fishing.

The Great Smoky Mountains National Park may be headquartered in Tennessee, but more of the park is on the North Carolina side. Here you'll find impressive peaks like Gregory Bald and Shuckstack, as well as Fontana Lake, which forms much of the park's southwestern boundary.

The land here is contained within three North Carolina counties—Haywood, which is home to more 6,000-foot-or-higher peaks than any other county in the eastern United States; Graham, which is more than two-thirds national forest and national park land; and Swain, which has the largest portion of the park than any other county. The small towns along the edge of the park—including Robbinsville, Bryson City, Dillsboro, and Sylva—sometimes bill themselves as "the quiet side of the park," and with good reason.

A little more than an hour's drive from the park's Oconaluftee entrance, the city of Asheville is nationally known for its art galleries, hip downtown scene, eclectic restaurants, and varied lodgings, including one of the largest collections of B&Bs in the Southeast. Near the town of Cherokee, the Blue Ridge Parkway begins its 469-mile meandering journey north through the North Carolina mountains to Virginia's Skyline Drive. Also adjoining the eastern side of the park is the Cherokee Indian Reservation, officially known as the Qualla Boundary.

But there's no reason for Carolinians and Tennesseans to get into a bragging match. Within the park itself, both sides are actually quite similar in terms of scenery, activities, flora and fauna, and historical sites. Indeed, you probably won't even know when you've gone from one side of the park to the other.

Planning

Getting Here and Around

Although there are numerous entrances to the North Carolina side of the park, the main entrance is via U.S. Route 441 near Cherokee and the Oconaluftee Visitor Center. Another pleasant (but slower) route to the Smokies is the Blue Ridge Parkway, which has its southern terminus in Cherokee.

There is no entrance fee, but the Park Service implemented a $5/day (or $15/week) parking fee in 2023. You can purchase a pass in advance at 🌐 *www.nps.gov/grsm/planyourvisit/fees.htm*or print one at a visitor center.

Great Itineraries

THE NORTH CAROLINA SIDE IN ONE DAY

Start early, pack a picnic lunch, and drive to the **Oconaluftee Visitor Center** to pick up orientation maps and brochures. While you're there, spend an hour or so exploring the **Mountain Farm Museum**. Drive the half mile to **Mingus Mill** and see corn being ground into meal in an authentic working gristmill. Head up Newfound Gap Road and Clingmans Dome Road to **Clingmans Dome**. The 25-mile drive takes you through a dizzying array of plants and trees. Stretch your legs and walk the half-mile paved, but fairly steep, trail to the observation tower on Clingmans Dome, the highest point in the Smokies. On a clear day you can see as far as 100 miles, though on most days air pollution limits views to about 20 miles. If you've worked up an appetite, head back down the mountain and stop for a leisurely picnic at **Collins Creek Picnic Area**. If you want a moderate afternoon hike, the four-mile round-trip **Kephart Prong Trail** is nearby and wanders along a stream to the remains of a Depression-era Civilian Conservation Corps camp. Alternatively, drive via the Blue Ridge Parkway and Heintooga Ridge Road to the **Heintooga Picnic Area** at Balsam Springs. At a mile high, this part of the Smokies is usually cool, even in mid-July. If you're up for it, you can hike all or part of the **Flat Creek Trail**, which begins near the Heintooga Picnic Area and is one of the hidden jewels of the park.

THE NORTH CAROLINA SIDE IN THREE DAYS

On Day 1, follow the one-day itinerary. On Day 2, drive to **Bryson City** and then three miles to **Deep Creek**. If you have children with you, or if you're a kid at heart, rent inner tubes and spend several hours tubing and swimming in Deep Creek. Have a picnic at Deep Creek Picnic Area, or drive into Bryson City for lunch. In the afternoon, take one of the nearby loop hikes to see waterfalls. If you want to do more driving, you can visit **Fontana Lake**, which hugs the southwestern border of the park. On Day 3, take I-40 to Cove Creek Road and drive to the **Cataloochee Valley**. Spend the morning spying elk and exploring the deserted homes, barns, and churches of the Cataloochee community. After a picnic by Cataloochee Creek, continue on Cove Creek Road, an unpaved, narrow park road, toward Big Creek. On the way, stop and hike at least a little of the **Mt. Sterling** trail—it's a strenuous, steep 5.4-mile hike to an old fire tower, so you may not have the time or the energy to hike the entire trail. Reconnect with I-40 and return home.

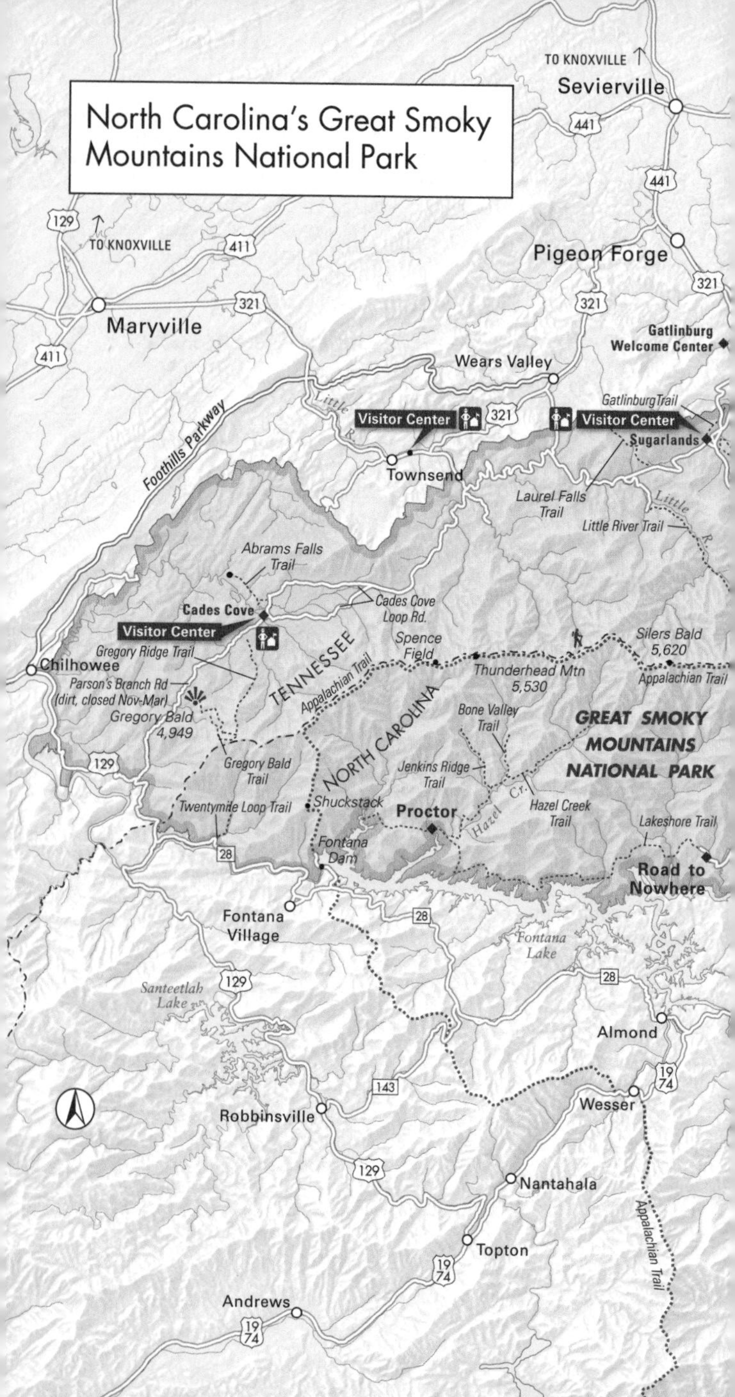

North Carolina's Great Smoky Mountains National Park
TO KNOXVILLE
Sevierville
441
129
TO KNOXVILLE
411
Pigeon Forge
321
Maryville
Gatlinburg Welcome Center
Wears Valley
Foothills Parkway
Little R.
Visitor Center
Visitor Center
Gatlinburg Trail
Sugarlands
Townsend
Laurel Falls Trail
Little River Trail
Little R.
Abrams Falls Trail
Cades Cove
Cades Cove Loop Rd.
Visitor Center
TENNESSEE
Spence Field
Silers Bald 5,620
Gregory Ridge Trail
Chilhowee
Thunderhead Mtn 5,530
Appalachian Trail
Parson's Branch Rd (dirt, closed Nov-Mar)
Appalachian Trail
Gregory Bald 4,949
Bone Valley Trail
GREAT SMOKY MOUNTAINS NATIONAL PARK
NORTH CAROLINA
Gregory Bald Trail
Jenkins Ridge Trail
Twentymile Loop Trail
Shuckstack
Proctor
Hazel Cr.
Hazel Creek Trail
Lakeshore Trail
Fontana Dam
Road to Nowhere
28
Fontana Village
Fontana Lake
Santeetlah Lake
Almond
143
Wesser
19 74
Robbinsville
Nantahala
Appalachian Trail
Topton
Andrews

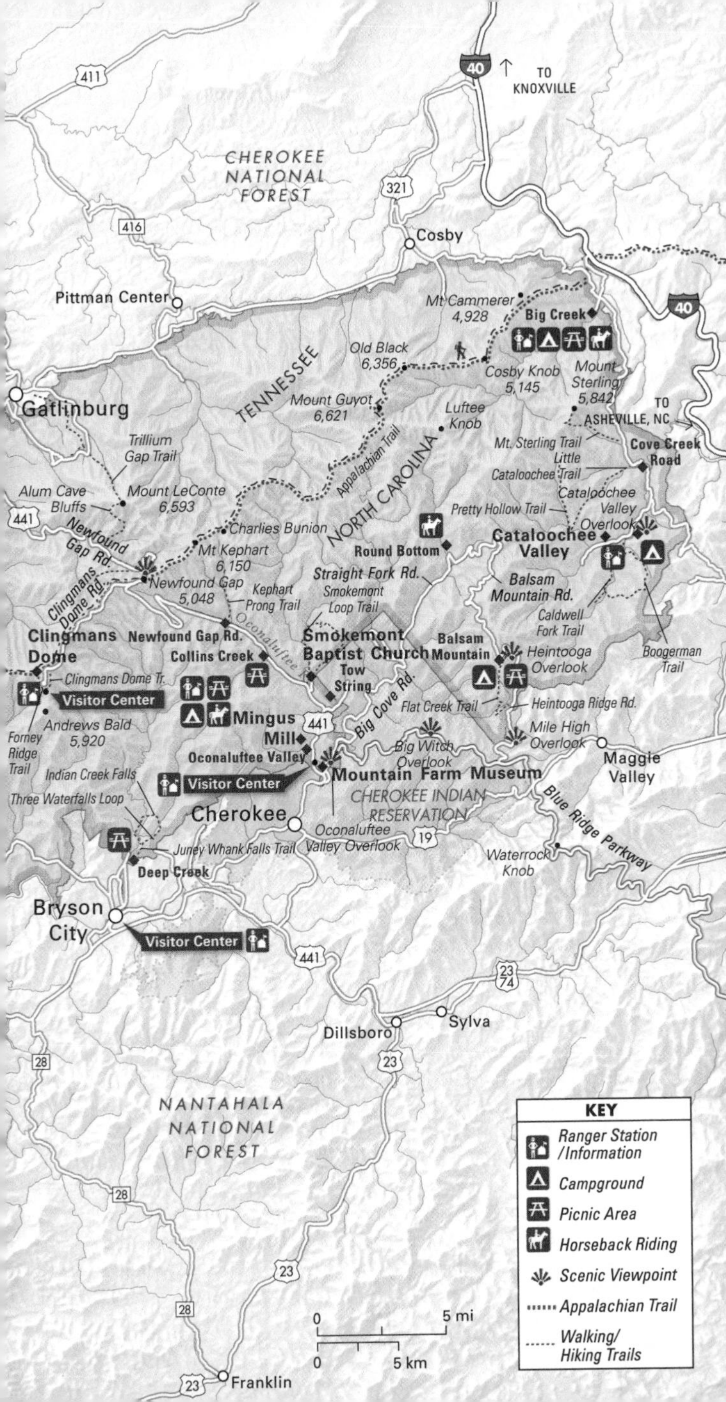

411
40
TO KNOXVILLE
CHEROKEE NATIONAL FOREST
321
416
Cosby
Pittman Center
Mt Cammerer 4,928
Big Creek
40
Old Black 6,356
TENNESSEE
Cosby Knob 5,145
Mount Sterling 5,842
Mount Guyot 6,621
Gatlinburg
Luftee Knob
TO ASHEVILLE, NC
Trillium Gap Trail
Appalachian Trail
Mt. Sterling Trail
Little Cataloochee Trail
Cove Creek Road
NORTH CAROLINA
Alum Cave Bluffs
Mount LeConte 6,593
Cataloochee Valley Overlook
Pretty Hollow Trail
441
Charlies Bunion
Newfound Gap Rd.
Mt Kephart 6,150
Round Bottom
Cataloochee Valley
Clingmans Dome Rd.
Newfound Gap 5,048
Straight Fork Rd.
Balsam Mountain Rd.
Kephart Prong Trail
Smokemont Loop Trail
Caldwell Fork Trail
Oconaluftee R.
Clingmans Dome
Newfound Gap Rd.
Smokemont Baptist Church
Balsam Mountain
Heintooga Overlook
Boogerman Trail
Collins Creek
Tow String
Clingmans Dome Tr.
Visitor Center
Big Cove Rd.
Heintooga Ridge Rd.
Flat Creek Trail
Mingus Mill
441
Andrews Bald 5,920
Mile High Overlook
Maggie Valley
Forney Ridge Trail
Oconaluftee Valley
Big Witch Overlook
Indian Creek Falls
Visitor Center
Mountain Farm Museum
Blue Ridge Parkway
Three Waterfalls Loop
CHEROKEE INDIAN RESERVATION
Cherokee
Oconaluftee Valley Overlook
19
Juney Whank Falls Trail
Waterrock Knob
Deep Creek
Bryson City
Visitor Center
441
23
74
Dillsboro
Sylva
23
28
NANTAHALA NATIONAL FOREST
KEY
Ranger Station /Information
Campground
Picnic Area
Horseback Riding
Scenic Viewpoint
Appalachian Trail
Walking/ Hiking Trails
28
23
0
5 mi
0
5 km
28
23
Franklin

Hotels

Other than campgrounds, there are no lodging options on the North Carolina side of the park. The closest accommodations are in Cherokee.

Restaurants

There are numerous picnic areas but no food service on the North Carolina side of the park. The visitor centers have some beverage vending machines.

Sights

The North Carolina side of the park provides a great variety of sights and experiences, from high peaks to historical houses. Near the Oconaluftee Visitor Center is the Mountain Farm Museum, one of the best-preserved collections of historic log buildings in the region. If you're interested in wildlife, Cataloochee is a beautiful valley where you can spot deer, wild turkey, and even elk. Even if you never leave your car, Newfound Gap Road offers plenty of scenic views. And if you're ready to lace up your hiking boots, there are hundreds of miles of hiking trails to be explored, from short walks near Bryson City to the Appalachian Trail, which skims 72 miles of the ridges along the North Carolina–Tennessee border.

HISTORIC SIGHTS

★ Cataloochee Valley

HISTORIC SIGHT | FAMILY | This is one of the most memorable and eeriest sights in all of the Smokies. At one time Cataloochee was a community of more than 1,200 people. After the land was annexed for the national park in 1934, the community dispersed. Although many of the original buildings are gone, more than a dozen houses, cabins, barns, and churches still stand. You can visit the Palmer Methodist Chapel, the Beech Grove School, and the Woody, Caldwell, and Messer homesteads. You have a good chance of spotting elk here, especially in the evening and early morning. You'll also likely see wild turkeys, deer, and perhaps bears. Cataloochee is one of the most remote parts of the Smokies, reachable by car via a narrow, winding gravel road that rises over a steep pass before dropping you into the isolated valley. Take the 5 mph speed limit seriously on the blind curves. At dawn and dusk, this uncrowded valley is pure beautiful magic. ✉ *Cove*

A water-powered turbine, rather than the more common wheel, grinds grain at the 19th-century Mingus Mill.

Creek Rd., off Rte. 276, Great Smoky Mountains National Park ☎ *865/436–1200* 🌐 *www.nps.gov/grsm* 🎫 *Free* 🕐 *Often closed in winter due to snow and ice.*

Mingus Mill

HISTORIC SIGHT | FAMILY | In the late 19th century this was a state-of-the-art gristmill, with two large grist stones powered by a store-bought turbine rather than a hand-built wheel. From mid-March to just after Thanksgiving, you can watch the miller make cornmeal and even buy a pound of it. ✉ *U.S. 441, Great Smoky Mountains National Park* ✥ *2 miles north of Cherokee* ☎ *865/436–1200* 🌐 *www.nps.gov/grsm/planyourvisit/mfm.htm* 🎫 *Free* 🕐 *Closed late Nov.–mid-Mar.*

★ Mountain Farm Museum

MUSEUM VILLAGE | FAMILY | This is perhaps the best re-creation anywhere of an Appalachian mountain farmstead. The nine farm buildings, all dating from the late 19th century, were moved in the 1950s to this site next to the Oconaluftee Visitor Center from various locations within the park. Besides a furnished two-story chestnut log cabin, there is a barn, apple house, corncrib, smokehouse, bee gums, springhouse, chicken coop, and other outbuildings. In season, corn, tomatoes, pole beans, squash, and other mountain crops are grown in the garden, and the park staff sometimes puts on demonstrations of pioneer activities, such as making apple butter and molasses. Two easy 1½-mile walking

Standing silent for more than a century, Palmer Methodist Chapel is one of the most moving sights in the Cataloochee Valley.

trails begin near the museum. Dogs on leashes are allowed on the trail but not within the farm grounds. Elk are sometimes seen grazing in the pastures adjoining the farm, and occasionally you may see white-tailed deer and wild turkeys. ■ **TIP→ This is an extremely popular place to visit, but in the evening after the visitor center closes, you're likely to have it to yourself.** ✉ *Oconaluftee Visitor Center, U.S. 441, Great Smoky Mountains National Park* ⊕ *1½ miles from Cherokee* ☎ *865/436–1200* 🌐 *www.nps.gov/grsm/planyourvisit/mfm.htm* 🎟 *Free.*

Proctor

HISTORIC SIGHT | Once a thriving lumber and copper mining town on Hazel Creek, Proctor has mostly been taken over by nature. Among the structures remaining are the white-frame Calhoun House, probably built in the early 1900s; the foundations of a church and of several other buildings; and bridges over Hazel Creek. About half a mile away is the Proctor cemetery. Proctor is best reached by boat across Fontana Lake. After arriving on the north shore of the lake, it's a short walk to the site of the old town. Fontana Marina offers daily boat transport across the lake. ✉ *Great Smoky Mountains National Park* ☎ *828/498–2017 for Fontana Marina* 🌐 *www.nps.gov/grsm/learn/historyculture/people.htm.*

Road to Nowhere

SCENIC DRIVE | **FAMILY** | Lakeview Drive was originally proposed as a way for local communities to reach their family cemeteries, after

Cataloochee, the Novel

Asheville native Wayne Caldwell's 2007 novel, *Cataloochee*, tells the story of three generations of mountain families in Cataloochee Valley. They came to this distant beautiful cove in search of a hardscrabble version of Eden. Some may have found it, but the idyll was not to last. As the government took steps to relocate the settlers out of Cataloochee to make room for Great Smoky Mountain National Park, a tragic act of violence touches the families.

Toward the end of the novel, a preacher at the Baptist church in Little Cataloochee says, "I heard Brother Smith over in Big Cataloochee preached about this land being Eden. I hope you see fit to forgive him, even if he is a Methodist. Because, Lord, this is pretty country right enough, but mankind tamed this forest and grubbed out these pastures, and that don't make it Paradise. You made Eden once and that's it."

being displaced from their homes for the Fontana Dam project in the 1940s. An environmental issue halted the construction of Lakeview Drive, earning it its nickname as the "Road to Nowhere." Today, the road begins at the park's entrance from Fontana Road in Bryson City, and ends at a tunnel six miles into the park. The drive is quite scenic, with an overlook of Fontana Lake and a few trailheads along the way. A network of hiking trails (including a 3.2-mile loop) begin at the tunnel. ⚠ **It's surprisingly dark and eerie in the tunnel, especially if you're there alone. If you end a loop hike at the tunnel and don't want to walk through it, there's a bypass trail.** ✉ *Lakeview Dr., Great Smoky Mountains National Park* ☎ *865/436–1200* 🌐 *www.nps.gov/grsm.*

Smokemont Baptist Church

CHURCH | Also known as the Oconaluftee Baptist Church, Smokemont Baptist Church is all that remains of the once-thriving lumbering community of Smokemont. Founded in 1832 and rebuilt in 1916, the church was added to the National Register of Historic Places in 1976. To get to this graceful white-frame church, turn off Newfound Gap Road at the Smokemont Campground, cross the Oconaluftee, and park in the area just past the bridge. The church is across the road and up the hill. An old cemetery, the Bradley Cemetery, is nearby. ✉ *Newfound Gap Rd., MM 17.2, Great Smoky Mountains National Park* ☎ *865/426–1200* 🌐 *www.nps.gov/grsm.*

PICNIC AREAS

★ Big Creek Picnic Area

BODY OF WATER | FAMILY | This is the smallest picnic area in the park, with only 10 picnic tables. The creek is wide and inviting, with small swimming holes and several channels that create tiny islands. The picnic area is accessible via Exit 451 off of Interstate 40 or the unpaved Cove Creek Road from Cataloochee. There's a small campground here and restrooms but no pavilion. Several good hiking trails begin here, and the Appalachian Trail crosses the road near the entrance at Davenport Gap. ✉ *Off I–40 at Exit 451, Great Smoky Mountains National Park* ☎ *865/436–1200* 🌐 *www.nps.gov/grsm.*

Collins Creek Picnic Area

OTHER ATTRACTION | FAMILY | The largest developed picnic area in the park, Collins Creek has 182 picnic tables. Collins Creek, which runs near the picnic area, is a small stream with above-average trout fishing (license required). The site has restrooms with flush toilets, potable water, and a 70-seat pavilion for groups that can be reserved in advance for $32. ✉ *Newfound Gap Rd., MM 25.4, Great Smoky Mountains National Park* ✥ *About 8 miles from Cherokee* ☎ *865/436–1200* 🌐 *www.nps.gov/grsm* ⏲ *Closed late Oct.–late Mar.*

★ Deep Creek Picnic Area

BODY OF WATER | FAMILY | Deep Creek offers more than picnicking. You can go tubing (rent a tube for the day for around $5 or $6 at nearby commercial tubing centers), hike about two miles to three pretty waterfalls, or go trout fishing. You can even go mountain biking here, as this is one of the few park trails where bikes are allowed. The picnic area, open year-round (but no running water in winter), has 58 picnic tables, plus a pavilion that seats up to 70 (reserve in advance, $32 fee). There's also a campground here. ✉ *1912 E. Deep Creek Rd., Great Smoky Mountains National Park* ☎ *865/436–1200* 🌐 *www.nps.gov/grsm.*

★ Heintooga Picnic Area

VIEWPOINT | FAMILY | Located at more than a mile high and set in a stand of spruce and fir, the picnic area has 41 tables. Nearby is Mile High Overlook, which offers one of the most scenic views of the Smokies and is a wonderful place to enjoy the sunset. For birders, this is a good spot to see golden-crowned kinglets, red-breasted nuthatches, and other species that prefer higher elevations. Nearby are a campground and trailheads for several good hiking trails, including Flat Creek. The disadvantage is that, due to the high elevation (and the risk of snow and ice), the picnic area is open only from late May to mid-October. ✉ *Heintooga Ridge Rd., Great Smoky Mountains National Park* ☎ *865/436–1200* 🌐 *www.nps.gov/grsm* ⏲ *Closed mid-Oct.–late May.*

SCENIC DRIVES

Heintooga Ridge Road–Balsam Mountain Road

SCENIC DRIVE | Begin this drive near mile marker 458 of the Blue Ridge Parkway, about 11 miles from Cherokee. Travel about 8 miles along the paved Heintooga Ridge Road, a mile-high drive that is lined with evergreens. At this elevation, you're often literally in the clouds. Near the Heintooga Picnic Area, take the narrow, unpaved 18-mile Balsam Mountain Road, sometimes called Roundbottom Road. Although it's only one lane wide and has many sharp curves, Balsam Mountain Road is well-maintained and does not require a four-wheel-drive vehicle. Travel trailers and other large vehicles are prohibited. The roadside scenery changes from firs and hemlocks as you descend from Balsam Mountain to the lowlands around Cherokee. There is a profusion of flowers along Balsam Mountain Road especially in the spring. If you tire of driving, there are plenty of nearby trails, including the 11-mile Balsam Mountain Trail and 3.3-mile Palmer Creek Trail. Another 12 miles on Big Cove Road, mostly through rural areas outside the park, gets you back to Cherokee. ✉ *Heintooga Ridge Rd., off Blue Ridge Pkwy., Great Smoky Mountains National Park.*

Newfound Gap Road

SCENIC DRIVE | **FAMILY** | Newfound Gap Road (U.S. 441) is by far the busiest road on the national park's North Carolina side, with more than a million vehicles making the 16-mile climb from an elevation of 2,000 feet near Cherokee to almost a mile high at Newfound Gap (and then down to Gatlinburg on the Tennessee side). It's the only paved road that goes all the way through the center of the park, so you definitely won't escape from the crowds. Mile markers run backward (as far as North Carolinians are concerned), starting at 31.1 where it intersects with the Blue Ridge Parkway near Cherokee. Among the sights on the road are the Oconaluftee Visitor Center and Mountain Farm Museum (mile marker 30.3); Mingus Mill (mile marker 29.9); Smokemont Campground and Nature Trail (mile marker 27.2); Web Overlook (mile marker 17.7), from which there's a good view almost due west of Clingmans Dome; and Newfound Gap (mile marker 14.7), the start of the seven-mile road to Clingmans Dome. The speed limit on Newfound Gap Road tops out at 45 mph. ✉ *Newfound Gap Rd., off Blue Ridge Pkwy., Great Smoky Mountains National Park* ☎ *865/436–1200* 🌐 *www.nps.gov/grsm/planyourvisit/nfg.htm.*

Did You Know?

An open-sided barn, a blacksmith shop, and a sorghum mill are among the beautifully preserved agricultural buildings at Mountain Farm Museum.

SCENIC STOPS

Big Witch Overlook

VIEWPOINT | **FAMILY** | This overlook on the Blue Ridge Parkway offers fine views of the eastern side of the Smokies, and in May and June the roadsides bloom with rosebay rhododendron. ✉ *Blue Ridge Pkwy., MM 461.9, Great Smoky Mountains National Park* ☎ *828/298–0398* 🌐 *www.nps.gov/blri.*

★ Cataloochee Valley Overlook

VIEWPOINT | This is a great spot to take in the broad expanse of Cataloochee Valley. Cataloochee comes from a Cherokee word meaning "row upon row" or "standing in rows," and indeed you'll see rows of mountain ridges here. The overlook is well marked and has a split-rail fence. ✉ *Cataloochee Entrance Rd., Great Smoky Mountains National Park* ☎ *865/436–1200* 🌐 *www.nps.gov/grsm.*

Heintooga Overlook

VIEWPOINT | One of the best spots to watch the sunset, Heintooga Overlook has sweeping views westward of the crest of the Great Smokies. ✉ *Heintooga Ridge Rd., Great Smoky Mountains National Park* ☎ *865/436–1200* 🌐 *www.nps.gov/grsm* ⏲ *Closed Nov.–late May.*

★ Newfound Gap Overlook

VIEWPOINT | At 5,048 feet, Newfound Gap is a drivable pass through the top of the park and provides excellent views of a broad swath of the Smokies. The ridge at Newfound Gap marks the North Carolina–Tennessee state line. If you want to say you've been on the Appalachian Trail, it's a short and easy walk away here. Franklin Delano Roosevelt officially dedicated the park at this site in 1940. ✉ *Newfound Gap Rd., MM 14.7, Great Smoky Mountains National Park* ☎ *865/436–1200* 🌐 *www.nps.gov/grsm.*

Oconaluftee Valley Overlook

VIEWPOINT | **FAMILY** | From atop the Thomas Divide, just a little below the crest of the Smokies, you can look down at winding Newfound Gap Road. This is also a good spot to view the sunrise. ✉ *Newfound Gap Rd., MM 15.4, Great Smoky Mountains National Park* ☎ *865/436–1200* 🌐 *www.nps.gov/grsm.*

TRAILS

★ Andrews Bald

TRAIL | From the Clingmans Dome parking, taking the trail less traveled to Andrews Bald feels like being in on a secret. To get there, walk the 1.8-mile Forney Ridge Trail, a rocky path with an elevation gain of almost 600 feet. The payoff is several acres of grassy bald at more than 5,800 feet, with stunning views of Fontana Lake and the southeastern Smokies. This is one of only two balds in the Smokies that the park service keeps clear (the other is Gregory Bald). *Difficult.* ✉ *Clingmans Dome Visitor Center, Clingmans Dome Rd., Great Smoky Mountains National Park* ☎ *865/436–1200* 🌐 *www.nps.gov/grsm/planyourvisit/forney-ridge-project-overview.htm.*

Flat Creek Trail

TRAIL | FAMILY | This is one of the hidden gems in the park. It's a little known but delightful hike, especially in summer when the higher elevation means respite from stifling temperatures. The 2.6-mile path stretches through pretty woodlands with evergreens, birch, rhododendron, and wildflowers. The elevation gain is about 570 feet. *Moderate.* ✉ *Heintooga Ridge Rd., MM 5.4, Great Smoky Mountains National Park* ☎ *865/436–1200* 🌐 *www.nps.gov/grsm* ☞ *Heintooga Ridge Rd. closed Nov.–late May.*

★ **Gregory Bald**

TRAIL | From almost 5,000 feet on Gregory Bald, you have a breathtaking view of Cades Cove and Rich Mountain to the north and Fontana Lake to the southeast. Gregory Bald is one of only two balds in the Smokies that are kept clear of tree growth by the Park Service. This is a view that just a few thousand people a year will see, as it's reachable only by a strenuous 11.2-mile roundtrip hike via the Gregory Ridge Trail, with 2,700 feet of elevation gain. The trailhead is at the end of Forge Creek Road in Cades Cove. In early summer, this difficult hike through old-growth forests to Gregory Bald offers an astounding display of hybrid flame azaleas. *Difficult.* ✉ *Forge Creek Rd., Great Smoky Mountains National Park* ☎ *865/436–1200* 🌐 *www.nps.gov/grsm.*

Kephart Prong Trail

TRAIL | A 4.2-mile round-trip woodland trail named for Horace Kephart, a writer and early promoter of the park, wanders beside a stream to the remains of a Civilian Conservation Corps camp. Close by, the trail takes a moderate slope to Mt. Kephart, gaining over 900 feet in elevation. *Moderate.* ✉ *Newfound Gap Rd., Great Smoky Mountains National Park* ✣ *5 miles north of Smokemont Campground* ☎ *865/436–1200* 🌐 *www.nps.gov/grsm.*

Lakeshore Trail

TRAIL | This hike begins with a boat ride across the lake from Fontana Marina. Your captain will give you directions on how to get from the docking point to the trailhead. A half-mile on the Lakeshore Trail will take you to the old lumber and mining town of Proctor. From there, walk 4.4 miles to Eagle Creek, where you can get picked up by the ferry or continue hiking. It's 5.2 miles more on the Lakeshore Trail to Fontana Dam, or you can climb the 2.7 miles up the Lost Cove Trail to Shuckstack, a peak with a climbable fire tower and sensational views of Fontana Lake. Then it's a 3.7-mile descent on the Appalachian Trail to the dam. *Moderate to Difficult.* ✉ *Great Smoky Mountains National Park* ✣ *Trailhead near Backcountry Campsite 86* ☎ *828/498–2129 for boat reservations* 🌐 *www.nps.gov/grsm.*

Little Cataloochee Trail

TRAIL | No other hike in the Smokies offers a cultural and historic experience quite like this one. In the early 20th century, Cataloochee Cove had the largest population of any place in the Smokies, around 1,200 people. Most of the original structures have been torn down or have succumbed to the elements, but a few historic frame buildings remain along this remote trail. Some have been restored by the park staff, such as the Cook Log Cabin near Davidson Gap, an apple house, and a church. You'll see several of these, along with rock walls and other artifacts, on the Little Cataloochee Trail. The trail is six miles each way, including a mile-long section of Pretty Hollow Gap Trail. Allow at least six hours for this hike. *Moderate.* ✉ *Little Cataloochee Trailhead, Old Cataloochee Tpke., Great Smoky Mountains National Park* ☎ *865/436–1200* 🌐 *www.nps.gov/grsm/planyourvisit/cataloochee.htm.*

★ Mt. Sterling

TRAIL | A 5.4-mile round-trip hike takes you to an old fire watchtower, rewarding you with amazing views. The route is steep, with an elevation gain of almost 2,000 feet, so you should consider this a strenuous challenging hike. *Difficult.* ✉ *Mt. Sterling Gap, Old Cataloochee Tpke., Great Smoky Mountains National Park* ☎ *865/436–1200* 🌐 *www.nps.gov/grsm.*

Smokemont Loop Trail

TRAIL | A 6.1-mile round-trip loop takes you by streams and, in spring and summer, lots of wildflowers, including trailing arbutus. At Smokemont Campground near Cherokee, this is an easy trail to access. The only downside is that there are no long-range views. *Moderate.* ✉ *Smokemont Campground, Newfound Gap Rd., Great Smoky Mountains National Park* ☎ *865/436–1200* 🌐 *www.nps.gov/grsm.*

★ Three Waterfalls Loop

TRAIL | **FAMILY** | For the effort of a 2.4-mile hike at the Deep Creek entrance to the park near Bryson City, this trail will reward you with three pretty waterfalls: Tom Branch, Indian Creek, and Juney Whank, which you can see close-up from a 90-foot-long wooden bridge that crosses directly over the falls. *Moderate.* ✉ *Deep*

Creek Rd., Great Smoky Mountains National Park ⊕ Near Bryson City entrance ☎ 865/436–1200 🌐 www.nps.gov/grsm ⊙ Campground closed Nov.–mid-Apr.

Twentymile Loop Trail

TRAIL | The national park's Twentymile entrance on the northern side of Cheoah Lake is its most difficult to reach, and thus the least crowded. This is an incredible area of the park, especially during spring when the flowers and wild azaleas bloom. An easily manageable 7.2-mile loop follows old logging roads along Twentymile Creek and Moore Springs Branch, connecting via the Twentymile Loop Trail. The elevation gain is minimal, but the solitude and serenity found along the creeks (there are multiple swimming holes) is a local secret. *Moderate.* ✉ *Great Smoky Mountains National Park ⊕ Via NC-28, 3 miles east from Tail of the Dragon.*

VISITOR CENTERS

★ Oconaluftee Visitor Center

VISITOR CENTER | FAMILY | The park's main information center on the North Carolina side is polished and inviting after a $3 million renovation and expansion. It is 1½ miles from Cherokee and offers interactive displays, a 20-minute film, a large book and gift shop, ranger-led programs, and assistance from helpful volunteers. There are restrooms and vending machines. Adjoining the visitor center, in a large level field next to the Oconaluftee River, is the Mountain Farm Museum, a reconstruction of an early 1900s mountain farmstead. Herds of elk are often seen here. ✉ *Newfound Gap Rd., MM 30.3, Great Smoky Mountains National Park* ☎ *865/436–1200.*

Activities

BICYCLING

The North Carolina side of the Smokies offers excellent cycling, and bicycles are permitted on most roads. Avoid Newfound Gap Road, which can be clogged with vehicular traffic. Instead, head to the (mostly) paved roads of Lakeview Drive—the so-called Road to Nowhere near Bryson City—and the Cataloochee Valley. Balsam Mountain Road and Cove Creek Road also offer pleasant biking with very little auto traffic. Since these roads are unpaved, with mostly gravel surfaces, you should use a mountain bike or an all-terrain hybrid. Helmets are not required in the park, but are strongly recommended. There are bike rental shops in Cherokee and Bryson City.

Did You Know?

Each turn of Newfound Gap Road reveals another stunning vista of the Oconaluftee River Valley.

Avoid the Crowds

Great Smoky Mountains gets twice as many visitors as any other national park. It's hard to commune with nature while you're searching for a parking place, dodging group photos, and stepping out of the way of strollers. However, this scenario is likely to occur only when fall foliage is at its brightest (October to early November) and on sunny weekends in July and August. Your best bet to beat the crowds is to visit during the spring, late summer, and even winter seasons. Any time of year, weekday crowds will be smaller than weekend ones.

Another trick is to avoid Newfound Gap Road, the main road through the park. Even if you want to stay in your car, back roads such as Balsam Mountain Road and Cove Creek Road have almost no traffic, even at peak times. In fact, you can usually drive for miles and not see another vehicle. Note that these back roads are generally unpaved, may be one-way, and might be closed in winter. From these windy routes, once you step onto a hiking trail, solitude is almost guaranteed.

BOATING

Fontana Lake

BOATING | FAMILY | Covering around 12,000 acres, Fontana Lake borders the southern edge of the Great Smokies. Unlike most other nearby lakes, Fontana's shoreline is almost completely undeveloped, since about 90% of it is owned by the federal government. Fishing here is excellent, especially for smallmouth bass, muskie, and walleye. On the downside, the Tennessee Valley Authority generates power at Fontana Dam, sometimes lowering the water level. Completed in 1944, the dam is the highest concrete dam east of the Rockies at 480 feet. The dam's visitor center gets about 50,000 visitors a year. The Appalachian Trail crosses the top of the dam. ✉ *Fontana Dam Visitor Center, 71 Fontana Dam Rd., Great Smoky Mountains National Park* ✥ *3 miles from Fontana Village off N.C. 28* ☎ *865/498–2234* 🌐 *www.visitnc.com/listing/UHdY/fontana-dam-visitors-center* ☞ *Visitor center closed Nov.–Mar.*

Fontana Marina

BOATING | FAMILY | Boat rentals—including kayaks, canoes, pontoon boats, and paddleboards—are available at Fontana Marina. The marina runs a shuttle service across the lake twice daily and can drop hikers, anglers, and campers at Hazel Creek, Eagle Creek, Pilkey Creek, Kirkland Branch, and other north-shore locations.

The footbridge is the perfect place to take in Juney Whank Falls, one of the trio of stunning sights along Three Waterfalls Trail.

A 90-minute tour aboard the *Miss Hazel* pontoon boat—grab a drink at the marina before you board—is an affordable and worthy excursion for an overview of the area's natural and human history. ✉ *300 Woods Rd., Great Smoky Mountains National Park* ✥ *Off N.C. 28 N* ☎ *828/498–2017* 🌐 *fontanavillage.com/marina* 🕙 *Closed Nov.–Apr.* ☞ *Shuttles to Hazel Creek $50 per person.*

CAMPING

All five developed campgrounds—Balsam Mountain, Big Creek, Cataloochee, Deep Creek, and Smokemont—require reservations. Only Smokemont is open year-round. Reservations are $30.

Balsam Mountain Campground. If you like camping among the evergreens, tent-only Balsam Mountain is for you. It's the highest campground in the park, at more than 5,300 feet. You may want to warm up in the evening with a campfire, even in summer. Due to its remote location off the Blue Ridge Parkway, this 64-site campground is rarely full, even on peak weekends. It's closed mid-October though late May. ✉ *Near end of Heintooga Ridge Rd., Cherokee* ☎ *865/436–1200* 🌐 *www.nps.gov/grsm/planyourvisit/balsam-mountain.htm.*

Big Creek Campground. With just a dozen campsites, Big Creek is the smallest campground in the park. This is a walk-in, not hike-in, campground. Five of the 12 sites sit beside Big Creek, which offers good swimming and fishing. Carefully observe bear protection rules, as a number have been spotted nearby. It's closed November through March. ✉ *Cove Creek Rd.,*

Newport ☎ *865/436–1200* 🌐 *www.nps.gov/grsm/planyourvisit/camping-at-big-creek.htm.*

Cataloochee Campground. The appeal of this 27-site campground is its location in the beautiful and historical Cataloochee Valley. Take care driving into the valley; Cove Creek Road is narrow with sharp curves, and in some places you hug the mountainside. It's closed late October through late March. ✉ *Cataloochee Valley, Cove Creek Rd., Waynesville* ☎ *877/444–6777* 🌐 *wwww.nps.gov/grsm/planyourvisit/cataloochee-campground.htm.*

Deep Creek Campground. This campground at the Bryson City entrance to the park is near the most popular tubing spot on the North Carolina side of the Smokies. There are also several swimming holes. Of the 92 sites here, 42 are for tents only. It's closed late October through late March. ✉ *1912 E. Deep Creek Rd., Bryson City* ☎ *865/436–1200* 🌐 *www.nps.gov/grsm/planyourvisit/deep-creek-campground.htm.*

Smokemont Campground. With 142 sites (98 for tents and 44 for RVs), Smokemont is the largest campground on the North Carolina side of the park. Some of the campsites are a little too close together, but the sites themselves are spacious. ✉ *Off Newfound Gap Rd., 6 miles north of Cherokee* ☎ *877/444–6777* 🌐 *www.nps.gov/grsm/planyourvisit/smokemont-campground.htm.*

EDUCATIONAL PROGRAMS

Discover the flora, fauna, and mountain culture of the Smokies with scheduled ranger programs and nature walks.

Interpretive Ranger Programs

HIKING & WALKING | FAMILY | The National Park Service organizes activities like daily guided hikes and talks from spring to fall. The programs vary widely, from presentations on mountain culture, blacksmithing, and old-time fiddle and banjo music to tours through historical areas of the park. Many of the programs are suitable for older children as well as adults. The Oconaluftee Visitor Center is a good place to learn about park events. ✉ *Great Smoky Mountains National Park* ☎ *865/436–1200* 🌐 *www.nps.gov/grca/planyourvisit/ranger-program.htm.*

Junior Ranger Program

HIKING & WALKING | FAMILY | Children ages 5 to 12 can take part in these hands-on educational programs. Kids can pick up a Junior Ranger booklet at the Oconaluftee Visitor Center. Spring through fall the park offers many age-appropriate demonstrations, classes, and programs, such as Stream Splashin', Critters and Crawlies, and—our favorite—Whose Poop's on My Boots? For kids 13 and older (including adults), look for events in the park's Not-So-Junior-Ranger Program. ✉ *Great Smoky Mountains National Park* ☎ *865/436–1200* 🌐 *www.nps.gov/grsm/learn/kidsyouth/beajunior-ranger.htm.*

FISHING

The North Carolina side of the Smokies has one of the best wild trout fisheries in the East. It has more than 1,000 miles of streams, and all are open to fishing year-round except Bear Creek where it meets Forney Creek. Native brook trout thrive in colder high-elevation streams, while brown and rainbow trout (not native but now widely present in the region) can live in somewhat warmer waters. Among the best trout streams on this side of the park are Deep Creek, Big Creek, Cataloochee Creek, Palmer Creek, Twentymile Creek, Raven Fork, Hazel Creek, and Noland Creek. Fishing licenses are available online at 🌐 *www.ncwildlife.org.*

To fish in the Cherokee Reservation (Qualla Boundary), everyone over 12 needs a separate tribal permit, available at 🌐 *ebcis.sovsportsnet.net*

North Carolina Wildlife Resources Commission

FISHING | You can order a North Carolina inland fishing license—valid throughout the park—online or at local fishing shops. A 10-day nonresident inland fishing license is $23, while an annual license is $45. North Carolina residents pay $9 for a 10-day license and $25 for an annual license. To fish for trout outside the park, you'll also need a trout stamp, which costs an extra $8 for three days for both North Carolina residents and non-residents. ✉ *1751 Varsity Dr., Raleigh, NC 27606* ☎ *833/950-0575* Hunting and fishing licenses 🌐 *ncwildlife.org.*

HIKING

Great Smoky Mountains National Park has over 800 miles of hiking trails, about equally divided between the North Carolina and Tennessee sides. The trails range from short nature walks to long, strenuous hikes that gain several thousand feet in elevation. Most hikers gravitate toward popular trails like Alum Cave and the Road to Nowhere, but take a chance on a lesser-known walk and you'll likely have the trail to yourself. The Little Cataloochee Trail is a favorite, but Flat Creek and Smokemont Loop are also extraordinary hikes.

Although permits are not required for day hikes, you must have a backcountry permit for overnight trips.

What's in a Name?

The Smoky Mountains have more than their fair share of odd and funny place names. Here are a few on the North Carolina side.

Bee Gum Branch, Noland Creek. A bee gum is a homemade bee hive, usually made from a hollowed-out black gum tree.

Big Butt, Luftee Knob. A "butt", in local vernacular, is a hillock or a broken-off end of a ridge. This one is pretty big.

Bone Valley, Hazel Creek. Named after the bones of cattle that froze to death in a spring snowstorm in 1888.

Boogerman Trail, Cataloochee. Named after Robert Palmer, who was nicknamed "Boogerman." The story goes that on his first day of school, little Robert was asked his name by the teacher to which he replied, "the boogerman" (or bogeyman), and the name stuck.

Fodderstack Rock, Thunderhead Mountain. Named after the rock's resemblance to a stack of chopped cornstalks or hay, called livestock fodder.

Hell Ridge, Luftee Knob. The ridge was logged, burned, and badly eroded.

Killpecker Ridge, Thunderhead Mountain. Named after the nickname given to the newest man on a logging crew, who tended to tire himself out chopping (or peckering) before he learned to pace himself.

Maggot Spring Branch, Bunches Bald. Named for small white worms that live in some cold mountain springs (they're not actually maggots).

Paw Paw Creek, Thunderhead Mountain. Named for the American pawpaw (*Asimina triloba*), a small tree that produces a large yellow-green berry.

Sweet Heifer Creek, Clingmans Dome. This refers to the young cows driven up these steep trails to summer pasture.

Twentymile, Fontana. Named because it was 20 miles from the town of Bushnell, now under the waters of Fontana Lake.

HORSEBACK RIDING

Get back to nature and away from the crowds with a horseback ride through the forest. Guided horseback rides are offered at Smokemont. Rides are at a walking pace, so they are suitable for even inexperienced riders.

Smokemont Riding Stable

HORSEBACK RIDING | FAMILY | The emphasis here is on a family-friendly horseback-riding experience, suitable even for novice riders. Choose either the one-hour trail ride or a 2½-hour waterfall ride. If you don't feel like saddling up, Smokemont also offers wagon rides. ✉ *135 Smokemont Riding Stable Rd., Great Smoky Mountains National Park* ✣ *Off U.S. 441* ☎ *828/497–2373* 🌐 *smokemontridingstable.com* ⏲ *Closed mid-Nov.–early Mar.* ☞ *1-hr rides $45.*

TUBING

On a hot summer's day there's nothing like hitting the water. On the North Carolina side, you can swim or go tubing on Deep Creek near Bryson City. The upper section is a little wild and woolly, with white water flowing from cold mountain springs. The lower section of Deep Creek is more suitable for kids. There are several tubing outfitters near the entrance to the park at Deep Creek. Some have changing rooms and showers. Wear a swimsuit and bring towels and dry clothes to change into. Most outfitters are open April through October. ⚠ **This isn't your usual lazy river tube trip! There's no shuttle, so you carry your tube up the creek. Several of the chutes above the campground include fun but eye-raising drops.**

Smoky Mountain Campground

WATER SPORTS | FAMILY | Just outside the Bryson City Entrance to the national park, look for a rustic structure with "TUBES" in huge red letters across the roof. This commercial operation rents tubes and sells camping supplies. It also has a campground and rental cabins. ✉ *1840 W. Deep Creek Rd., Great Smoky Mountains National Park* ☎ *828/488–3302* 🌐 *www.smokymtncampground.com* ⏲ *Closed Nov.–Mar.*

Chapter 5

5

THE TENNESSEE GATEWAYS

Updated by
Stratton Lawrence

Sights	Restaurants	Hotels	Shopping	Nightlife
★★★★☆	★★★★☆	★★★★☆	★★★☆☆	★★★☆☆

WELCOME TO THE TENNESSEE GATEWAYS

TOP REASONS TO GO

★ **Family-Friendly Fun.** Sevierville and Pigeon Forge offer an endless array of mini golf, go-kart tracks, and thrill rides.

★ **Ride to the Mountaintops.** Three competing chairlift, trams, and gondola rides whisk you to scenic vistas in Gatlinburg.

★ **Southern Appalachian Cuisine.** Chef-driven restaurants elevate locally grown produce and mountain favorites like trout.

★ **Five-Star Relaxation.** The sleepy destination of Townsend is worlds away from the faster pace across the mountains.

★ **Water Parks Galore.** The waterslides keep getting taller and faster in splashy Pigeon Forge.

1 Knoxville. The quintessential college city, Knoxville's culture is rooted in its history yet feels modern and alive.

2 Sevierville. A revitalized walkable downtown now boasts many of the area's best restaurants.

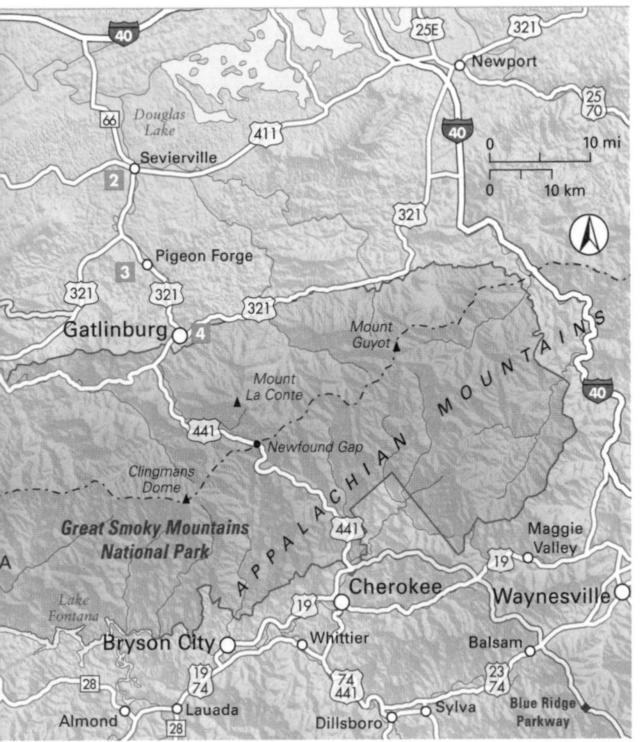

3 **Pigeon Forge.** The mountains are an afterthought in this brightly lit strip of amusement parks, outlet malls, dinner theaters, and theme restaurants.

4 **Gatlinburg.** Set in a gorgeous mountain valley, Gatlinburg is a classic tourist town that manages to retain a kitschy charm.

5 **Townsend.** If you came to the Smokies to hike, fish, or float down the river, laid-back Townsend offers easy access to nature.

When you're exploring the Tennessee side of Great Smoky Mountains National Park, chances are you won't actually be staying within its borders. Most visitors opt for one of the touristy towns just outside the major gateways: Gatlinburg, Pigeon Forge, and Sevierville are boisterous, while Townsend is a bit quieter. Those in the know escape the crowds a bit farther away in the college town of Knoxville.

Set in the foothills of the Great Smokies, Knoxville is about an hour from the western entrances to the park. There are numerous museums, a thriving dining scene, and a lovely downtown filled with public art. The University of Tennessee campus, home to more than 28,000 students, is just west of downtown and includes Neyland Stadium, one of the largest college football stadiums in the United States. If you're in Knoxville on a fall weekend when the Volunteers have a home game, the city will be a sea of bright orange.

Close to the park, Gatlinburg is a compact chunk of everything you'd expect in a town built on tourism, with a panoply of candy shops, gift stores, and flashy restaurants lining the walkable main street. A chairlift and tramway take visitors to the tops of nearby peaks. Millions visit Gatlinburg each year, and some 600,000 of them are here to get married (no blood test or waiting period required, and the 15 wedding chapels accept walk-ins), making the Gatlinburg area the "Wedding Capital of the South."

About seven miles northwest, Pigeon Forge isn't the quaint village that the name suggests. It sprawls along a multilane parkway lined with motels, go-kart tracks, video game arcades, fudge shops, comedy theaters, and Las Vegas–inspired architecture (but without the gambling). In the summer and fall tourist season, Pigeon Forge's population of around 6,000 can swell tenfold to more than 60,000.

Sevierville, the next town over, is constantly adding new tourist attractions and taking down old ones. Townsend, about 18 miles southwest of Pigeon Forge, feels like a throwback to a quieter era. It's much smaller and less developed and calls itself the "peaceful side of the Smokies."

Planning

Hotels

In the larger communities around the mountains, such as Knoxville, Gatlinburg, and Pigeon Forge, you can find the usual chain motels and hotels. For more of a local flavor, look at the many mountain lodges and country inns—some with just a few rooms with simple comforts and others with upmarket amenities like tennis courts, golf courses, and spas.

Restaurants

Although restaurants in Gatlinburg and Pigeon Forge put the emphasis on inexpensive meals that appeal to middle-of-the-road tastes, some cooks in eastern Tennessee—many of whom are products of the lauded Blackberry Farm resort—are offering more sophisticated fare. You can find nearly every world cuisine somewhere in the region, and plenty of spots still offer authentic mountain food like Smoky Mountain trout, often served family-style.

⇨ *Hotel prices in the reviews are the lowest cost of a standard double room in high season. Restaurant prices in the reviews are the average cost of a main course at dinner, or if dinner is not served, at lunch.*

What It Costs

$	$$	$$$	$$$$
RESTAURANTS			
under $15	$15–$25	$26–$235	over $35
HOTELS			
under $150	$150–$225	$226–$300	over $300

Knoxville

45 miles northwest of the Gatlinburg entrance to Great Smoky Mountains National Park.

Arriving in Knoxville after a few days in tourist-driven Gatlinburg or Pigeon Forge feels like taking a refreshing drink of authentic Tennessee culture. The city finds the sweet spot between the buzzy energy of a college town and a bustling modern metropolis. On summer evenings, Market Square fills with street musicians and diners enjoying meals on breezy patios. One block away, Gay Street is a quintessential American thoroughfare, with marquees for the Tennessee and Bijou theaters inviting patrons inside for concerts or theatrical performances. The nearby Old City district is a neighborhood of former warehouses converted to hip nightlife spots and funky shops (with names like Good Golly Tamale, Betty Lou's Fabulous Gift Store, and Pretentious Beer Co.). Just south of downtown, the vast Urban Wilderness invites mountain bikers, hikers, and climbers to explore the Tennessee River's headwaters. And in the spring, drive through the Sequoyah Hills to see the dogwoods in bloom in front of stately mansions fronting the river.

Few cities have a history this rich. In 1786, patriot general James White and a few pioneer settlers built a fort here beside the Tennessee River. A few years later, territorial governor William Blount selected White's fort as capital of the newly formed Territory of the United States South of the River Ohio and renamed the settlement Knoxville after his longtime friend, Secretary of War Henry Knox. It flourished from its beginning as the gateway to the frontier and became the state capital when Tennessee was admitted into the Union in 1796.

GETTING HERE AND AROUND

Knoxville sits at the intersection of Interstate 40, which runs east–west through miles of commercial development on the west side of the city, and Interstate 75, which runs north–south. To get to the national park, take Exit 407 off Interstate 40, where you'll find handy tourist information centers.

VISITOR INFORMATION

Visit Knoxville Visitor Center. ✉ *301 S. Gay St., Knoxville* ☎ *865/523–7263* 🌐 *www.visitknoxville.com.*

A brilliant butterfly alights on a black-eyed Susan in the 315-acre Ijams Nature Center.

Sights

Downtown Knoxville is fairly easy to explore on foot, with Gay Street stretching downhill from the visitor center and passing Market Square before ending at the Tennessee River. The Old City, an industrial neighborhood reborn as a restaurant and bar district, lies just north of downtown. The sprawling campus of the University of Tennessee is just west of downtown, off Cumberland Avenue. The free Knoxville Trolley runs several lines through downtown, stopping at downtown hotels.

The rest of Knoxville sprawls along Interstate 40 west of downtown, a jumble of malls, fast-food restaurants, and hotels. The Knoxville Zoo is just off Interstate 40 east of downtown.

Beck Cultural Exchange Center

HISTORY MUSEUM | Commemorating Knoxville's African-American history with photographs, art, and a large archive of newspapers, this center is located in the former home of one of the city's most prominent Black families. In nearby Morningside Park is a statue of the late Alex Haley, a one-time Knoxville resident and author of the book *Roots.* ✉ *1927 Dandridge Ave., Knoxville* ☎ *865/524–8461* 🌐 *www.beckcenter.net* 🎫 *Free* 🕓 *Closed Sun. and Mon.*

Blount Mansion

HISTORIC HOME | In this modest structure dating from 1792, Territorial Governor William Blount, a signer of the Constitution, planned the admission of Tennessee as the 16th state in the Union. The

Knoxville
KEY
Exploring Sights
Restaurants
Hotels
0
1,000 ft
0
200 m
North Broadway
West 5th Avenue
N. Central Street
Lamar St. NE
Hall of Fame Drive
East Depot Ave.
Randolph St.
East Magnolia Ave.
East Jackson Ave.
Richards St.
West 5th Avenue
Cooper St.
Avenue
West Depot
North Gay Street
East Jackson Ave.
Willow Ave.
S. Central St.
West Jackson Avenue
West Vine Avenue
Oak Avenue
Hall of Fame Drive
South Gay St.
Wall Ave. SW.
Walnut Street
State Street
South Central Street
Locust Street Southwest
Union Ave.
Market St. SW.
Clinch Avenue
West Church Avenue
11th Street
Forest Ave.
Highland Avenue
Bridge Ave. SW.
12th Street
13th Street
Laurel Avenue
Clinch Avenue
White Avenue
Henley Street
Cumberland Avenue
Main Street West
West Hill Avenue
11th Street
Estabrook Road
Poplar St. SW.
West Hill Ave.
Neyland Drive
South Gay Street
Cumberland Avenue
Circle Drive
Middle Drive
Middle Drive
Volunteer Blvd.
Volunteer Blvd.
Phillip Fulmer Way
Henley Street
Neyland Drive
West Blount Ave.
Mimosa Ave. SE.
Hawthorne Ave. SE
Volunteer Blvd.
Volunteer Blvd.
Lake Loudoun Blvd. SW.
Phillip Fulmer Way

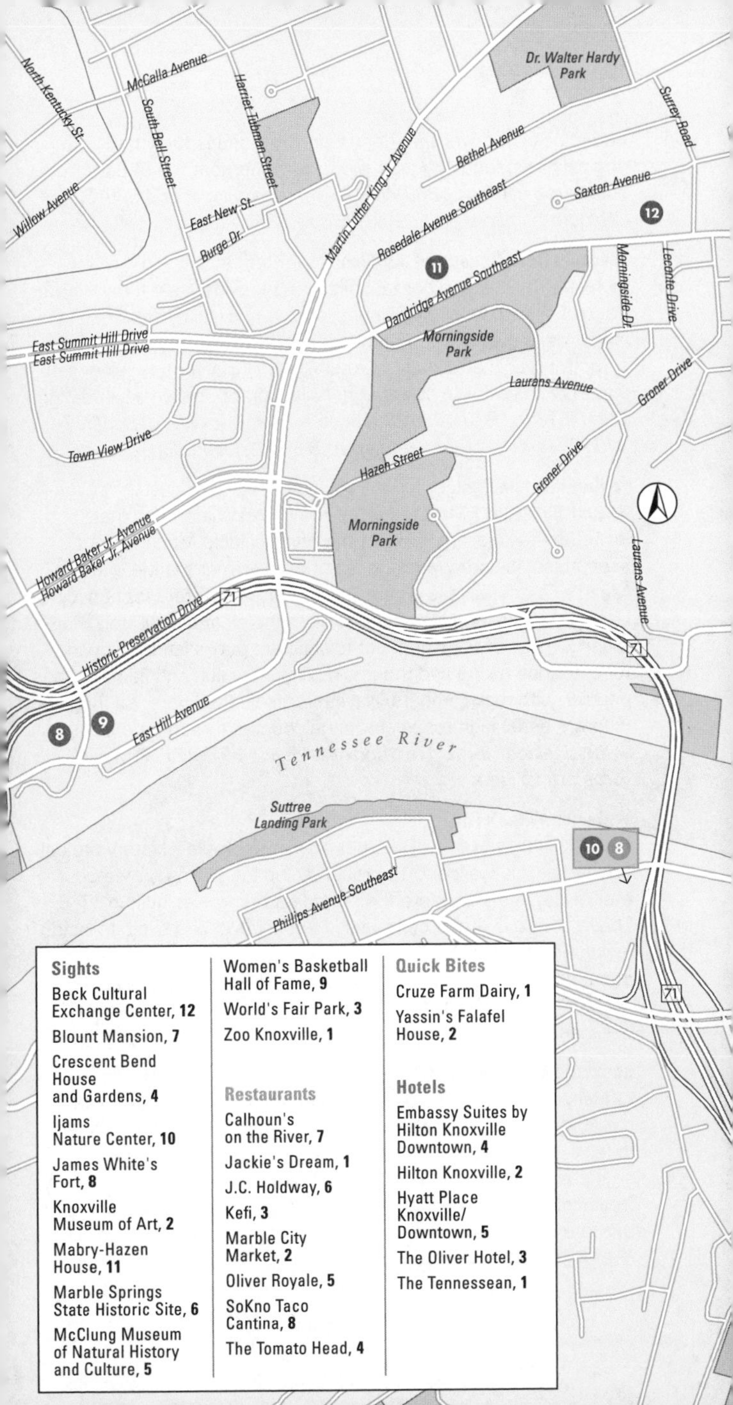

North Kentucky St.
McCalla Avenue
South Bell Street
Harriet Tubman Street
Dr. Walter Hardy Park
Surrey Road
Martin Luther King Jr Avenue
Bethel Avenue
Willow Avenue
East New St.
Burge Dr.
Rosedale Avenue Southeast
Saxton Avenue
12
11
Morningside Dr.
Leconte Drive
Dandridge Avenue Southeast
East Summit Hill Drive
East Summit Hill Drive
Morningside Park
Laurans Avenue
Groner Drive
Town View Drive
Hazen Street
Groner Drive
Morningside Park
Howard Baker Jr. Avenue
Howard Baker Jr. Avenue
Laurans Avenue
71
Historic Preservation Drive
71
8
9
East Hill Avenue
Tennessee River
Suttree Landing Park
10
8
Phillips Avenue Southeast
71
Sights
Beck Cultural Exchange Center, 12
Blount Mansion, 7
Crescent Bend House and Gardens, 4
Ijams Nature Center, 10
James White's Fort, 8
Knoxville Museum of Art, 2
Mabry-Hazen House, 11
Marble Springs State Historic Site, 6
McClung Museum of Natural History and Culture, 5
Women's Basketball Hall of Fame, 9
World's Fair Park, 3
Zoo Knoxville, 1
Restaurants
Calhoun's on the River, 7
Jackie's Dream, 1
J.C. Holdway, 6
Kefi, 3
Marble City Market, 2
Oliver Royale, 5
SoKno Taco Cantina, 8
The Tomato Head, 4
Quick Bites
Cruze Farm Dairy, 1
Yassin's Falafel House, 2
Hotels
Embassy Suites by Hilton Knoxville Downtown, 4
Hilton Knoxville, 2
Hyatt Place Knoxville/Downtown, 5
The Oliver Hotel, 3
The Tennessean, 1

home looks out over the Tennessee River and is furnished with original and period antiques, along with memorabilia of Blount's checkered career. ✉ *200 W. Hill Ave., Knoxville* ☎ *865/525–2375* 🌐 *blountmansion.org* 🎫 *$10* ⏲ *Closed Sun.–Tues.*

Crescent Bend House and Gardens

GARDEN | This historic home, built in 1834, is just past the western edge of the University of Tennessee campus. Its nine formal Italian gardens overlook the Tennessee River. The home includes the Armstrong-Lockett House Museum, with 18th-century American and English furniture and a large collection of English silver dating from 1610 to 1830. ✉ *2728 Kingston Pike, Knoxville* ☎ *865/637–3163* 🌐 *www.crescentbend.com* 🎫 *$7* ⏲ *Closed Sun.–Thurs.*

★ Ijams Nature Center

NATURE PRESERVE | FAMILY | Part of the Urban Wilderness that includes the adjacent Forks of the River Wildlife Management Area, this 315-acre woodland is home to former marble quarries. Mead's Quarry Lake is where River Sports Outfitters rents paddleboards, kayaks, and canoes to explore the clear blue water. More than 12 miles of trails connect to adjacent public lands, allowing for extended hiking and mountain biking circuits, and Ijams Crag is popular with rock climbers. Navitat is also based here, offering six different aerial high-ropes challenge courses through the treetops. ✉ *2915 Island Home Ave., Knoxville* ☎ *865/577–4717* 🌐 *www.ijams.org* 🎫 *Free.*

★ James White's Fort

HISTORIC SIGHT | FAMILY | Different eras of Knoxville's history are celebrated at this walled fort of rough-hewn log cabins on the perimeter of downtown, where the city's first home was built in 1786. Their survival over the centuries is remarkable, and exhibits inside include pioneer artifacts, authentic furnishings, and information about James White's role in the American Revolution. ✉ *205 E. Hill Ave., Knoxville* ☎ *865/525–6514* 🌐 *jameswhitesfort.org* 🎫 *$10* ⏲ *Closed Sun.; closed Sat. Dec.–Mar.*

Knoxville Museum of Art

ART MUSEUM | Designed by renowned museum architect Edward Larrabee Barnes, the four-level concrete-and-steel building is faced in Tennessee pink marble. It devotes ample space to regional artists and includes four exhibition galleries, an exploratory gallery for children, a great hall, an auditorium, a museum store, and an outdoor sculpture garden. ✉ *1050 World's Fair Park Dr., Knoxville* ☎ *865/525–6101* 🌐 *knoxart.org* 🎫 *Free* ⏲ *Closed Mon.*

The Sunsphere, a gold-domed observation tower with 360-degree views of the skyline, is the centerpiece of Knoxville.

Mabry-Hazen House

HISTORIC HOME | Wraparound porches and towering magnolias frame this 1858 home that served as headquarters for both Confederate and Union forces during the Civil War. Built by prominent Knoxvillian Joseph A. Mabry Jr., the home's exhibits trace the history of Knoxville through the expansive collections of the Mabry and Hazen families. ✉ *1711 Dandridge Ave., Knoxville* ☎ *865/522–8661* 🌐 *www.mabryhazen.com* 🎫 *$10* 🕓 *Closed Sun. Open Sat. by appointment only.*

Marble Springs State Historic Site

HISTORIC SIGHT | **FAMILY** | About 10 minutes south of the city, this collection of log cabins was the summer home of John Sevier, Tennessee's first governor. Tours of the property are offered, as well as craft demonstrations. Hiking trails meander along the adjacent creek, which includes the namesake spring. ✉ *1220 W. Governor John Sevier Hwy., Knoxville* ☎ *865/573–5508* 🌐 *www.marblesprings.net* 🎫 *Free. Tours $10* 🕓 *Closed Mon. and Tues.*

McClung Museum of Natural History and Culture

HISTORIC HOME | **FAMILY** | On the University of Tennessee campus, this museum has diverse collections of dinosaur fossils and exhibits on geology, archaeology of native peoples, the Civil War, and fine arts. Of special note is a room devoted to ancient Egyptian artifacts. ✉ *1327 Circle Park Dr., Knoxville* ☎ *865/974–2144* 🌐 *mcclungmuseum.utk.edu* 🎫 *Free* 🕓 *Closed Sun. and Mon.* ✍ *Advance reservations may be required—call first.*

Women's Basketball Hall of Fame

OTHER MUSEUM | It's easy to find this museum dedicated to all things women's basketball—just look for the 30-foot-wide basketball sitting atop a metal cage on the edge of the city's skyline. Exhibits include jerseys from WNBA All-Stars, a locker room with recordings of inspirational half-time talks from top coaches, and play courts where you can test your skills against those of the game's top players. ✉ *700 Hall of Fame Dr., Knoxville* ☎ *865/633–9000* 🌐 *www.wbhof.com* 🎟 *$8* ⏲ *Closed Sun; closed Mon. from Sep.–April.*

World's Fair Park

CITY PARK | **FAMILY** | Knoxville hosted the World's Fair in 1982, and the legacy is a green space maintained in the heart of the city. The centerpiece is the Sunsphere, a gold-domed observation tower with 360-degree views of the city. Below, there's a splash pad that's popular with children during summer and a festival lawn and amphitheater that host events throughout the year. ✉ *963 World's Fair Park Dr., Knoxville* ☎ *865/314-0660* 🌐 *www.worldsfairpark.org* 🎟 *Sunsphere observation deck, $5* ⏲ *Sunsphere closed Mon.*

Zoo Knoxville

ZOO | **FAMILY** | Concise enough to see in a morning but big enough to fill a full day, this top-notch zoo is home to more than 800 animals, including elephants, giraffes, lions, and gorillas. A highlight is the sprawling gibbon exhibit with rope bridges that stretch over pedestrian paths. The petting zoo, miniature train, and splash pad are hits with kids. A permanent exhibit with 22 realistic dinosaurs opened in 2023. ✉ *3500 Knoxville Zoo Dr., Knoxville* ☎ *865/637–5331* 🌐 *zooknoxville.org* 🎟 *$27.*

Restaurants

Calhoun's on the River

$$ | **BARBECUE** | **FAMILY** | A perennial favorite, this barbecue joint and steak house draws crowds for its hickory-smoked ribs and its views of the action on the Tennessee River. There's a dedicated dock for the restaurant, and many locals arrive by water to take in the scenery on the spacious deck. **Known for:** parties whenever the University of Tennessee Volunteers play at home; wings drenched in the signature Thunder Road sauce; meats slow-smoked over a hickory fire. 💲 *Average main: $15* ✉ *400 Neyland Dr., Knoxville* ☎ *865/673–3355* 🌐 *calhouns.com.*

Jackie's Dream

$ | **SOUTHERN** | Make the drive to this soul food joint in North Knoxville and you'll feel like you've discovered a local secret. Jackie serves up daily specials like smothered pork chops and fried tilapia, with sides like "Mama's Cabbage" and candied yams. **Known for:** Knoxville hot chicken; meat-and-three feasts; authentic laid-back atmosphere. *Average main: $12 ✉ 1008 E. Woodland Ave., Knoxville ☎ 865/219–5789 🌐 jackiesdreamknoxville.com ⏲ Closed Mon. and Tues.*

> **Tip**
>
> If you plan to visit multiple historic sites and houses, a combination ticket is available for $25 at the Mabry-Hazen House, Crescent Bend, Marble Springs, James White's Fort, or the Blount Mansion.

★ J.C. Holdway

$$$$ | SOUTHERN | The seasonal flavors of eastern Tennessee's farms come to life over the wood-fired grill at this chef-owned ode to Southern cuisine, where the menu changes weekly. One decadent constant is a sous-vide farm egg appetizer with gnocchi and chicken confit. **Known for:** floor-to-ceiling windows create an open airy environment; a small but thoughtfully curated wine list; impeccable and enthusiastic service. *Average main: $38 ✉ 501 Union Ave., Knoxville ☎ 865/312–9050 🌐 www.jcholdway.com*  *Closed Sun. and Mon.*

Kefi

$$$ | GREEK FUSION | Greek meets fine dining at this trendy spot for Mediterranean-style mezze like grilled octopus, lamb chops, and beef short ribs. An extensive cocktail menu, highlighted by anise liqueurs from Lebanon and Turkey, invites diners to relax and settle in for the evening. **Known for:** group dining with tables full of shared plates; saganaki "flaming cheese" mezze; informed passionate servers. *Average main: $28 ✉ 120 E. Jackson Ave., Knoxville ☎ 865/474–1492 🌐 www.kefiknox.com.*

Marble City Market

$ | INTERNATIONAL | FAMILY | Big and bright, this newcomer food hall has room for a dozen vendors, ranging from vegan soul food to Korean fusion to street tacos. There's a bar, a coffee shop, and plenty of room to hang with friends. **Known for:** sidewalk seating; wide variety of ethnic fare; craft cocktails at Frank & George's bar. *Average main: $10 ✉ 333 W. Depot Ave., Suite 110, Knoxville ☎ 865/240–3796 🌐 www.marblecitymarket.com.*

★ Oliver Royale

$$$ | CONTEMPORARY | Dining outside at this swank bistro feels like settling into a sidewalk café in France with a Southern twist. The extensive whiskey menu tempts you to order an old-fashioned—with sugar muddled slow to perfection—before digging into a plate of local rainbow trout with aged ham and whipped polenta, all sourced sustainably from regional farms. **Known for:** decadent burger topped with Welsh cheddar, Benton's ham crisps, and tomato-apple chutney; atmospheric dining; confit short rib Benedict at weekend brunch. *Average main: $33 5 Market Sq., Knoxville 865/622–6434 www.oliverroyale.com.*

★ SoKno Taco Cantina

$ | **MEXICAN FUSION** | **FAMILY** | Minutes from Ijams Nature Center, this bustling taco joint fills up on weekends with bicyclists, climbers, hikers, and paddlers scarfing down tortillas stuffed with ground beef and chorizo and slugging crisp margaritas. **Known for:** a lively outdoor scene on three patios; massive Nasty Nachos; late-night grub all week long. *Average main: $12 3701 Sevierville Pike, Knoxville 865/851–8882 soknota.co.*

The Tomato Head

$ | **PIZZA** | **FAMILY** | This perennially popular (and affordable!) spot features carefully sourced comfort food with ample vegetarian options. The extensive menu includes generously sized salads and pizzas with toppings like basil ricotta, house-pickled banana peppers, and sun-dried tomato pesto. **Known for:** bacon salad with spinach and poppy-seed dressing; fast friendly service; house-made pesto. *Average main: $14 12 Market Sq., Knoxville 865/637–4067 thetomatohead.com.*

Coffee and Quick Bites

Cruze Farm Dairy

$ | **ICE CREAM** | **FAMILY** | The throwback vibe at this downtown creamery—complete with staff wearing signature red-and-white checkered blouses—makes ordering a cookies-and-cream shake feel like the wholesome Americana it should be. Ice-cream flavors are simple and straightforward—sweet cream, chocolate, strawberry—but do include dairy-free options like raspberry Dole Whip. **Known for:** waffle cones dipped in chocolate, peanut butter, or toasted coconut syrup; toppings like cookie dough and graham crackers; vintage '50s vibes. *Average main: $6 445 S. Gay St., Knoxville 865/333–1265 www.cruzefarm.com.*

★ Yassin's Falafel House

$ | **MEDITERRANEAN** | Yassin Terou and his family quickly became local legends after opening their falafel joint, thanks to infallibly friendly service and quick-serve Mediterranean cuisine that begs for a repeat visit. There are additional locations in West Knoxville and Alcoa. **Known for:** juicy, perfectly flaked gyro meat; excellent house-made tahini; decadently sweet baklava. *Average main: $10 706 Walnut St., Knoxville 865/219–1462 yassinsfalafelhouse.com Closed Sun.*

Hotels

Embassy Suites by Hilton Knoxville Downtown
$$ | **HOTEL** | **FAMILY** | Dwarfing its downtown competitors in height and style, this stylish high-rise features a coffee shop, a taco joint, and a Mediterranean eatery, KoPita, with a glass porch overlooking Gay Street. **Pros:** views from the rooftop lounge and pool are unparalleled in the city; gorgeous central lobby; generous made-to-order breakfast included. **Cons:** some living room areas lack natural light; suites lack kitchenettes; small fitness center. *Rooms from: $199 ✉ 507 S. Gay St., Knoxville ☎ 865/544–8502 🌐 www.hilton.com/en/hotels/tysxdes-embassy-suites-knoxville-downtown 176 suites Free Breakfast.*

Hilton Knoxville
$$ | **HOTEL** | Originally built for the 1982 World's Fair, some rooms in this high-rise hotel feature views of the mountains and Neyland Stadium. **Pros:** Starbucks in the lobby; cozy outdoor seating at the Firefly bar; five-minute walk to Market Square. **Cons:** exterior architecture is utilitarian and dreary; self-parking is a bit pricey; breakfast not included. *Rooms from: $169 ✉ 501 W. Church Ave., Knoxville ☎ 865/523–2300 🌐 www.hilton.com/en/hotels/knxkhhf-hilton-knoxville 320 rooms No Meals.*

Hyatt Place Knoxville/Downtown
$$$ | **HOTEL** | This prominent South Gay Street building was once home to the Farragut Hotel, where James Brown owned a soul music radio station in the basement and college sports's Southeastern Conference was founded in 1932. **Pros:** rooftop bar got a makeover in 2020; spacious gym includes a yoga room; pets are welcome. **Cons:** some rooms lack a view; valet parking only; no pool. *Rooms from: $270 ✉ 530 S. Gay St., Knoxville ☎ 865/544–9977 🌐 www.hyatt.com/en-US/hotel/tennessee/hyatt-place-knoxville-downtown/tyszd 165 rooms Free Breakfast.*

★ **The Oliver Hotel**
$$ | **HOTEL** | Tucked into a historic 1876 building, steps from Market Square, this trendy boutique hotel offers sophisticated, thoughtful luxury. **Pros:** free French-style bicycle rentals; proximity to Market Square; courteous front desk staff. **Cons:** no pool or gym (although guests have access to YMCA next door); some rooms are small, with a single queen bed; books up quickly. *Rooms from: $225 ✉ 407 Union Ave., Knoxville ☎ 865/521–0050 🌐 www.theoliverhotel.com 28 rooms No Meals.*

The Tennessean
$$$ | **HOTEL** | Looking out over World's Fair Park, the upscale Tennessean embraces its local origins, from the maritime maps of

the Tennessee River over each bed to the flowing water-themed carpets. **Pros:** creative cocktails at the elegant Drawing Room restaurant; walking distance to both the university and downtown; modern gym with city views. **Cons:** off-site valet parking only; most suites lack kitchen; gets crowded on University of Tennessee game weekends. *Rooms from: $229* *531 Henley St., Knoxville* *865/232–1800* *www.thetennesseanhotel.com* *82 suites* *No Meals.*

Nightlife

Brother Wolf

COCKTAIL LOUNGES | Teleport to Italy at this cocktail bar specializing in aperitivo cocktails, with an inventive selection of Negronis and spritzes. There's an inviting menu of antipasti and pastas, or move next door to their sister Italian restaurant, Osteria Stella. *108 W. Jackson Ave., Knoxville* *865/247-4729* *brotherwolf.com.*

Crafty Bastard Brewery

BREWPUBS | Helping to lead Knoxville's charge to compete with Asheville's beer scene, this scrappy brewhouse opens its garage doors to create an indoor/outdoor scene that often includes live music and sometimes even pick-up basketball games. It's all washed down by a selection of small-batch brews heavy on sours and hoppy IPAs. There's a second taproom on the west side of town (*9937 Kingston Pike). 6 Emory Pl., Knoxville* *865/333–4760* *www.craftybastardbrewery.com.*

Schulz Brau Taproom and Biergarten

BEER GARDENS | Beer tastes better inside a castle, served in a heavy glass mug and backed by Bavarian oompah music. That's the scene at this German-inspired beer hall and outdoor biergarten inside a towering gate and turreted walls. *126 Bernard Ave., Knoxville* *800/245–9764* *www.schulzbraubrewing.com* *Closed Mon.*

Tern Club

COCKTAIL LOUNGES | Order a tiki cocktail and step into the mid-20th-century at this throwback lounge with a Polynesian theme. The tucked-away courtyard out back is a cozy place to sip and smile. *135 S. Gay St., Knoxville* *865/312–5530* *ternclub.com* *Closed Mon.*

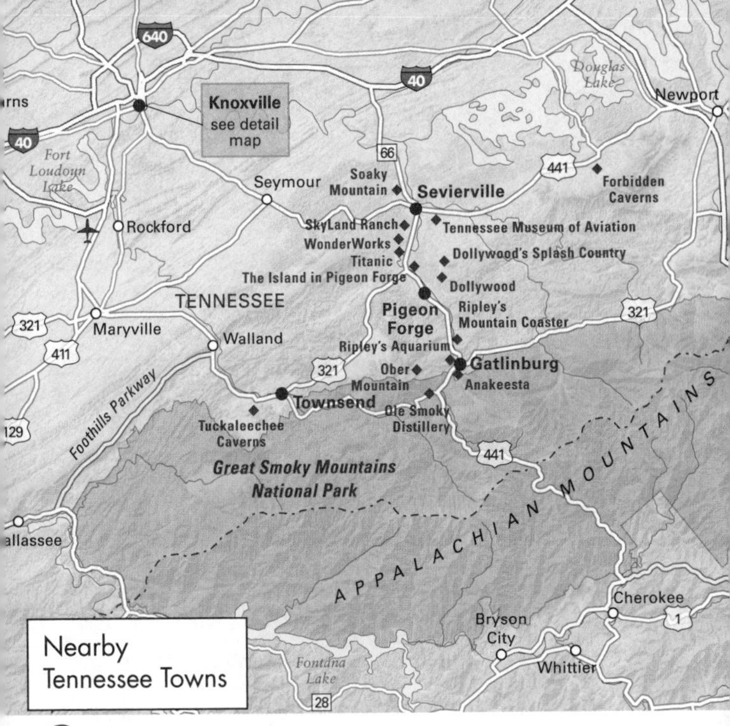

Performing Arts

The Tennessee Theatre

LIVE MUSIC | This ornate 1,600-seat former movie house serves as the city's performing arts center, hosting comedians, touring musicals, and live bands. Its marquee is a landmark on South Gay Street. ✉ *604 S. Gay St., Knoxville* ☎ *865/684–1200* 🌐 *www.tennesseetheatre.com.*

Sevierville

27 miles southeast of Knoxville.

Named for John Sevier, Tennessee's first governor, Sevierville (Suh-VEER-Vul) sits just north of Pigeon Forge, although there's no visible transition amidst the franchise restaurants, motels, and outlet malls along the main drag (U.S. 441). The tiny rejuvenated downtown has some charm, including several intimate restaurants, a duckpin bowling alley, and a statue of a young Dolly Parton playing her guitar. Just outside of town, you can find quieter accommodations and a boutique distillery, Shine Girl, owned by Dolly's niece.

Once a source of flint for Native American arrowheads, Forbidden Caverns is one of the region's most stunning sights.

GETTING HERE AND AROUND

When you're coming from Knoxville, Sevierville is the first town you'll reach after taking Exit 407 off of Interstate 40. Great Smoky Mountains National Park is about 16 miles south of Sevierville.

VISITOR INFORMATION

Sevierville Convention and Visitors Bureau. ✉ *110 Gary Wade Blvd., Sevierville* ☎ *865/453–6411* 🌐 *visitsevierville.com.*

Sights

Forbidden Caverns

CAVE | FAMILY | A beautiful and surreal crystal-clear stream runs through this underworld of grottoes and natural chimneys. This cave was a source of flint for Native American arrowheads and later served as a clandestine site for moonshine production. A stereophonic sound system adds to the experience. Pack a jacket even if it's sweltering outside. Temperatures inside the cavern hold steady year-round at 58 degrees. ✉ *455 Blowing Cave Rd., Sevierville* ☎ *865/453–5972* 🌐 *forbiddencavern.com* 🎫 *$20* ⏲ *Closed Dec.–Mar.*

SkyLand Ranch

AMUSEMENT PARK/CARNIVAL | FAMILY | Sevierville's newest major attraction includes the Southeast's longest mountain coaster and a hilltop village with farm animals and a restaurant accessed via chairlift. The Western-themed complex includes two attractive white barns framing a courtyard where live bluegrass musicians and rodeo-style lasso experts perform. ✉ *1620 Parkway, Sevierville* ☎ *865/737-2624* 🌐 *www.skylandranch.com* 🎟 *$34.*

Soaky Mountain

WATER PARK | FAMILY | Massive waterslides abound at this modern water park with thrill rides that include the Avalaunch Watercoaster, the Whoop! and Holler! body slides, and a new dueling watercoaster, The Edge. There's also a surf wave, a 35,000-square-foot wave pool, and an extensive water playground called The Hive. ✉ *175 Gists Creek Rd., Sevierville* ☎ *833/687–6259* 🌐 *soakymountainwaterpark.com* 🎟 *$48* 🕒 *Closed Oct.–May.*

Tennessee Museum of Aviation

OTHER MUSEUM | FAMILY | Vintage warplanes fill the hangar at this attraction that celebrates the history of flight. The collection includes early-20th-century warplanes, helicopters, and amphibious aircraft. The runway just outside means that some lucky guests witness unscheduled flight demonstrations. ✉ *135 Air Museum Way, Sevierville* ☎ *866/286–8738* 🌐 *www.tnairmuseum.com* 🎟 *$16* 🕒 *Closed Sun. and Mon.*

Restaurants

★ The Appalachian

$$$ | SOUTHERN | Downtown Sevierville's transformation feels complete with the opening of this fine-dining twist on traditional mountain cuisine. If you're feeling adventurous, try the seared headcheese or the buffalo frog legs, but there's plenty of comfort dishes like hanger steak with hen-of-the-woods mushrooms to fall back on. **Known for:** inventive small plates like fried chicken skins with honey; steaks ranging up to a 48 oz tomahawk rib eye; patio dining. 💲 *Average main: $32* ✉ *133 Bruce St., Sevierville* ☎ *865/505–0245* 🌐 *www.theappalachianrestaurant.com* 🕒 *Closed Sun. and Mon.*

Applewood Farmhouse Restaurant

$$ | SOUTHERN | FAMILY | Even if it plays up the "good 'ol days" kitsch, the Applewood is a welcome respite from the other places on the parkway. The two restaurants at either end of the complex have nearly identical menus that feature family recipes developed over time, perfected with effort, and prepared with fresh ingredients. **Known for:** homemade apple butter and apple fritters; chicken and dumplings; cider from the on-site general store. 💲 *Average main: $17* ✉ *240 Apple Valley Rd., Sevierville* ☎ *865/428–1222* 🌐 *www.applewoodfarmhouserestaurant.com.*

Graze Burgers

$$ | **BURGER** | **FAMILY** | The grass-fed beef patties here are gussied up with style. The unconventional options include the Last Frontier, topped with house-smoked salmon, capers, and lemon dill on a brioche bun. **Known for:** a solid whiskey selection; hand-cut fries; grass-fed beef with creative toppings. *Average main: $16* ✉ *125 Bruce St., Sevierville* ☎ *865/366–3775* 🌐 *grazeburgers.com.*

Trotter's Whole Hog BBQ

$ | **BARBECUE** | **FAMILY** | If you can drag yourself away from the pulled pork, smoked out back and served on a potato bun, this inviting new downtown joint offers a full menu that includes house-made smoked sausage and fried catfish. Two dozen beers and ciders are sold by the ounce from a pour-it-yourself wall of taps. **Known for:** laid-back vibe; ribs, dry-rubbed chicken, and whole hogs smoked on the premises; impressive draft beer selection. *Average main: $14* ✉ *127 Bruce St., Sevierville* ☎ *865/263–2103* 🌐 *www.trottersbbq.com.*

Hotels

The Ridge Outdoor Resort

$$ | **RESORT** | **FAMILY** | Choose from eight glamping tents and five tiny homes at this sprawling RV resort with amenities like a zero-entry pool and an on-site café. **Pros:** everything you'd expect in a luxury cabin; playground and basketball court; the feel of camping with none of the unpleasantness. **Cons:** some tents overlook the parking lot; noise transfers through canvas walls; almost all trees were removed from the site. *Rooms from: $199* ✉ *1250 Middle Creek Rd., Sevierville* ☎ *865/505–3111* 🌐 *theridgeoutdoorresort.com* *13 cabins* *No Meals.*

Sanctuary Treehouse Resort

$$$$ | **APARTMENT** | **FAMILY** | The first six treehouses at this new resort opened in 2023, and within a few years, they aim to be the largest treehouse resort in the world. **Pros:** lots to explore, including hidden ladders and slides; big porches and hanging beds underneath; thoughtful tasteful decor. **Cons:** pricey for a glorified cabin rental; not all units have luxury fixtures and tile; buildout of shared amenities is ongoing. *Rooms from: $390* ✉ *163 Pheasant Ridge Rd., Sevierville* ☎ *423/873–3386* 🌐 *www.treehouseresort.com* *6 treehouses* *No Meals.*

Smoky Hollow Outdoor Resort

$ | **RESORT** | **FAMILY** | If the bustle of the Parkway feels overwhelming, this family-run gem a few miles off the main drag will remind you why you came to the mountains. **Pros:** chickens and goats that live on-site are a hit with kids; balance of novelty and luxury are on point; peace, quiet, and starry skies. **Cons:** shared bathrooms in the barn; space may feel cramped for longer stays; parking is a quarter-mile walk or golf cart ride away. *Rooms from: $99 660 Gists Creek Rd., Sevierville 865/446–2043 smokyhollowoutdoorresort.com 6 units No Meals.*

Wilderness at the Smokies

$$ | RESORT | FAMILY | You won't find mountains, forests, or wildlife at this sprawling family-friendly resort, but there is a 66,000-square-foot indoor water park (open year round) with a wave pool and waterslides. **Pros:** the massive water-park complex can entertain children for days; it's possible to park the car for an entire vacation; indoor ropes course and laser tag arena. **Cons:** it's a 30-minute drive to the national park; crowded during summer; no pets. *Rooms from: $160 1424 Old Knoxville Hwy., Sevierville 877/325–9453 www.wildernessatthesmokies.com 632 rooms No Meals.*

Nightlife

The Pines

GATHERING PLACES | FAMILY | The site of the historic Pines Theater, where Dolly Parton played her first paying gig, is now an entertainment-focused bar and restaurant with duckpin bowling lanes, shuffleboard, foosball, and retro video games. The kitchen serves burgers and ramen bowls, and there's also a top-notch sushi and lobster roll joint, Pinchy's, directly across the street. *230 Court Ave., Sevierville 865/366–1471 www.thepinesdowntown.com Closed Mon. and Tues.*

Gatlinburg

8 miles southeast of Pigeon Forge.

The main gateway to Great Smoky Mountains National Park, Gatlinburg is a bona fide tourist town packed with amusement parks, oddball museums, family-style eateries, and "shoppes" peddling souvenirs of all types. Popular with honeymooners and families, the town's narrow streets are clogged with tourists during summer, crowding sidewalks and packing restaurants. There's plenty of kitsch—museums dedicated to everything from celebrity cars to salt and pepper shakers—but it can feel charming after driving through Pigeon Forge. It's at the entrance to the national park, meaning you can chow down at a pancake house for breakfast,

The flashiest and most polished of the three mountaintop attractions around Gatlinburg, Anakeesta is known for its hanging bridges through the trees.

sweat it off with a long hike, and be back in time for a round of mini golf at sunset.

GETTING HERE AND AROUND

Parkway is the main drag running through town, leading back to Pigeon Forge and becoming U.S. 441 to head into the national park. Heading out of town to the north, U.S. 321 splits to the northeast, and after a few miles, Glades Road branches off and swiftly leaves behind the commercialism of Gatlinburg for a winding journey past bucolic mountain landscapes and log cabins interspersed with the workshops of local artisans.

VISITOR INFORMATION

Gatlinburg Welcome Center. ✉ *1011 Banner Rd., Gatlinburg* ☎ *865/436–4178* 🌐 *www.gatlinburg.com.*

Sights

★ **Anakeesta**

AMUSEMENT PARK/CARNIVAL | FAMILY | Of the three attractions that whisk visitors to the top of nearby mountains from downtown (Ober Mountain and SkyLift Park are the others), Anakeesta is the flashiest and most polished. Choose between an enclosed gondola and a chairlift for the 600-foot elevation gain, arriving at a ridge-top village featuring 16 hanging bridges, two mountain coasters, dueling zip lines, and an observation tower at the summit. There are elaborate rope-bridge-and-tree-house play areas for kids, a pleasant garden, and three restaurants, including Smokehouse, on an outside porch with million-dollar views of the mountains, and Cliff Top, which serves entrées like a rib-eye steak and soy-ginger trout. ■ TIP→ **A 2023 addition, Astra Lumina, is a stunningly beautiful nighttime walk through a synchronized light show and soundscape.** ✉ *576 Parkway, Gatlinburg* ☎ *865/325–2400* 🌐 *anakeesta.com* 🎫 *$35.*

Ober Mountain

MOUNTAIN | FAMILY | Generations of visitors have ridden the 120-passenger tramway up the 2.1-mile ascent to Ober Mountain, a ski resort in winter and amusement park in summer. Attractions include indoor ice skating, bumper cars, and a small zoo featuring black bears, bobcats, and otters. In warm weather there are waterslides, a roller coaster, and daily live bluegrass music. Even when the crowds are heaviest, there's plenty to do at the restaurants and shops "up top." ■ TIP→ **The attraction changed hands in 2022, rebranding to Ober Mountain, and upgrades to the attractions are underway.** ✉ *1001 Parkway, Suite 2, Gatlinburg* ☎ *865/436–5423* 🌐 *obergatlinburg.com* 🎫 *$49.*

Ole Smoky Distillery

DISTILLERY | You don't have to whisper anymore to find moonshine in Gatlinburg—you can visit the state's first legal moonshine distillery. Take a tour to see the painstaking production process, then let the spirit of recipes 200 years old trickle down your throat as you sample these magical mountain elixirs made with local corn. Just down the street, the "Barrelhouse" tasting room shows off their white oak barrel-aged whiskey. ✉ *903 Parkway, Unit 128, Gatlinburg* ☎ *865/436–6995* 🌐 *olesmoky.com* 🎫 *Free tours; $5 tastings.*

Ripley's Aquarium of the Smokies

AQUARIUM | FAMILY | This 1.4-million-gallon saltwater aquarium highlights the wonders of the underwater world. You can get up close and personal with a penguin, pet a stingray, share space with 12-foot-long sharks swimming in overhead tunnels, and stick around for the dive and feeding shows. ■ TIP→ **Groups that include 10 or more children can schedule a sleepover with the sharks!** ✉ *88 River Rd., Gatlinburg* ☎ *865/430–8808* 🌐 *www.ripleyaquariums.com/gatlinburg/* 🎫 *$40.*

Ripley's Mountain Coaster

AMUSEMENT RIDE | FAMILY | Gatlinburg has several "mountain coasters" (gravity-controlled, single-car coasters), including options at Anakeesta and Ober Mountain. But to experience one without a huge time commitment—and that the operators claim goes a little bit faster, thanks to banked turns—this smooth double track is a winner that loops through the forest and tops out at 35 mph. There's also a mountain glider, where riders descend while suspended from a track in a harness. ✉ *386 Parkway, Gatlinburg* ☎ *865/430-7800* 🌐 *ripleys.com/gatlinburg/ripleys-mountain-coaster* 🎫 *$25 for two rides.*

Restaurants

Crockett's Breakfast Camp

$ | **AMERICAN** | **FAMILY** | Heaping plates of flapjacks aren't hard to come by in Gatlinburg, but they're not all served on rough-hewn tables in a dining room modeled after an early-20th-century logging camp. But the rustic digs and taxidermied animals—including a coyote lying over the fireplace—aren't the primary appeal: that's the skillets of sausage, scrambled eggs, and towering "griddle cakes." **Known for:** pancakes guaranteed to spark a morning food coma; menus that look like a century-old newspaper; massive fried cinnamon rolls. 💲 *Average main: $12* ✉ *1103 Parkway, Gatlinburg* ☎ *865/325–1403* 🌐 *crockettsbreakfastcamp.com.*

★ **Delauder's BBQ**

$ | **BARBECUE** | In these parts, BBQ means just one thing—pulled pork. And while many spots in town may serve shredded pig, they're not serving a sandwich that makes you want to buy a T-shirt to prove you've been there; for that experience, head to this unassuming old-school joint that'll leave you full but drooling for more. **Known for:** the Holy Bologna is a beast of pulled pork, grilled bologna, and nacho cheese; dining room that feels like an antique shop; tasty fried mac and cheese. 💲 *Average main: $10* ✉ *1875 E. Parkway, Gatlinburg* ☎ *865/325–8682* 🕒 *Closed Mon.-Wed.*

★ **The Greenbrier**

$$$ | **STEAKHOUSE** | It's well worth the five-minute drive from town to this haven in the hills for prime beef steaks and inspired seafood. The stone-and-log entryway is a clue that you've left the touristy part of the Parkway behind and entered a dining room with a talented chef calling the shots on the ever-changing menu. **Known for:** creative cocktails that use Bob Dylan's Heaven's Door bourbon; lively scene in the Walkers Union bar; 18-ounce porterhouse. 💲 *Average main: $35* ✉ *370 Newman Rd., Gatlinburg* ☎ *865/412–1576* 🌐 *greenbrierrestaurant.com* 🕒 *Closed Mon.*

The Peddler Steakhouse

$$$ | **AMERICAN** | **FAMILY** | It's not every day in the Smokies you walk past an 80-foot-high redwood tree to eat at a riverfront steak house comprising five historic log cabins. And it's probably just as unusual to have your steak brought table-side and custom cut before being sizzled over Texas hickory charcoal while you graze on hot homemade bread and items from the salad bar. **Known for:**

reasonably priced children's menu; laid-back atmosphere; well-stocked bar. *Average main: $31 ✉ 820 River Rd., Gatlinburg ☎ 865/436–5794 🌐 peddlergatlinburg.com.*

Whole Earth Grocery & Café

$ | **VEGETARIAN** | If you're packing a picnic for the park—or if you just need a meal that's not fried—this long-standing organic spot is an outlier in a town built on pancakes and pizzas. The simple menu of wraps, sandwiches, and salads is made to order but ready almost as fast as grab-and-go. **Known for:** organic items that are nearly impossible to find anywhere else in town; surprisingly good veggie burgers made with lentils; house-made chicken salad. *Average main: $8 ✉ 446 E. Parkway, Gatlinburg ☎ 865/436–6967 🌐 www.wholeearthgrocery.net ⊙ Closed Sun. No dinner.*

Wild Plum Tea Room

$$ | **SOUTHERN** | Enjoy an idyllic stream-side setting that's just right to sip the signature sweet tea (served sweet, either hot or cold). Savor the sherried tomato bisque, or sample creative salads like dill pea or arugula tossed with strawberries and feta with a citrus vinaigrette. **Known for:** a delicate spin on Southern cuisine; salmon burger made with flaky whole fish; citrusy tea that's deceivingly sweet. *Average main: $20 ✉ 555 Buckhorn Rd., Gatlinburg ☎ 865/436–3808 🌐 www.wildplumtearoom.com ⊙ Closed Sun.–Wed.*

Hotels

The Appy Lodge

$ | **HOTEL** | **FAMILY** | This comfortable hotel—an old Fairfield Inn redone with an Appalachian Trail theme—has attractive woodsy decor, easy parking, and a complimentary breakfast. **Pros:** indoor and outdoor pools; some rooms have fireplaces; free downtown parking pass. **Cons:** tiny gym; it's a drive to Gatlinburg's main strip; crowded at high season. *Rooms from: $104 ✉ 168 Parkway, Gatlinburg ☎ 865/430–3659 🌐 theappylodge.com 101 rooms Free Breakfast.*

Buckhorn Inn

$ | **B&B/INN** | Opened in 1938, this venerable (and affordable) lodging's Southern charm has kept visitors returning for nearly a century. **Pros:** quiet location away from town but close to the national park; almond-crusted French toast for breakfast; views of the mountains. **Cons:** books up quickly in high season; furniture is a bit dated; no swimming pool. *Rooms from: $125 ✉ 2140 Tudor Mountain Rd., Gatlinburg ☎ 866/941–0460 🌐 www.buckhorninn.com 9 rooms and 10 cottages Free Breakfast.*

Greystone Lodge on the River

$$ | **HOTEL** | **FAMILY** | One of the oldest hotels in Gatlinburg and still one of its finest, the family-owned Greystone Lodge commands a heart-of-town location that's walkable to anything along the main road, yet feels tucked away from the traffic. **Pros:** convenient location; free covered garage parking with easy room access; excellent value. **Cons:** pool is on the small side; some of the decor feels dated; no pets. *Rooms from: $180 559 Parkway, Gatlinburg 800/451–9202 greystonelodgetn.com 247 rooms Free Breakfast.*

Hilton Garden Inn Gatlinburg

$$ | **HOTEL** | Contemporary design and an eco-friendly vibe take top billing at this LEED-certified hotel. **Pros:** indoor saltwater pool doesn't use harsh chemicals; outdoor hot tub and cozy patio seating; convenient location. **Cons:** can book up fast on holiday weekends; pricier than similar options; gym is a bit cramped. *Rooms from: $199 635 River Rd., Gatlinburg 865/436–0048 hilton.com/en/hotels/gatgigi-hilton-garden-inn-gatlinburg 118 rooms No Meals.*

Margaritaville Resort

$$$ | **HOTEL** | **FAMILY** | There's nothing tropical about Gatlinburg, but that didn't stop the Jimmy Buffett empire from taking over a chain motel and giving it an upscale overhaul, including the stand-alone St. Somewhere Spa. Featuring one of the town's bigger pools and a waterslide, it's an inviting place to wile away the afternoon. **Pros:** three pools, including an indoor pool and a kids' wading area; the best rooms have porches overlooking the pool and mountains; gorgeous lobby area decked out with lush plants. **Cons:** not as expansive as other Margaritaville resorts; no swim-up or outdoor bar at the pool; no complimentary breakfast. *Rooms from: $259 539 Parkway, Gatlinburg 865/430–4200 www.margaritavilleresorts.com/margaritaville-resort-gatlinburg 163 rooms No Meals.*

Shopping

★ **Great Smoky Arts & Crafts Community**

ART GALLERIES | **FAMILY** | It's worth driving the eight-mile loop road through the arts and crafts community, even if you don't plan to stop. But you probably will—these mountain craftspeople do more than carve chainsaw sculptures (although they do that, too). Along the way, you'll find the works of world-class painters like Jim Gray, whose gallery is housed in a century-old former church. Just behind the gallery, Ogle's Broom Shop is home to third-generation broom makers whose functional and decorative brooms and hiking sticks are treasured by craft aficionados. There are also spots to stop for a meal, a cold drink, or ice cream. ✉ *668 Glades Rd., Gatlinburg* ☎ *865/412–1012* 🌐 *greatsmokyartsandcrafts.com.*

Nantahala Outdoor Center Gatlinburg

SPORTING GOODS | FAMILY | If your plans include outdoor adventure in the Smokies, consider this your base camp, where you'll find expertise, apparel, gear, and guides—all under 18,000 square feet of retail space. There's so much here—for hiking, fishing, whitewater rafting, canoeing, and camping—the store actually schedules guided orientation tours. And to keep it fun for the whole family, you'll also find a kids' play area, a rock-climbing wall, and a swinging rope bridge. ✉ *1138 Parkway, Gatlinburg* ☎ *865/277–8209* 🌐 *noc.com.*

Pigeon Forge

25 miles southeast of Knoxville; 5 miles south of Sevierville.

Dolly Parton's namesake theme park, Dollywood, has long been the most famous attraction in Pigeon Forge. Although the town intentionally plays up its cornpone image, the attractions along the main drag, Parkway, don't reflect the quiet folksiness of the smaller communities scattered throughout these parts. Pigeon Forge has exploded with enough heavy-duty outlet shopping and children's entertainment—from indoor skydiving simulators to laser tag—to keep families busy for days on end.

GETTING HERE AND AROUND

Pigeon Forge begins at the southern border of Sevierville and stretches for about five miles along U.S. 441, a multilane parkway that is an endless row of tourist attractions, franchise restaurants, and motels before abruptly narrowing back into a pretty wooded road running alongside the Little Pigeon River. The entrance to Great Smoky Mountains National Park is about 8 miles south of Pigeon Forge.

Pigeon Forge Trolley

TRANSPORTATION | Each year, millions of visitors to Pigeon Forge happily "park their cares and ride with the bears," taking advantage of the hop-on, hop-off privileges on the city's fleet of more than 40 trolley buses that travel designated routes about every 15 to 30 minutes. Day passes are $3, while individual trips are $1. ✉ *186 Old Mill Ave., Pigeon Forge* ☎ *865/453–6444* 🌐 *www.cityofpigeonforge.com/routes-and-schedules.aspx.*

The most popular tourist destination in Tennessee, Dollywood is just one of country singer Dolly Parton's many Pigeon Forge attractions.

VISITOR INFORMATION

Pigeon Forge Welcome Center. ✉ *1950 Parkway, Pigeon Forge* ☎ *865/453–8574* 🌐 *www.mypigeonforge.com.*

Sights

★ Dollywood

AMUSEMENT PARK/CARNIVAL | FAMILY | More than three million visitors a year walk through the gates of Dollywood, Tennessee's most popular attraction. The 150-acre theme park includes roller coasters, thrill rides, a steam locomotive, and live concerts at the Back Porch Theater. A $37-million expansion, Wildwood Grove, includes two new coasters: Dragonflier, a suspended family coaster, and Big Bear Mountain, which debuted in 2023 as the park's longest coaster. There are also craft displays, lots of mountain music, and a replica of Dolly's "Tennessee Mountain Home."

■ TIP→ **Wheelchairs and electric convenience vehicles are available to rent—reserve online 48 hours in advance.**

✉ *2700 Dollywood Parks Blvd., Pigeon Forge* ☎ *800/365–5996* 🌐 *www.dollywood.com* 🎟 *$89* 🕒 *Closed Jan.–Mar.*

Dollywood's Splash Country

WATER PARK | FAMILY | More than a dozen waterslides and thrill rides make up this expansion of Dollywood, including the corkscrew tunnels of the Mountain Scream slide and the 1,500-foot Downbound Float Trip lazy river. There's also the Mountain Waves pool and Little Creek Falls kids' area. ✉ *2700 Dollywood Parks Blvd., Pigeon Forge* ☎ *865/365–5996* 🌐 *www.dollywood.com* 🎫 *$55* 🕑 *Closed mid-Sept.–May.*

The Island in Pigeon Forge

AMUSEMENT PARK/CARNIVAL | **FAMILY** | A 200-foot Ferris wheel, a giant state-of-the-art arcade, and a flying-horse carousel anchor this 22-acre complex. There's also a high-ropes course, bumper cars, and Alcatraz East, a museum devoted to crime and criminals. The complex is home to two Margaritaville hotels, an Ole Smoky Moonshine tasting barn, and more than two dozen shops. Don't miss the multimillion-dollar "mini-Bellagio" dancing water fountain that comes to life for 20 minutes at the top of every hour. ✉ *131 The Island Dr., Pigeon Forge* ☎ *865/286–0119* 🌐 *islandinpigeonforge.com* 🎫 *Free; unlimited rides wristbands from $40.*

Titanic

HISTORY MUSEUM | **FAMILY** | Costing $25 million for construction—and filled with artifacts valued at more than $4.5 million—this half-scale replica of the *Titanic* is designed to give you an idea of what it may have felt like to be a passenger aboard the sinking ship on that fateful night during her maiden voyage. You'll have the opportunity to climb the grand staircase, touch an iceberg, and try to stand on sloped decks. ✉ *2134 Parkway, Pigeon Forge* ☎ *800/381–7670* 🌐 *titanicpigeonforge.com* 🎫 *$32.*

WonderWorks

SCIENCE MUSEUM | **FAMILY** | In an upside-down world, this is the sort of wacky, interactive learning museum that will help make sense of life's lingering questions like: What does it feel like to be shaken by an earthquake? Can you really move an object with nothing but brain power? How do you design a roller coaster? Schedule at least two hours to move through the activities and exhibits, or longer if you really want to dig into learning. ✉ *100 Music Rd., Pigeon Forge* ☎ *865/868–1800* 🌐 *www.wonderworksonline.com* 🎫 *$33.*

Restaurants

Local Goat

$$ | **AMERICAN** | The menu at this laid-back pub and sports bar touts its sustainable, locally sourced ingredients, but you wouldn't call the generously sized burgers or full racks of ribs health food. Tucked away off the highway, the dining room and Billy Goat Tavern live up to their "local" moniker—this is a welcome escape from Pigeon Forge's onslaught of tourist-oriented eateries. **Known for:** chicken wings glazed in Jack Daniels sauce; impressive beer list heavy on Tennessee brews; homemade bread and buns. 💲 *Average main: $19* ✉ *2167 Parkway, Pigeon Forge* ☎ *865/366–3035* 🌐 *www.localgoatpf.com.*

The Old Mill

$$ | SOUTHERN | FAMILY | If your idea of homestyle Southern cooking includes entrées like chicken and dumplings, sugar-cured ham and turnip greens, or chicken-fried steak and mashed potatoes, you're in the right spot. The grains and grits originate next door at the mill that has been in continuous operation since the 1830s. **Known for:** heritage cuisine; signature corn bread; views of the river passing below. 💲 *Average main: $25* ✉ *175 Old Mill Ave., Pigeon Forge* ☎ *877/653–6455* 🌐 *www.old-mill.com.*

Hotels

★ **Dollywood's DreamMore Resort**

$$ | RESORT | FAMILY | Dollywood visitors who want the full experience can stay put and skip the traffic of Pigeon Forge. **Pros:** priority access to the theme parks; rooms are bright and airy and feel brand new; nightly storytelling. **Cons:** rooms are not huge for the price; can feel overrun with kids; no complimentary breakfast. 💲 *Rooms from: $220* ✉ *2525 DreamMore Way, Pigeon Forge* ☎ *865/365–1900* 🌐 *www.dollywood.com* *307 rooms* 🍽 *No Meals.*

The Inn at Christmas Place

$$$ | HOTEL | FAMILY | From the stockings hung by the chimney with care to the carols that never, ever stop, this cheerful hotel celebrates the sights, sounds, and smells of Christmas all year long. **Pros:** Santa Claus and his elves greet you at check in; Christmas spirit extends to every corner; the lights at night are magical. **Cons:** except for the red and green, rooms are pretty standard; the extra holiday touches are baked into the price; street-facing rooms get some traffic noise. 💲 *Rooms from: $239* ✉ *119 Christmas Tree Ln., Pigeon Forge* ☎ *865/868–0525* 🌐 *innatchristmasplace.com* *145 rooms* 🍽 *Free Breakfast.*

Under Canvas

$$ | RESORT | FAMILY | A 10-minute drive down winding roads, this idyllic glamping spot is perfect for people who say things like, "I don't camp." The canvas walls let you hear the crickets chirping, and the zip-down windows give a view of the starry night, but you're in a comfy bed with a wood-burning stove to stay warm (and for those who upgrade to a deluxe tent, there's even a hot shower and toilet). **Pros:** sleeping "outside" has never been easier or more comfortable; summer camp vibe around the two shared campfires; thoughtful design and creative flourishes. **Cons:** popular with families, so this isn't really a place for honeymooners; voices carry, even with generous spacing between tents; isolated from other attractions. *Rooms from: $189* *1015 Laurel Lick Rd., Pigeon Forge* *888/496–1148* *www.undercanvas.com* *Closed Dec.–Mar.* *41 tents* *No Meals.*

Performing Arts

The Comedy Barn Theater

COMEDY CLUBS | FAMILY | Live country music, spirited dancing, and a whole lot of slapstick comedy can be found at this *Hee Haw*–esque variety show, part of Dolly Parton's empire. The jokes are clean, so it's safe to bring the kids. *2775 Parkway, Pigeon Forge* *865/428–5222* *comedybarn.com* *From $45.*

★ **Dolly Parton's Stampede**

CIRCUSES | FAMILY | This is dinner theater on steroids—you (and several thousand other people) get to eat a finger-lickin' good (silverware is optional) four-course meal while animals kick up the dust on the arena floor to the accompaniment of dramatic music, lighting, and pyrotechnics. The pace is quick, and the service is quicker. In a sequence timed as tight as a traffic signal on a four-lane highway, you'll watch rodeo clowns picking on cute girls in the audience, kids chasing chickens running in all different directions, knights jousting on horseback, and a chorus of costumed singers belting out rousing patriotic songs. Vegetarian and gluten-free meals are available by advance request. *3849 Parkway, Pigeon Forge* *865/453–4400* *dpstampede.com.*

Shopping

Christmas Place

SOUVENIRS | FAMILY | This village of shops is the go-to shopping destination for everything holiday-related, including personalized ornaments, strings of novelty lights, and a sleigh-load of designer-decorated trees. *2470 Parkway, Pigeon Forge* *865/453–0415* *www.christmasplace.com.*

Townsend

33 miles southeast of Knoxville, 26 miles west of Gatlinburg/Pigeon Forge.

Townsend, population about 600, sits in a mist-shrouded valley about an hour south of Knoxville. Like Gatlinburg, Townsend is right outside the entrance to Great Smoky Mountains National

Park, but there the similarities end, because this is the "peaceful side of the Smokies." There's no defined downtown—it's a string of businesses along the highway—but there's still a noticeably slower pace to life here. Townsend's tourist development is geared toward tubing on the Little River that parallels town. A handful of shops, restaurants, and motels make it an ideal base for exploring the Tremont and Cades Cove areas of the park.

GETTING HERE AND AROUND

To get to Townsend from downtown Knoxville, take U.S. 129 off of Interstate 40, exit 387, to Alcoa/Maryville, where U.S. 321/T.N. 73 leads to Townsend. Once in Townsend, the road continues through town to the entrance to Great Smoky Mountains National Park, while another road branches off and heads east to Pigeon Forge, about 20 miles away.

Great Smoky Mountains Heritage Center is just about a mile inside Townsend from the entrance to the national park. The beautiful scenic Cades Cove is 10 miles into the park.

Sights

Great Smoky Mountains Heritage Center

HISTORIC SIGHT | Exhibits on Native American and pioneer culture, including plenty of artifacts, demonstrate how people subsisted in these mountains in centuries past. The grounds include a historic log cabin and an amphitheatre that hosts live bluegrass and mountain music on Friday night. ✉ *123 Cromwell Dr., Townsend* ☎ *865/448–0044* 🌐 *gsmheritagecenter.org* 🎫 *$12.*

Tuckaleechee Caverns

CAVE | FAMILY | In addition to intricate cave formations, the 1.25-mile tour of this subterranean world includes 210-foot Silver Falls, the tallest underground waterfall in the eastern United States. The well-lit caverns, including a massive one measuring more than 100 feet, are home to a seismic station used to detect earthquakes and rocket launches all over the world. ✉ *825 Cavern Rd., Townsend* ☎ *865/448–2274* 🌐 *tuckaleecheecaverns.com* 🎫 *$22.*

Restaurants

The Abbey

$ | AMERICAN | Set in an old wooden church smack dab on the Little River, this idyllic craft-beer-and-pizza joint attracts a post-tubing crowd and weekend revelers. The beer selection includes 10 Tennessee brews on tap, and the menu of flatbreads is rounded out by steamed subs, wings, and pulled pork BBQ. **Known for:** rib dinners on Friday night; live music most weekends; fun scene on the river. *Average main: $11* *7765 River Rd., Townsend* *865/448–1924* *www.townsendabbey.com* *Closed Mon. and Tues.*

★ Appalachian Bistro

$$$ | **SOUTHERN** | Much of the produce used at this fine-dining outpost at Dancing Bear Lodge is grown from seeds at the on-site garden, resulting in explosive flavors like a summer squash soup with bacon and seared scallops or pan-seared salmon over corn, okra, and sausage succotash. The monthly changing menu is aided by the custom-built smokehouse behind the kitchen, fueled by firewood from the property. **Known for:** charcuterie platter with pickled veggies, deviled eggs, and country ham biscuits; friendly knowledgeable service; eight beers and ciders on tap. *Average main: $32* *7140 E. Lamar Alexander Pkwy., Townsend* *865/448–6000* *dancingbearlodge.com/dining* *Closed Mon.*

Apple Valley Café

$ | **AMERICAN** | **FAMILY** | A stop at this mercantile to browse the locally made crafts and kitschy mountain trinkets is almost a requisite when passing through Townsend, but don't pass up a visit to the cozy café for a sandwich, burger, or salad enjoyed on the rustic shaded porch. **Known for:** the 1-pound Grand Godfather Angus burger; delicious apple pie milkshakes; hearty pancake platters. *Average main: $10* *7138 E Lamar Alexander Pkwy, Townsend* *865/448–1232* *www.applevalleystores.com.*

Peaceful Side Social

$ | **PIZZA** | Peaceful Side quickly became a prime local hangout when it opened in 2022, thanks to its comfortable outdoor seating area and an appealing menu of sourdough pizzas and a solid local beer selection. They've since opened an adjacent taco bar and have announced plans to brew their own beer on the premises. **Known for:** local beer list; tacos and pizza tend to please; local gathering spot. *Average main: $14* *7967 E. Lamar Alexander Pkwy., Townsend* *865/518–6300* *peacefulsidesocial.com.*

Hotels

Blackberry Farm

$$$$ | **RESORT** | **FAMILY** | Sprawling over more than 4,200 acres with fantastic views of the Smokies, this rustic estate, complete with a photo-ready red barn, hides a luxurious country retreat with refined service. **Pros:** plenty of activities, including children's programs; wonderful setting and hospitality; huge wine cellar. **Cons:** long drive to the national park; books up far in advance; luxury doesn't come cheap. *Rooms from: $845* *1471 W. Millers*

Cove Rd., Townsend ☎ *865/984–8166* 🌐 *www.blackberryfarm.com* *68 rooms* *All-Inclusive.*

Blackberry Mountain

$$$$ | **ALL-INCLUSIVE** | Blackberry Farm expanded their empire in 2022 with this 5,200-acre property, where the all-inclusive experience begins at $1,000/night; for many, that's worth it to sleep in luxury and dine on meals from some of the country's top budding chefs. **Pros:** you'll be pampered by the staff; unparalleled luxury; incredible array of wellness and adventure options. **Cons:** steep pricetag; many activities require an additional fee; it's a long drive from the national park. *Rooms from: $1,000* ✉ *1507 E. Millers Cove Rd., Townsend* ☎ *865/518–0900* 🌐 *www.blackberrymountain.com* *38 cottages* *All-Inclusive.*

★ **Dancing Bear Lodge**

$$$ | **RESORT** | **FAMILY** | Thoughtful architecture that melds modern amenities with rustic accents (and plenty of natural light streaming through the windows) is first among the many reasons this family-owned collection of cottages inspires and rejuvenates its guests. **Pros:** the Dancing Bean coffee shop is an excellent workspace; s'mores around the fire pit in the evenings; frequent wildlife sightings. **Cons:** books up far in advance; not all units have hot tubs; no pool. *Rooms from: $260* ✉ *7140 E. Lamar Alexander Pkwy., Townsend* ☎ *865/448–6000* 🌐 *dancingbearlodge.com* *26 cottages* *No Meals.*

Talley Ho Inn

$ | **HOTEL** | **FAMILY** | A mile from the entrance to the national park, this low-key roadside motel features rooms with balconies and gas fireplaces. **Pros:** spacious rooms, some with jetted tubs; outdoor saltwater pool with mountain views; cottages can accommodate larger groups. **Cons:** often at full capacity during summer; some rooms face the highway; no fitness center. *Rooms from: $129* ✉ *8314 State Hwy. 73, Townsend* ☎ *865/448–2465* 🌐 *www.talleyhoinn.com* *48 rooms* *No Meals.*

Activities

Smoky Mountain Outdoor Center

BIKING | **FAMILY** | Tubing outfitters line the Little River, but this small outpost just off Highway 321 stands out for its high-quality canvas tubes, sparkling shuttle vehicles, and well-stocked store that sells name brands like Costa Del Mar and Patagonia. It also rents bicycles to ride the paved trail through Townsend or to take to Cades Cove. ✉ *209 Wears Valley Rd., Townsend* ☎ *865/448–1232* 🌐 *www.smoctn.com.*

Chapter 6

THE NORTH CAROLINA GATEWAYS

Updated by
Stratton Lawrence

Sights	Restaurants	Hotels	Shopping	Nightlife
★★★★★	★★★★★	★★★★☆	★★★☆☆	★★★☆☆

WELCOME TO THE NORTH CAROLINA GATEWAYS

TOP REASONS TO GO

★ **Biltmore Estate.** Imagine yourself in the Gilded Age at this 250-room showplace.

★ **Cherokee Heritage.** History comes alive at the Museum of the Cherokee Indian.

★ **Blue Ridge Parkway.** Experience one of North America's iconic drives.

★ **Mt. Mitchell State Park.** Treat yourself to stunning views from this towering peak.

★ **Nantahala River.** The most accessible whitewater rafting in the area.

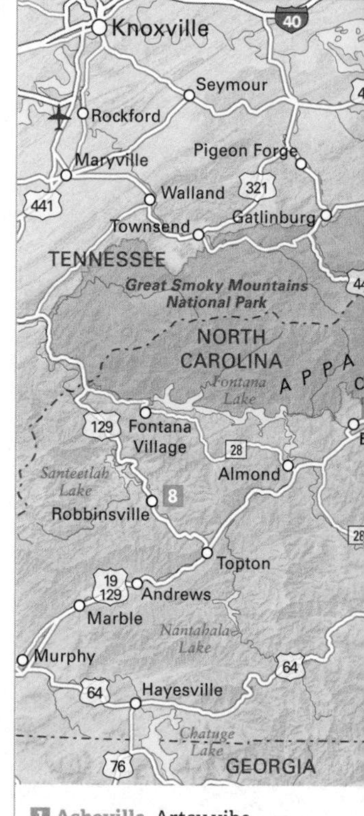

1 Asheville. Artsy vibe, sophisticated dining scene.

2 Blue Ridge Parkway. One stunning view after another.

3 Brevard. A must-see for music fans and outdoors lovers.

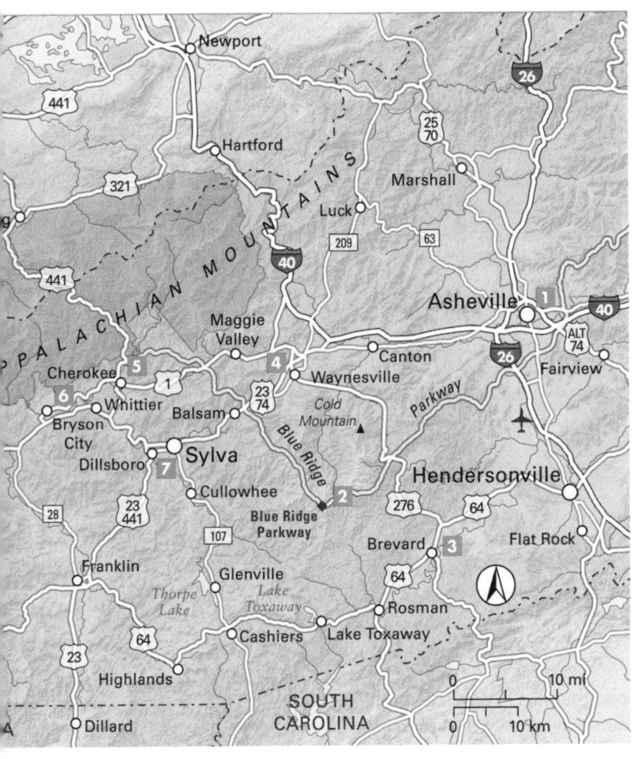

4 Waynesville. Home to Cold Mountain and mountain cuisine.

5 Cherokee. North Carolina's main gateway to the Smokies.

6 Bryson City. Thrills aboard the railroad or on the river.

7 Sylva and Dillsboro. Breweries, bookstores, and incredible dining abound.

8 Robbinsville. Stare up at gorgeous old-growth forests.

Asheville, the hub of western North Carolina about an hour from the east side of the Smokies, is one of the biggest small cities you'll ever visit, with the artsy élan and dynamic downtown of a much larger burg. Here you can tour America's largest home, the Biltmore Estate, and discover why Asheville has a national reputation for its arts, crafts, and music scenes.

Set in a valley surrounded by the highest mountains in Eastern America, Asheville is a base for exploring the park, but it is also a destination in itself. Coffeehouses, brewpubs, sidewalk cafés, clubs, boutiques, galleries, and antiques shops are everywhere in the city's Art Deco downtown. Just a short drive away are inviting small mountain towns, mile-high vistas that will take your breath away, and enough high-energy outdoor fun to keep your heart rate up.

Around the eastern edge of the park are a number of small Carolina towns. The best known is Cherokee, North Carolina's main entrance to the national park. Although it's the most touristy town on this side, it has much to offer in terms of history, such as the Museum of the Cherokee Indian, the Oconaluftee Indian Village, and the outdoor drama *Unto These Hills.* One of the lesser-known gateways to the park is Bryson City, which is great for whitewater rafting trips on the Nantahala River. Sylva and Dillsboro, sister cities 10 minutes south of Cherokee, boast funky downtowns and the region's highest concentration of notable restaurants. Robbinsville and Santeetlah Lake are popular with anglers, while Waynesville is short on glitz but long on charm. Brevard is further afield but worth the visit for its charming downtown and proximity to Pisgah National Forest. The towns all share the same backdrop: the beautiful Blue Ridge and Smoky Mountains.

Planning

Hotels

You can find the usual chain motels and hotels here, though not as many as on the Tennessee side of the park. Bed-and-breakfasts bloom in the mountains like wildflowers, and Asheville alone has more than three dozen. There are also a few large resorts, including the Omni Grove Park Inn.

Restaurants

At many places in the rural mountains, the emphasis is on "slow food," made with locally grown, often organic ingredients. Asheville is the place to go for innovative cuisine, but the smaller mountain towns like Sylva turn out reliable and hearty mountain favorites.

⇨ *Hotel prices in the reviews are the lowest cost of a standard double room in high season. Restaurant prices in the reviews are the average cost of a main course at dinner, or if dinner is not served, at lunch.*

What It Costs

$	$$	$$$	$$$$
RESTAURANTS			
under $15	$15–$25	$26–$35	over $35
HOTELS			
under $150	$150–$225	$226–$300	over $300

Asheville

Approx. 42 miles east of Catalochee; approx. 52 miles east of Cherokee (main North Carolina entrance for Great Smoky Mountains National Park).

Asheville is the hippest city in the South. At least that's the claim of its fans, who are legion. Visitors flock to Asheville for its arts, culture, breweries, and restaurants, which rival that of much larger metropolitan areas. The downtown is built around a hilltop, with myriad coffeehouses, cocktail lounges, museums, galleries, bookstores, antique shops, and boutiques.

An Italian Renaissance-style landmark has been transformed into the Asheville Art Museum.

The city has a much more cosmopolitan and diverse population than most others its size (90,000 people in the city, almost half a million in the metro area). There's a thriving gay community, many self-described hippies and hipsters, young-at-heart retirees, and alternative-lifestyle seekers. *Rolling Stone* once called Asheville the "U.S. capital of weird" (sorry, Austin), but with more than 60 microbreweries and brewpubs in the area—and two large national craft breweries, New Belgium and Sierra Nevada, with their East Coast operations here—Asheville prefers the title of "Beer City, USA." Breweries go out of their way to accommodate families with playgrounds, yard toys, and arcade games, so it's common to see dozens of children running around while Patagonia-clad parents sip IPAs on a weekend afternoon. ■ TIP→ **Many of the bigger breweries have both a primary location and a taproom in another neighborhood, so make sure you're headed to the location you intend to visit.**

Asheville is also one of the best places in the South to sample ethnic fare, with casual and fine-dining restaurants spanning the world for inspiration. The city really comes alive at night, so visit after dark to see downtown at its best. Especially on summer and fall weekends, Pack Square, Biltmore Avenue, the South Slope area, Haywood Street, Wall Street, the Grove Arcade, Pritchard Park (site of a popular drum circle on Friday night), and Battery Park Avenue are busy until late.

GETTING HERE AND AROUND

From the east and west, the main route to Asheville is Interstate 40. Interstate 26 brings you from southwest Virginia in the north or the coast of South Carolina in the south. The most scenic route to Asheville is via the Blue Ridge Parkway, which meanders between Shenandoah National Park in Virginia and Cherokee, North Carolina. Interstate 240 forms a freeway perimeter around Asheville, and Pack Square is the center of the city.

Although a car is virtually a necessity to explore Asheville thoroughly, the city does have a metropolitan bus system with nearly 20 routes radiating from the Asheville Rides Transit (ART) Station downtown. Asheville also has a hop-on, hop-off sightseeing trolley service and other tour services; tickets are available at the Asheville Visitor Center. The city is highly walkable, and the best way to see downtown is on foot.

VISITOR INFORMATION

Asheville Visitor Center. ✉ *36 Montford Ave., Downtown* ☎ *828/258–6129* 🌐 *www.exploreasheville.com.*

TOURS

LaZoom Comedy Tours

BUS TOURS | **FAMILY** | Get on the bus—even if you're someone who would never consider a bus tour. This quirky Asheville institution since 2007 offers an array of tours in their purple people mover, including a Lil' Boogers ride for kids and a haunted tour. You're buying tickets to a comedy show that just happens to be rolling around, using Asheville as its inspirational canvas. ✉ *76 Biltmore Ave., Downtown* ☎ *828/225–6932* 🌐 *www.lazoomtours.com* 🎟 *From $27.*

Downtown

A city of neighborhoods, Asheville rewards careful exploration, especially on foot. You can break up your sightseeing with stops at the more than 100 restaurants and bars in downtown alone and at scores of unique shops (only a couple of downtown Asheville stores are national chains).

Asheville has the largest extant collection of Art Deco buildings in the South outside Miami Beach, most notably the S&W Cafeteria (completed 1929), Asheville City Hall (1928), First Baptist Church (1927), and Asheville High School (1929). It's also known for its architecture in other styles: Battery Park Hotel (1924) is neo-Georgian; the Flatiron Building (1924) is neoclassical; the Basilica of St. Lawrence (1909) is Spanish baroque; the 15-story Jackson

Building (1924), Asheville's first skyscraper, is neo-Gothic; the Grove Arcade Building (1929) is Tudor and Late Gothic Revival; and the old Pack Library (1926), now part of the Asheville Art Museum, is in the Italian Renaissance style. The Eagle–Market Street District, also known as "The Block," was the heart of Black business and culture in Downtown Asheville until the 1960s and is seeing some revitalization efforts today.

Sights

★ Asheville Art Museum

ART MUSEUM | Established in 1948, this architectural centerpiece of downtown incorporates the footprint of the old Pack Library—a 1926 Italian Renaissance–style building—and a recently completed $24 million addition that includes a contemporary glass entrance, a sunny atrium, and a rooftop sculpture garden and café. Expanded galleries display more of the museum's permanent collection of American art since 1860, with an emphasis on Southeast regional artists, including those from Black Mountain College. ✉ *2 S. Pack Sq., Downtown* ☎ *828/253–3227* 🌐 *www.ashevilleart.org* 🎫 *$15* 🕙 *Closed Tues.*

Asheville Museum of Science

SCIENCE MUSEUM | **FAMILY** | Exhibits at the small but worthwhile AMOS include a large collection of North Carolina gems and minerals, interactive astronomy and climate displays, and a *Teratophoneus* dinosaur skeleton. ✉ *43 Patton Ave., Downtown* ☎ *828/254–7162* 🌐 *ashevillescience.org* 🎫 *$10* 🕙 *Closed Tues.*

Asheville Pinball Museum

OTHER MUSEUM | **FAMILY** | A favorite of locals and visitors alike, this museum/arcade features 70 vintage pinball machines and video games. Bring the kids, who'll probably ignore the modern machines in favor of those from the 1930s. There's also a bar serving snacks and craft beers and restrooms labeled Pac Man and Ms. Pac Man. ✉ *1 Battle Sq., Downtown* ✥ *Just north of Grove Arcade* ☎ *828/776–5671* 🌐 *ashevillepinball.com* 🎫 *Museum free, unlimited play $15* 🕙 *Closed Tues.*

Basilica of St. Lawrence

CHURCH | A collaboration of Biltmore House head architect Richard Sharp Smith and the Spanish engineer-architect Rafael Guastavino, this elaborate Catholic basilica was completed in 1909. It follows a Spanish Renaissance design, rendered in brick and polychrome tile, and has a large self-supporting dome with Catalan-style vaulting. Take a self-guided tour with one of the free brochures in the vestibule, or book a 25- to 45-minute guided tour at least two weeks in advance. ✉ *97 Haywood St., Downtown* ☎ *828/252–6042* 🌐 *www.saintlawrencebasilica.org* 🎫 *Free* ☞ *Open for self-guided tours Mon. 11am–12pm; Tues.–Thurs. 11am–1pm and 3–5pm.*

Black Mountain College Museum and Arts Center

ART MUSEUM | Although it was around less than 25 years in the mid-20th century, the famed Black Mountain College was important in the development of several groundbreaking art, dance, and literary movements. Some of the maverick spirits it attracted in its short lifetime were artists Willem and Elaine de Kooning, Robert Rauschenberg, Josef and Anni Albers, and Kenneth Noland; dancer Merce Cunningham; composer John Cage; filmmaker Arthur Penn; futurist Buckminster Fuller; and writers M. C. Richards, Charles Olson, and Robert Creeley. This museum celebrates their historic work alongside modern exhibitions and performances. ✉ *120 College St., Downtown* ☎ *828/350–8484* 🌐 *www.blackmountaincollege.org* 🎫 *Free, special exhibits from $5* ⏲ *Closed Sun. and between exhibitions.*

★ **Thomas Wolfe Memorial**

HISTORIC HOME | Asheville's most famous son, novelist Thomas Wolfe (1900–1938), grew up in a 29-room Queen Anne–style home that his mother ran as a boardinghouse. In his prime in the 1930s, Wolfe was widely viewed as one of the best writers America had ever produced. The house—memorialized as "Dixieland" in Wolfe's novel *Look Homeward, Angel*—has been restored to its original 1916 condition, including the canary-color (Wolfe called it "dirty yellow") exterior. Guided tours of the house and heirloom gardens begin at half past each hour. ✉ *52 N. Market St., Downtown* ☎ *828/253–8304* 🌐 *www.wolfememorial.com* 🎫 *$5* ⏲ *Closed Sun. and Mon.*

Restaurants

Bouchon

$$$ | **FRENCH** | A French-style bistro, Bouchon ("cork" in French, and a type of Lyonnaise restaurant) serves simple Gallic comfort food, such as steak frites, bouillabaisse, and a version of chicken cordon bleu in a lemon juice, white wine, and butter reduction. The owner is from Lyon, and the casual spot fills up due to its prime location on Lexington Avenue. **Known for:** French fare like steak frites and escargots in garlic butter; steak tartare and ris de veau (sautéed sweetbreads) on Thursdays; all-you-can-eat mussels in savory sauces. $ *Average main: $27* ✉ *62 N. Lexington Ave., Downtown* ☎ *828/350–1140* 🌐 *www.ashevillebouchon.com* ⏲ *Closed Mon. and Tues. No lunch.*

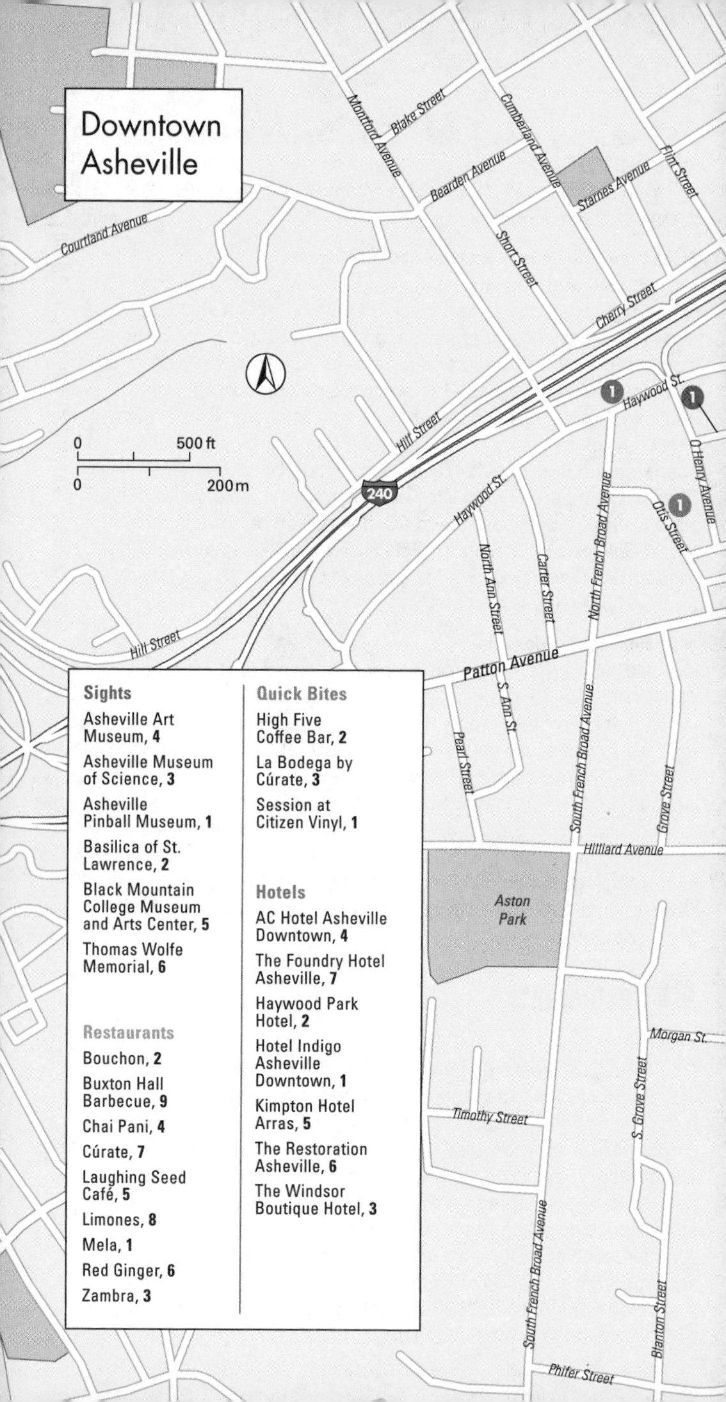

Downtown Asheville
Courtland Avenue
Montford Avenue
Blake Street
Cumberland Avenue
Bearden Avenue
Starnes Avenue
Flint Street
Short Street
Cherry Street
Haywood St.
Hill Street
O'Henry Avenue
Otis Street
240
0
500 ft
0
200 m
Haywood St.
North Ann Street
Carter Street
North French Broad Avenue
Hill Street
Patton Avenue
S. Ann St.
Pearl Street
South French Broad Avenue
Grove Street
Hilliard Avenue
Aston Park
Morgan St.
S. Grove Street
Timothy Street
South French Broad Avenue
Blanton Street
Phifer Street
Sights
Asheville Art Museum, 4
Asheville Museum of Science, 3
Asheville Pinball Museum, 1
Basilica of St. Lawrence, 2
Black Mountain College Museum and Arts Center, 5
Thomas Wolfe Memorial, 6
Restaurants
Bouchon, 2
Buxton Hall Barbecue, 9
Chai Pani, 4
Cúrate, 7
Laughing Seed Café, 5
Limones, 8
Mela, 1
Red Ginger, 6
Zambra, 3
Quick Bites
High Five Coffee Bar, 2
La Bodega by Cúrate, 3
Session at Citizen Vinyl, 1
Hotels
AC Hotel Asheville Downtown, 4
The Foundry Hotel Asheville, 7
Haywood Park Hotel, 2
Hotel Indigo Asheville Downtown, 1
Kimpton Hotel Arras, 5
The Restoration Asheville, 6
The Windsor Boutique Hotel, 3

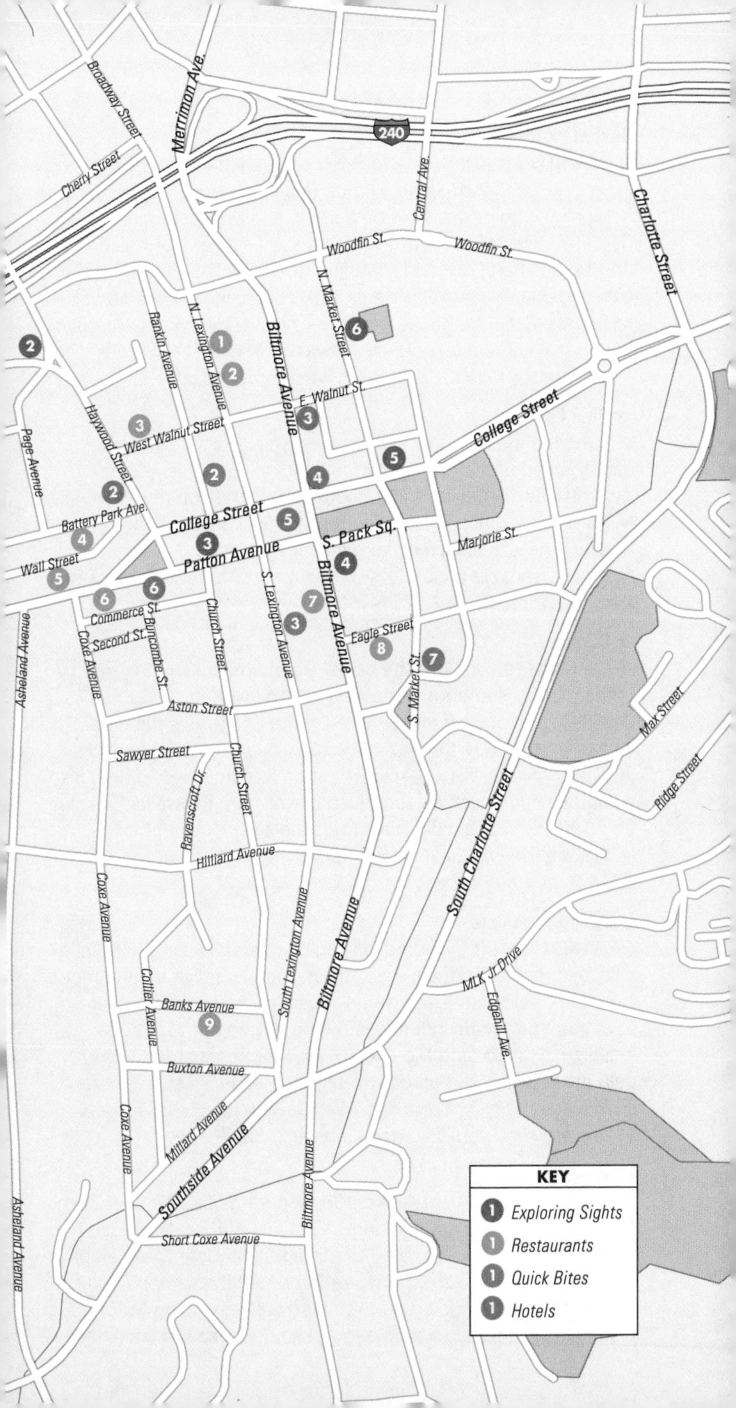

Broadway Street
Merrimon Ave.
240
Cherry Street
Central Ave.
Charlotte Street
Woodfin St.
Woodfin St.
N. Market Street
Rankin Avenue
N. Lexington Avenue
Biltmore Avenue
E. Walnut St.
College Street
Haywood Street
West Walnut Street
Page Avenue
Battery Park Ave.
College Street
S. Pack Sq.
Marjorie St.
Patton Avenue
Wall Street
Commerce St.
Buncombe St.
Church Street
S. Lexington Avenue
Biltmore Avenue
Eagle Street
S. Market St.
Second St.
Coxe Avenue
Asheland Avenue
Aston Street
Max Street
Sawyer Street
Church Street
Ravenscroft Dr.
Ridge Street
South Charlotte Street
Hilliard Avenue
Coxe Avenue
South Lexington Avenue
Biltmore Avenue
MLK Jr Drive
Edgehill Ave.
Collier Avenue
Banks Avenue
Buxton Avenue
Millard Avenue
Southside Avenue
Coxe Avenue
Biltmore Avenue
Asheland Avenue
Short Coxe Avenue
KEY
Exploring Sights
Restaurants
Quick Bites
Hotels

Buxton Hall Barbecue

$$ | **BARBECUE** | **FAMILY** | In what was once a wood-floored skating rink in the South Slope district, this sprawling eatery serves traditional whole-hog, slow-pit barbecue in the eastern North Carolina style, infused with vinegar-based sauce. The pulled pork is king here, but don't overlook the BBQ hash poutine with pimento cheese or the mussels with bacon and roasted lemon. **Known for:** Catawba Brewing in the same building; industrial-chic decor; banana pudding pie. *Average main: $17 32 Banks Ave., Downtown 828/232–7216 www.buxtonhall.com.*

★ **Chai Pani**

$$ | **INDIAN** | In 2022, this unassuming storefront Indian street food eatery stunned the culinary world by winning the James Beard Award for Most Outstanding Restaurant in the country. Fortunately, the accolade hasn't changed the laid-back delightful experience of dining here. **Known for:** shareable dishes; vegetarian-friendly menu; reasonable prices. *Average main: $15 22 Battery Park Ave., Downtown 828/254–4003 www.chaipani.com.*

★ **Cúrate**

$$ | **SPANISH** | If you have the blahs, Cúrate, with its extraordinary authentic tapas and fun atmosphere (they won the 2022 James Beard Award for Best Hospitality—in the country) is the cure. The kitchen showcases the flavors of Spain over two dozen snacks and small plates, with special attention to cured Iberian ham dishes and seafood such as octopus and calamari. **Known for:** Spanish sherries and wines; convivial atmosphere; selection of hams. *Average main: $24 13 Biltmore Ave., Downtown 828/239–2946 curatetapasbar.com Closed Mon.*

Laughing Seed Café

$$ | **VEGETARIAN** | This vegetarian-vegan eatery is a longtime Asheville favorite on charming Wall Street. The extensive menu ranges from banh mi sandwiches and a vegan sweet potato Reuben to dinner specialties influenced by the flavors of India, Cuba, Thailand, Mexico, and Morocco. **Known for:** Thai panang curry; cold-press juices and other beverages; breads baked in-house. *Average main: $17 40 Wall St., Downtown 828/252–3445 laughingseed.com Closed Tues. and Wed.*

Limones

$$$ | **MODERN MEXICAN** | Three components—a talented chef from Mexico City, locally sourced ingredients, and a San Francisco bistro atmosphere—combine to make this modern Mexican place a standout. Whet your appetite with the ceviche sampler and lobster nachos before going on to the regularly changing list of main dishes like carne asada with a romesco mole. **Known for:** extensive

margarita menu; smart unobtrusive service; airy and open space. *Average main: $29* *15 Eagle St., Downtown* *828/252–2327* *limonesrestaurant.com* *Closed Sun.*

Mela

$$ | **INDIAN** | Rather than specialize in one type of Indian cuisine, Mela offers dishes from across the country. The traditionally prepared tandoori dishes (chicken, shrimp, and lamb) are especially delicious, and at lunch there's an inexpensive buffet. **Known for:** classic dishes nicely presented; bright and airy dining room; vegetarian and vegan options. *Average main: $18* *70 N. Lexington Ave., Downtown* *828/225–8880* *melaasheville.com.*

Red Ginger

$$ | **CHINESE FUSION** | Dim sum becomes an all-day affair at this upscale Chinese eatery. The menu of farm-to-table small plates—don't miss the black truffle *shumai* (open-faced dumplings), crispy fish, or pork dumplings—is a feast for the eyes and the stomach. **Known for:** Asheville's best Chinese restaurant; farm-fresh ingredients; creative cocktails. *Average main: $18* *82 Patton Ave., Downtown* *828/505–8688* *www.redgingerasheville.com.*

Zambra

$$ | **TAPAS** | Sophisticated tapas—think grilled octopus in black ink sauce, pistachio-crusted veal sweetbreads with blackberries, and squash gnocchi—have made Zambra one of the most interesting restaurants in Asheville. Moorish colors, dim lighting, and an underground setting create a romantic atmosphere. **Known for:** Spanish and North African tapas; intimate romantic atmosphere; 200 Spanish wines and sherries. *Average main: $23* *85 W. Walnut St., Downtown* *828/232–1060* *zambratapas.com.*

Coffee and Quick Bites

High Five Coffee Bar

$ | **CAFÉ** | With exposed brick walls and antique wood floors, this is a staple haunt for fresh-brewed coffees and teas, plus pastries and free Wi-Fi. There are also locations in North Asheville and Woodfin. **Known for:** silky coffee and tea lattes; skilled baristas; laid-back atmosphere. *Average main: $4* *13 Rankin Ave., Downtown* *828/713–5291* *www.highfivecoffee.com.*

La Bodega by Cúrate

$$ | **SPANISH** | The perfect stop for chic picnic provisions, a memorable lunch, or a lively *pintxos* (small bar snacks) dinner with friends, fans of Cúrate are thrilled to find many of its specialties available at this sister establishment, including cured meats, cheeses, sangria—even paella. The "La Bodega Experience" is

This gracious Queen Anne-style home has been lovingly preserved as the Thomas Wolfe Memorial.

one of the best prix-fixe menus in town. **Known for:** nicely curated selection of European foodstuffs; gourmet sandwiches; perfect for picnics. *Average main: $16* *32 S. Lexington Ave., Downtown* *828/630–0330* *labodegabycurate.com.*

★ Session at Citizen Vinyl

$$ | SANDWICHES | Set in the ground floor of the historic Asheville Citizen Times Building, Citizen Vinyl is one of the South's foremost vinyl record producers. It's also a lounge, bar, coffee shop, and an excellent café, Session. **Known for:** biscuits-and-gravy specials on Mondays; Amaro cocktails; former home of WWNC Radio, where Bill Monroe popularized bluegrass. *Average main: $15* *14 O'Henry Ave., Downtown* *828/515–3090* *citizenvinyl.com.*

Hotels

AC Hotel Asheville Downtown

$$$$ | HOTEL | With a distinctively modern facade, this polished hotel has a prime central location just north of Pack Square, within walking distance of most downtown restaurants, bars, galleries, and shops. **Pros:** unbeatable views from the rooftop terrace and bar; one of the city's sleekest lodgings; favorite of business travelers. **Cons:** priced like a premium brand; less local charm than nearby alternatives; more of a big-city vibe. *Rooms from: $340* *10 Broadway St., Downtown* *828/258–2522* *www.marriott.com/en-us/hotels/avlac-ac-hotel-asheville-downtown/overview* *132 rooms* *No Meals.*

★ The Foundry Hotel Asheville

$$$$ | **HOTEL** | This boutique downtown lodging occupies a former steel foundry and several other industrial buildings around a central courtyard. **Pros:** complimentary Champagne on arrival; Tesla car service to nearby attractions; pet-friendly for a $150 fee. **Cons:** not as central as other downtown hotels; near the top end in terms of prices; $30 valet parking only. *Rooms from: $300* *51 S. Market St., Downtown* *828/552–8545* *foundryasheville.com* *87 rooms* *No Meals.*

Haywood Park Hotel

$$ | **HOTEL** | Location is the biggest draw of this all-suites downtown hotel within walking distance of many shops, restaurants, and galleries. **Pros:** small shopping mall and café; Isa's Bistro has sidewalk seating; large and comfortable rooms. **Cons:** not as high-end as other nearby hotels; pricey in high season; no pool. *Rooms from: $199* *1 Battery Park Ave., Downtown* *828/232–8217* *www.haywoodpark.com* *33 suites* *No Meals.*

Hotel Indigo Asheville Downtown

$$$ | **HOTEL** | With views of the Blue Ridge Mountains from many of the rooms in this 12-story tower (especially the 16 upper-floor suites with floor-to-ceiling windows), Hotel Indigo is done up in striking colors like teal and aubergine and features furnishings and artworks by local craftspeople. **Pros:** short walk to Grove Arcade and many restaurants; nice extras like walk-in showers; better views the higher you go. **Cons:** some noise from nearby expressway; can be pricey in high season; no pool. *Rooms from: $239* *151 Haywood St., Downtown* *828/239–0239* *www.ashevilleindigo.com* *100 rooms* *No Meals.*

Kimpton Hotel Arras

$$$ | **HOTEL** | Replacing an office building at the most prominent corner in town, this gleaming hotel tower is downtown's new centerpiece. **Pros:** complimentary bicycles, with helmets; open pet policy; modern gym with Peloton equipment. **Cons:** $29/day valet parking only; some rooms are small for the price; no pool. *Rooms from: $269* *7 Patton Ave., Downtown* *828/255–0303* *www.hotelarras.com* *128 rooms* *No Meals.*

★ The Restoration Asheville

$$$$ | **HOTEL** | This newer luxury hotel has an enviable central location overlooking Pritchard Park. **Pros:** luxurious accents and amenities; top-notch in-house dining; pet-friendly. **Cons:** some smaller rooms; rooftop and basement bars can be crowded; self-parking in an offsite garage. *Rooms from: $469* *68 Patton*

Ave., Downtown ☎ *828/220–0368* 🌐 *therestorationhotel.com/asheville-nc-restoration-hotel* 🛏 *60 rooms* 🍽 *No Meals.*

★ **The Windsor Boutique Hotel**
$$$$ | APARTMENT | Built in 1907, the Windsor Hotel shook off any signs of age with a top-to-bottom renovation. **Pros:** large beautifully designed suites; perfect location in heart of downtown; washer/dryer and a kitchen in each room. **Cons:** two-night minimum stay in high season; parking is around the block; not pet-friendly. 💲 *Rooms from: $300* ✉ *36 Broadway St., Downtown* ☎ *844/494–6376* 🌐 *www.windsorasheville.com* 🛏 *14 suites* 🍽 *No Meals.*

Nightlife

Capella on 9
COCKTAIL LOUNGES | Asheville's primo rooftop bar, Capella on 9 has expansive indoor and outdoor spaces tastefully designed and filled with local artworks. It offers dramatic views of downtown Asheville and the surrounding mountains, as well as a first-rate selection of craft cocktails and small plates. ✉ *AC Hotel by Marriott, 10 Broadway St., Downtown* ☎ *828/258–2522* 🌐 *www.capellaon9.com.*

The Crow and Quill
BARS | This speakeasy is one of Asheville's best-kept secrets; there's no sign on the door, and inside it's so dimly lit you could go incognito. The bar offers more than 600 whiskeys, and a ragtime band makes surprise appearances. ✉ *106 N. Lexington Ave., Downtown* 🌐 *www.thecrowandquill.com.*

The Orange Peel
LIVE MUSIC | Bob Dylan, Modest Mouse, and the Beastie Boys have played at this now-legendary venue. There's a great dance floor with springy wood slats, two bars serving wine and beer, and a speakeasy-style bourbon bar, PULP, on the bottom floor. ✉ *101 Biltmore Ave., Downtown* ☎ *828/398–1837* 🌐 *theorangepeel.net.*

Sovereign Remedies
COCKTAIL LOUNGES | Offering creative craft cocktails and a classed-up cool atmosphere (though it's still Asheville casual), this is one of the city's best spots for locally sourced farm-to-glass delights. The light-filled space boasts high ceilings, large mirrors, locally built furnishings, and a huge array of spirits. Servers and bartenders are friendly and knowledgeable. ✉ *29 N. Market St., Downtown* ☎ *828/919–9518* 🌐 *www.sovereignremedies.com.*

Shopping

Grove Arcade

MALL | Nearing a century old, this stunning historic building's glass roof fills its corridors with light on sunny days—and is a welcome escape during a summer thunderstorm. It's home to restaurants, a bookstore with a bar inside, and shops that include a wooden instrument maker and an apothecary. ✉ *1 Page Ave., Downtown* ☎ *828/252–7799* 🌐 *grovearcade.com.*

Activities

BASEBALL

Asheville Tourists

BASEBALL & SOFTBALL | **FAMILY** | A Class A farm team of the Houston Astros, the Asheville Tourists typically play April to early September at McCormick Field, the oldest minor league park in regular use. It appears briefly in the 1988 movie *Bull Durham.* ✉ *McCormick Field, 30 Buchanan Pl., Downtown* ☎ *828/258–0428* 🌐 *www.milb.com* 🎫 *$12.*

River Arts District

Asheville's former industrial area, just southwest of downtown along the French Broad River, is now an arts district liberally decorated with murals and graffiti. As industrial companies moved out, artists moved in, seeking cheaper rents for studios and lofts. Today the district is home to some 200 working artists—mainly pottery and ceramics artists, fabric designers, painters, and sculptors—and this doesn't include students taking courses. Around 75 studios in 20 late-19th- and early-20th-century industrial buildings are open to the public, and in early November just about all of them throw open their doors for Studio Stroll. The district abounds with restaurants, breweries, a skate park, performance spaces, and even a small movie theater. A greenway along the river makes it possible to explore the entire area on foot or bicycle.

Restaurants

★ **The Bull and Beggar**

$$$ | **FRENCH FUSION** | The Bull and Beggar is decidedly warehouse hip, with brick walls, old wood floors, and high ceilings. The French-inspired menu plays like an upscale steakhouse, and the surf-and-turf theme extends to the mollusks, which include raw oysters and escargot. **Known for:** an incredible 34-oz. dry-aged ribeye; excellent surf, as well as turf; sunny patio. [$] *Average main: $32 ✉ 37 Paynes Way, No. 007, River Arts District ☎ 828/575–9443 🌐 www.thebullandbeggar.com ⊙ Closed Wed.*

12 Bones Smokehouse
$$ | BARBECUE | FAMILY | The lively crowds at this BBQ hot spot range from hippie potters to downtown suits—former president Barack Obama made 12 Bones his first stop on multiple trips to Asheville—who come for the ribs, pulled pork, beef brisket, sweet vinegar slaw, and corn pudding. On a sunny day, grab a seat at the picnic tables outside and take in the murals that cover every wall in the vicinity. **Known for:** smoky baby back ribs; waitresses who call you "sweetie"; collard greens and other Southern sides. [$] *Average main: $15 ✉ 5 Foundy St., River Arts District ☎ 828/253–4499 🌐 www.12bones.com ⊙ Closed Sat. and Sun.; closes at 4:30 on weekdays.*

Vivian
$$$ | CONTEMPORARY | The emphasis is on the cooking at this dimly lit, painted-cinder-block eatery that blends French techniques with Southern ingredients like mountain trout and North Carolina shrimp. Vivian's service is top-notch, making it ideal for a date night. **Known for:** creative versions of contemporary dishes; interesting craft cocktails; unpretentious setting. [$] *Average main: $28 ✉ 348 Depot St., Suite 190, River Arts District ☎ 828/225–3497 🌐 vivianavl.com ⊙ Closed Mon. and Tues. No dinner Sun.*

Nightlife

Bottle Riot
WINE BARS | In a city of breweries, this is the place to bring your friend who only drinks wine—although there's also one of the city's best European beer selections and a few charcuterie plates. Sit inside the brick warehouse interior or snag a picnic table outside by the river. *✉ 37 Paynes Way, No. 009, River Arts District ☎ 828/505–8606 🌐 bottleriot.com.*

Crucible
COCKTAIL LOUNGES | There's no sign outside this speakeasy serving both classic and off-the-wall cocktails. It's equally dark and shady inside, but the bartenders are top-notch. Order a signature cocktail or tell the bartender what you like and trust them—they won't fail you. *✉ 140A Roberts St., River Arts District ☎ 828/575–9995.*

The Grey Eagle
LIVE MUSIC | This venerable Asheville institution features popular regional and national bands on its intimate stage, with contra dancing and patio concerts on certain nights. During the day the

space doubles as a taqueria. ✉ *185 Clingman Ave., River Arts District* ☎ *828/232–5800* 🌐 *www.thegreyeagle.com.*

Shopping

The Asheville Cotton Mill
SHOPPING CENTER | This 1887 brick building, one of the oldest industrial buildings in Asheville, is a former factory once owned by Moses H. Cone, whose family mansion is on the Blue Ridge Parkway. With an exterior covered by a colorful mural, it's home to a music venue, photographers, boutique seamstresses, and a trendy tattoo studio. ✉ *122 Riverside Dr., River Arts District* ☎ *305/968–1300* 🌐 *www.cottonmillasheville.com.*

★ **Marquee Asheville**
ANTIQUES & COLLECTIBLES | Somewhere between an art gallery, an antique mall, and a craft fair, a stroll through Marquee is like touring a museum of Asheville's most creative visual artists. Offerings range from whimsical decor to functional furniture. There's an on-site bar to sip while you browse, and leashed dogs are welcome. ✉ *36 Foundy St., River Arts District* ☎ *828/989–1069* 🌐 *marqueeasheville.com.*

West Asheville

Across the French Broad River, West Asheville has transformed from a sleepy industrial suburb into the city's cultural nexus. Haywood Road, the walkable main artery, offers interesting restaurants, edgy stores, and popular clubs.

Sights

New Belgium Brewing
BREWERY | New Belgium's beautiful expansive deck overlooks the French Broad River, making it a major draw for afternoon libations. Excellent 45-minute tours of this state-of-the-art brewery are free every day at 1:30 and 4:30. Tastings of several beers are included. ✉ *21 Craven St., West Asheville* ☎ *828/333–6900* 🌐 *www.newbelgium.com.*

Restaurants

The Admiral
$$$ | **MODERN AMERICAN** | This tiny restaurant disguised as a dive bar helped transform West Asheville into a dining destination. The buzz around their charcuterie program, house-made pasta, and

entrées like a confit duck leg continues today. **Known for:** dark hip interior; creative plates that please both vegetarians and omnivores; inspiring service. *Average main: $32* *400 Haywood Rd., West Asheville* *828/252–2541* *www.theadmiralasheville.com* *Closed Tues.*

Gan Shan West

$ | **ASIAN FUSION** | Inspired by the food of Southeast Asia, China, and Japan, Gan Shan West has an eclectic and inventive menu of house-made dumplings, ramen, soups, and noodles. Choose a table in the colorful petite dining room or sit on the breezy patio. **Known for:** pleasant outdoor dining; cool and casual vibe; tasty creative specials. *Average main: $14* *285 Haywood St., Suite 20, West Asheville* *828/417–7402* *www.ganshangroup.com* *Closed Sun. and Mon.*

★ **Jargon**

$$$$ | **ECLECTIC** | This charming intimate space features handmade shadow-box art from the 1950s, a collection of mirrors, and retro lava lamps above the bar. The menu is equally eclectic, with small and large plates, including deep-fried deviled eggs, calamari in a garlic marinara sauce, roasted octopus with fava beans, duck and andouille gumbo, elk meatballs, and trout with fennel. **Known for:** creative takes on traditional dishes; craft cocktails like the Ice Breaker; outdoor courtyard. *Average main: $36* *715 Haywood Rd., West Asheville* *828/785–1761* *jargonrestaurant.com.*

Sunny Point Café

$$ | **SOUTHERN** | **FAMILY** | Sunny Point serves food that's simple, well prepared, and not too expensive. Herbs and some veggies come from the restaurant's organic garden next door. **Known for:** perfect intro to West Asheville; great breakfasts served all day; covered outdoor patio dining. *Average main: $16* *626 Haywood Rd., West Asheville* *828/252–0055* *sunnypointcafe.com* *No dinner Sun. and Mon.*

Hotels

★ **Wrong Way River Lodge & Cabins**

$$ | **APARTMENT** | **FAMILY** | Each of the 16 A-frame cabins in this inviting complex features a private porch and vintage touches like a record player and classic games. **Pros:** friendly staff with insider recommendations; fun spacious alternative to a hotel room; walk or bike directly onto the trail along the river. **Cons:** 10-minute drive to downtown; busy road in between cabins and the river; less head space in the standard cabins. *Rooms from: $188* *9*

Midnight Dr., West Asheville ☎ *828/771–6771* 🌐 *www.wrongway-campground.com* 16 cabins No Meals.

Nightlife

One World Brewing West

LIVE MUSIC | One World's wide-open space hosts live music nearly every night of the week. Order a pint and boogie onto the dance floor for Grateful Dead covers and Latin Night dance parties or kick back for the Sunday Jazz Jam. ✉ *520 Haywood Rd., West Asheville* ☎ *828/575–9992* 🌐 *oneworldbrewing.com.*

Biltmore Village

Across from the main entrance to the Biltmore Estate, Biltmore Village is a highly walkable collection of restored English village–style houses dating from the turn of the 20th century, along with some newer buildings designed to blend with the original architecture. Stroll the brick sidewalks and tree-lined streets and visit antiques stores, art galleries, and restaurants.

Sights

★ **Biltmore House and Estate**

HISTORIC HOME | Built in the 1890s as the home of George Vanderbilt, this astonishing 250-room, 175,000-square-foot French Renaissance château is America's largest private house and the number one attraction of its kind in North Carolina. Richard Morris Hunt designed it, and Frederick Law Olmsted landscaped the original 125,000-acre estate (now 8,000 acres). It took 1,000 workers five years to complete the gargantuan project. On view are the antiques and art collected by the Vanderbilts, including notable paintings by Renoir and John Singer Sargent, along with 75 acres of gardens, formally landscaped grounds, and hiking and biking trails. You can also see the on-site Biltmore Winery, the most visited winery in America.

Also on the grounds are a deluxe hotel, a more moderately priced hotel, many restaurants, and an equestrian center. Antler Hill Village includes a hotel, shops, restaurants, farm buildings, and crafts demonstrations. Most people tour the house on their own, but guided tours are available. Candlelight tours of the house are offered at Christmastime. Note that there are a lot of stairs to climb, but much of the house is accessible for guests in wheelchairs or with limited mobility. Pricing is complex, varying by month and day of the week, and not inexpensive, but a visit is well worth the cost for its access to the house, gardens, winery, and extensive grounds. If time allows, a bike rental from the Bike Barn in Antler Hill Village allows you to fully explore the pastoral countryside that feels miles from the nearby city.

■ TIP→ **Self-guided visits to the interior of the house typically require advance reservations.** ✉ *1 Lodge St., Biltmore Village* ☎ *828/225–1333* 🌐 *www.biltmore.com* 🎫 *From $79.*

Cathedral of All Souls

CHURCH | One of the most beautiful churches in America, the Episcopal Cathedral of All Souls was designed by Richard Morris Hunt following the traditional Greek Cross plan and inspired by abbey churches in northern England. It opened in 1896. ✉ *9 Swan St., Biltmore Village* ☎ *828/274–2681* 🌐 *www.allsoulscathedral.org.*

Restaurants

Corner Kitchen

$$$ | MODERN AMERICAN | Entrées such as pecan-crusted mountain trout with ginger sweet potatoes grace the frequently changing new American menu at this charmingly renovated Victorian cottage with wood floors, plaster walls painted in serene colors, and a fireplace in one dining room. **Known for:** innovative versions of Southern and American favorites; charming Biltmore Village location; farm-to-table menu. 💲 *Average main: $27* ✉ *3 Boston Way, Biltmore Village* ☎ *828/274–2439* 🌐 *thecornerkitchen.com.*

★ **Dining Room at the Inn on Biltmore Estate**

$$$$ | MODERN AMERICAN | Romantic, impressive, delightful: that just begins to describe the field-to-white-linen-tablecloth dining experience at the Inn on Biltmore Estate, featuring lamb and beef from the estate's own farm and vegetables from its gardens. Afternoon tea is a favorite event. **Known for:** Asheville's most elegant dining; impeccable service; estate-grown ingredients. 💲 *Average main: $42* ✉ *1 Antler Hill Rd., Biltmore Village* ☎ *828/225–1699* 🌐 *www.biltmore.com.*

Hotels

Grand Bohemian Hotel

$$$$ | HOTEL | As close as you can get to the main gate of the Biltmore Estate and steps from all the best local shops and restaurants, this Tudor-style lodging is designed to blend in beautifully with the architecture of Biltmore Village. **Pros:** rooms are spacious and graciously appointed; a great location if you're touring the estate; very good on-site restaurant. **Cons:** in an area with many

The 250-room Biltmore House, still the largest privately owned house in the United States, epitomizes Gilded-Age glamour.

tourists; very pricey in high season; over-the-top decor isn't for everyone. *Rooms from: $455* ✉ *11 Boston Way, Biltmore Village* ☎ *828/505–2949* 🌐 *www.kesslercollection.com/bohemian-asheville* *104 rooms* *No Meals.*

The Inn on Biltmore Estate

$$$$ | **HOTEL** | Many visitors to the Biltmore Estate long to stay overnight; if you're one of them, your wish is granted at this posh property perched on a nearby hilltop. **Pros:** excellent romantic restaurant; gorgeous vistas and outdoor terraces; shuttle to the Biltmore Estate. **Cons:** expensive rates (though there are off-season discounts); may feel too formal for some travelers; some rooms are on the small side. *Rooms from: $495* ✉ *1 Antler Hill Rd., Biltmore Village* ☎ *828/225–1660* 🌐 *www.biltmore.com* *210 rooms* *No Meals.*

Village Hotel on Biltmore Estate

$$$ | **HOTEL** | **FAMILY** | The Biltmore Estate's less pricey—though hardly inexpensive—lodging sits in a prime location at Antler Hill, putting you near the winery, restaurants, and shops. **Pros:** in the middle of the Biltmore Estate; free shuttle around the property; walking distance to winery. **Cons:** atmosphere is more like a midpriced chain hotel; you'll still be spending a lot of cash; the village gets busy with tourists during the day. *Rooms from: $270* ✉ *297 Dairy Rd., Biltmore Village* ☎ *866/799–9228* 🌐 *www.biltmore.com* *209 rooms* *No Meals.*

Forestry Camp

BREWPUBS | Burial Beer Co. transformed their Biltmore-area production facility—once the building that housed laborers constructing the Blue Ridge Parkway—into this casual hangout spot known for wild and sour beers and a kitchen dishing out entrées like cassoulet and pan-roasted sea trout. ✉ *10 Shady Oak Dr., Biltmore Village* 🌐 *burialbeer.com* ⏲ *Closed Mon.*

Biltmore Equestrian Center

HORSEBACK RIDING | **FAMILY** | The Biltmore Estate offers guided hour-long horseback rides on the estate trails as well as longer private rides, which usually must be reserved at least two days in advance. ✉ *Biltmore Estate, Deer Park Rd., Biltmore Village* ☎ *800/411–3812* 🌐 *www.biltmore.com* 🎫 *From $115.*

Montford, Grove Park, and North Asheville

The area north of Downtown Asheville is largely residential and comprised of several smaller neighborhoods. Historic Montford and Grove Park are the closest to downtown and are home to fine Victorian-era houses, including many remarkable Queen Anne homes from the late 19th century. North of Montford is the campus of UNC Asheville, nationally known for its liberal arts focus.

Sights

North Asheville Tailgate Market

MARKET | **FAMILY** | On Saturday morning from 8 to noon, the UNC Asheville campus fills with produce, crafts, baked goods, and flower stands from the best small farm and organic vendors in the region. Expect crowds of in-the-know locals. There are typically several food trucks selling breakfast items. ✉ *UNC Asheville Lot P28, 3300 University Heights, North Asheville* ✣ *Southeast of Owen Hall* 🌐 *northashevilletailgatemarket.com* ⏲ *Closed Jan.*

★ **All Day Darling**

$ | **DINER** | Breakfast is the champ at this bright and airy in-demand spot for biscuits, smashed avocado toast, and frittatas, but it's also worth a visit later in the day for delicious bites like fried halloumi with honey and capers. **Known for:** quick counter service; hemp lattes; breakfast sandwiches overflowing with goodness. *Average main: $14 102 Montford Ave., Montford 828/505–3701 alldaydarlingavl.com.*

★ Plant

$$ | **VEGETARIAN** | Don't let the pig statue out front full you—this is sophisticated vegan dining with a menu of frequently changing dishes from different cultures and cuisines. A typical menu might include seitan chili with cheese, lasagna with raw vegetables, smoked portobello mushrooms, and delicious coconut milk ice cream for dessert. **Known for:** biodynamic cooking methods; industrial-chic setting; organic wines and local beers. *Average main: $20 165 Merrimon Ave., Chestnut Hill 828/258–7500 plantisfood.com Closed Mon. and Tues. No lunch.*

Tall John's

$$$ | **MODERN EUROPEAN** | One of Asheville's hottest dinner spots, this neighborhood tavern serves elevated but approachable fare like pork schnitzel with fennel salad and striped bass with harissa. **Known for:** bustling weekend brunch; convivial atmosphere; steak tartare with saltines. *Average main: $31 152 Montford Ave., Montford 828/782–5514 talljohns.com Closed Mon.*

Hotels

Albemarle Inn

$$$ | **B&B/INN** | This 1909 Greek Revival home in the upscale Grove Park residential area was home to Hungarian composer Béla Bartók when he wrote his famous "The Asheville Concerto." You can stay in his room on the third floor, although other rooms with private balconies overlooking lovely gardens or working fireplaces may appeal more to modern Romeos and Juliets. **Pros:** lovely residential neighborhood; lots of historic details; excellent breakfast. **Cons:** old-fashioned claw-foot tubs; not within easy walking distance of downtown; some steps to climb. *Rooms from: $245 86 Edgemont Rd., Grove Park 828/255–0027 www.albemarleinn.com 11 rooms Free Breakfast.*

Chestnut Street Inn

$$$ | **B&B/INN** | Even in a city with no shortage of excellent B&Bs, this 1905 Colonial Revival–style inn stands out for its location—walking distance of downtown, yet tucked away in the quiet charming Chestnut Hill Historic District. **Pros:** award-winning restoration of a historic house; local beer on tap; complimentary ice cream. **Cons:** just-baked cookies will ruin your diet; a couple of rooms on the small side; children only allowed in one

suite. $ *Rooms from: $255 ✉ 176 E. Chestnut St., Chestnut Hill ☎ 828/989–1729 ⊕ www.chestnutstreetinn.com ⇌ 9 rooms ¶◎| Free Breakfast.*

1900 Inn on Montford

$$$ | B&B/INN | Guests are pampered at this Arts and Crafts–style B&B, where all rooms have huge beds and most have whirlpool tubs and handsome fireplaces. **Pros:** three-course breakfast; lots of modern amenities; live music on Saturday evenings. **Cons:** children under 12 not allowed; a bit of a hike from downtown; decor not for everyone. $ *Rooms from: $287 ✉ 296 Montford Ave., Montford ☎ 828/254–9569 ⊕ www.innonmontford.com ⇌ 8 rooms ¶◎| Free Breakfast.*

★ **Omni Grove Park Inn**

$$$$ | RESORT | This massive resort has hosted 10 U.S. presidents, from Woodrow Wilson to Barack Obama, and with grand views of downtown and the Blue Ridge Mountains, a challenging golf course, and a variety of dining options, it's easy to see why. **Pros:** imposing and historic property; magnificent mountain views; top-notch amenities. **Cons:** sometimes fills up with groups; expensive during high season; some small rooms. $ *Rooms from: $315 ✉ 290 Macon Ave., Grove Park ☎ 828/252–2711 ⊕ www.omnihotels.com/hotels/asheville-grove-park ⇌ 514 rooms ¶◎| No Meals.*

The Reynolds Mansion

$$$ | B&B/INN | In a beautifully restored Colonial Revival mansion, this inn dating from the 1840s has two levels of wraparound porches and a dozen fireplaces. **Pros:** handsome and historic building; gracious and friendly service; quiet setting. **Cons:** in a mixed-use neighborhood; not close to many restaurants; swimming pool has short season. $ *Rooms from: $249 ✉ 100 Reynolds Heights, North Asheville ☎ 828/258–1111 ⊕ thereynoldsmansion.com ⇌ 13 rooms ¶◎| Free Breakfast.*

Nightlife

Asheville Pizza and Brewing Company

BEER GARDENS | FAMILY | The combination of a movie theater, pizza joint, and a brewery makes this a popular spot to catch new releases while lounging on a sofa, drinking a microbrew, and scarfing a slice. Kids and dogs are welcome, but movies are often sold out, so buy tickets before the show. *✉ 675 Merrimon Ave., North Asheville ☎ 828/254–1281 ⊕ www.ashevillebrewing.com.*

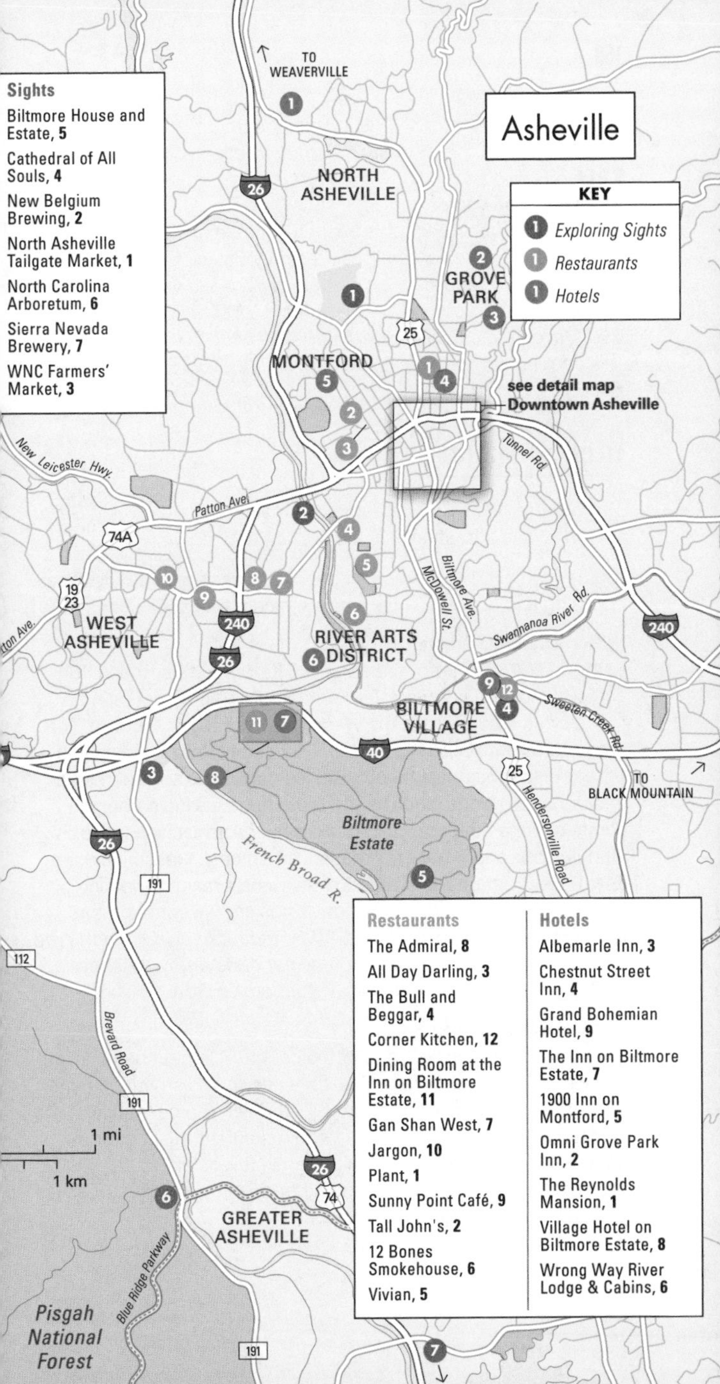
Asheville
KEY
Exploring Sights
Restaurants
Hotels
Sights
Biltmore House and Estate, 5
Cathedral of All Souls, 4
New Belgium Brewing, 2
North Asheville Tailgate Market, 1
North Carolina Arboretum, 6
Sierra Nevada Brewery, 7
WNC Farmers' Market, 3
Restaurants
The Admiral, 8
All Day Darling, 3
The Bull and Beggar, 4
Corner Kitchen, 12
Dining Room at the Inn on Biltmore Estate, 11
Gan Shan West, 7
Jargon, 10
Plant, 1
Sunny Point Café, 9
Tall John's, 2
12 Bones Smokehouse, 6
Vivian, 5
Hotels
Albemarle Inn, 3
Chestnut Street Inn, 4
Grand Bohemian Hotel, 9
The Inn on Biltmore Estate, 7
1900 Inn on Montford, 5
Omni Grove Park Inn, 2
The Reynolds Mansion, 1
Village Hotel on Biltmore Estate, 8
Wrong Way River Lodge & Cabins, 6
TO WEAVERVILLE
NORTH ASHEVILLE
GROVE PARK
MONTFORD
see detail map Downtown Asheville
New Leicester Hwy.
Patton Ave.
Tunnel Rd.
WEST ASHEVILLE
RIVER ARTS DISTRICT
Biltmore Ave.
McDowell St.
Swannanoa River Rd.
BILTMORE VILLAGE
Sweeten Creek Rd.
TO BLACK MOUNTAIN
Hendersonville Road
Biltmore Estate
French Broad R.
Brevard Road
1 mi
1 km
GREATER ASHEVILLE
Blue Ridge Parkway
Pisgah National Forest
26
240
40
25
74A
19 23
191
112
74

GOLF

Grove Park Golf Course

GOLF | Dating from 1899, this beautiful course has been played by several U.S. presidents, most recently Barack Obama. Flocks of wild turkeys regularly visit the fairway. The views of the Blue Ridge Mountains are well worth the trip. ✉ *Omni Grove Park Inn, 290 Macon Ave., Grove Park* ☎ *800/438–5800* 🌐 *www.omnihotels.com/hotels/asheville-grove-park/golf* *$90-$190, 18 holes, 6400 yds, par 70.*

Greater Asheville

The Greater Asheville area turns mountainous quite quickly. Several worthwhile attractions sit just outside downtown.

★ **North Carolina Arboretum**

GARDEN | FAMILY | Part of the original Biltmore Estate, these 434 acres completed Frederick Law Olmsted's dream of creating a world-class arboretum in the western part of North Carolina. The arboretum is affiliated with the University of North Carolina and is part of Pisgah National Forest. Highlights include southern flora in stunning settings, such as the Blue Ridge Quilt Garden, with plants arranged in patterns reminiscent of Appalachian quilts. A 10-mile network of trails is great for hiking or mountain biking. The 16,000-square-foot Baker Exhibit Center hosts traveling shows on art, science, and history. Dogs are welcome on the grounds but must be leashed. ✉ *100 Frederick Law Olmsted Way, Greater Asheville* ✥ *10 miles southwest of downtown Asheville* ☎ *828/665–2492* 🌐 *www.ncarboretum.org* *Free.*

Sierra Nevada Brewery

BREWERY | Sierra Nevada, one of the country's largest national craft breweries, situated its East Coast brewery and distribution center on a 190-acre site on the French Broad River. The beautifully landscaped complex includes a good restaurant, tasting room, gift shop, and hiking and biking trails. Sierra Nevada offers the best brewery tours in the region, ranging from a 45-minute brewhouse tour to a three-hour Beer Geek tour.

■ TIP→ **Tours book up quickly, so reserve as far in advance as possible.** ✉ *100 Sierra Nevada Way, Greater Asheville* ✣ *Near Asheville Regional Airport* ☎ *828/681–5300* 🌐 *www.sierranevada.com* 🎫 *Tours $9–$75.*

WNC Farmers' Market

MARKET | FAMILY | The highest-volume farmers' market in North Carolina may not have the prettiest exterior, but it's a good place to buy local jams, jellies, honey, stone-ground grits and cornmeal, and, in season, local fruits and vegetables. It's open every day, year-round, except for major holidays. On the grounds of the market is a Southern-style restaurant, Moose Café. ✉ *570 Brevard Rd., Greater Asheville* ☎ *828/253–1691* 🌐 *www.ncagr.gov/markets/facilities/markets/asheville.*

Activities

ZIP LINING

Navitat Canopy Adventures

ZIP LINING | FAMILY | Zip through the treetops on two different zipline complexes in Madison County, about 25 miles north of Asheville. One has ziplines up to 1,250 feet in length, with hiking trails. The other has three "racing style" ziplines as long as 3,600 feet. You need to be able to walk about a mile and be in generally good health.

■ TIP→ **Navitat at Night offers a memorable evening alternative to the typical zipline experience.** ✉ *242 Poverty Branch Rd., Barnardsville* ☎ *828/626–3700* 🌐 *navitat.com/asheville-nc* 🎫 *Tours from $70.*

Blue Ridge Parkway

Entrance 2 miles east of Asheville; ends at Cherokee at the Oconaluftee entrance to the national park.

The Blue Ridge Parkway's 252 miles within North Carolina wind down the High Country through Asheville and on to the Smokies. Highlights on and near the parkway include Mt. Mitchell (the highest mountain peak east of the Rockies), Grandfather Mountain, and Linville Falls.

VISITOR INFORMATION

Blue Ridge Parkway Visitor Center

✉ *195 Hemphill Knob Rd., Asheville.*

Sights

Craggy Gardens

TRAIL | FAMILY | At an elevation of 6,000 feet, Craggy Gardens has some of the Blue Ridge Parkway's most colorful displays of rhododendrons, usually blooming in June. You can also hike trails and picnic here. Craggy Pinnacle trail offers stunning 360-degree views. ✉ *364 Blue Ridge Pkwy.* ✥ *Exit at MM 344.1* ☎ *828/775–0976* 🌐 *www.blueridgeparkway.org/poi/craggy-gardens* 🎟 *Free.*

Folk Art Center

ART GALLERY | FAMILY | As the headquarters of the prestigious Southern Highland Craft Guild, the Folk Art Center includes shops and daily craft demonstrations from March to December. It regularly hosts exceptional quilting, woodworking, and pottery shows. ✉ *Blue Ridge Pkwy., MM 382, Asheville* ☎ *828/298–7928* 🌐 *www.southernhighlandguild.org.*

★ Grandfather Mountain

MOUNTAIN | FAMILY | Soaring to almost 6,000 feet, Grandfather Mountain is famous for its Mile-High Swinging Bridge, a 228-foot-long footbridge that sways over a 1,000-foot drop into the Linville Valley. There are 13 miles of hiking trails and some 100 picnic tables. Part of the area is a state park with free admission, and part is private land—including the swinging bridge—with a $15 admission fee. ✉ *Blue Ridge Pkwy. and U.S. 221, Linville* ☎ *828/963–9522* 🌐 *www.ncparks.gov/grandfather-mountain-state-park/home* 🎫 *Free for state park; $15 for private area of park.*

Linville Falls

WATERFALL | FAMILY | A half-mile hike winds through evergreens and rhododendrons to overlooks with views of cascades tumbling into Linville Gorge. There's a visitor center, a campground, and a picnic area. ✉ *U.S. 221, Spruce Pine* ✣ *Off Blue Ridge Pkwy.* ☎ *828/765–1045* 🌐 *www.blueridgeparkway.org/poi/linville-falls* 🎫 *Free.*

Linville Gorge Wilderness

CANYON | Some of the most challenging hikes and climbs in the South are in Linville Gorge, often called "the Grand Canyon of the East." The gorge is part of a 12,000-acre federal wilderness area in the Pisgah National Forest, and there are about 39 miles of trails here. Free backcountry camping permits are available from the Grandfather Mountain ranger's office in Nebo, which also has maps of the gorge and its trails. ✉ *Blue Ridge Pkwy., MM 317, Nebo* ☎ *828/652–2144* 🌐 *www.fs.usda.gov/recarea/nfsnc/recarea/?recid=48974* 🎫 *Free.*

Moses H. Cone Memorial Park

HISTORIC HOME | FAMILY | On the grounds of this turn-of-the-20th-century estate known as Flat Top Manor are about 100 picnic sites. The park has an apple orchard and hiking and cross-country skiing trails. The Southern Highland Craft Guild often hosts traditional craft demonstrations and sales here. ✉ *Blue Ridge Pkwy., MM 292.7–295* ☎ *828/348–3400* 🌐 *www.nps.gov/blri/planyourvisit/moses-h-cone-memorial-park-mp-294.htm* 🎫 *Free.*

★ Mt. Mitchell State Park

STATE/PROVINCIAL PARK | FAMILY | This park—established in 1915 as North Carolina's first state park—includes the 6,684-foot Mt. Mitchell, the highest mountain peak east of the Rockies. At the 1,946-acre park you can drive nearly to the summit, where an observation tower provides panoramic views to as far as Clingmans Dome in the Smokies if clouds and haze aren't obscuring the horizon. The summit was named after Elisha Mitchell, a professor at the University of North Carolina at Chapel Hill, who died from a fall while trying to prove the mountain's true height. ✉ *2388 NC 128, Burnsville* ✣ *Off Blue Ridge Pkwy.* ☎ *828/675–4611* 🌐 *www.ncparks.gov/state-parks/mount-mitchell-state-park* 🎫 *Free.*

Did You Know?

An easy half-mile hike takes you to the overlook for Linville Falls, one of the most photographed sights in North Carolina.

Mt. Pisgah

MOUNTAIN | **FAMILY** | The 5,721-foot Mt. Pisgah is one of the most easily recognized peaks around Asheville due to the television tower installed here in the 1950s. It has walking trails, a picnic area, and an amphitheater where nature programs are offered most evenings from June through October. There is an inn, a restaurant, and a small grocery a short distance away. Nearby Graveyard Fields is popular for blueberry picking in midsummer. ✉ *Blue Ridge Parkway MM 408.6, Waynesville* ☎ *828/271–4779* 🌐 *www.nps.gov/blri/planyourvisit/mount-pisgah.htm* 🎫 *Free.*

Waterrock Knob

MOUNTAIN | **FAMILY** | You don't have to walk the 1.2-mile round-trip trail to the summit of Waterrock Knob for a view—the vistas from the visitor center are also wonderful—but a trip to the top for sunrise or sunset can be stunning. Heading northeast from Cherokee on the Parkway, this is the first trail and notable summit. ✉ *Blue Ridge Pkwy., MM 451.2, Balsam* ☎ *828/348–3400* 🌐 *www.blueridgeparkway.org/poi/waterrock-knob* 🎫 *Free.*

Hotels

★ **Pisgah Inn**

$$$ | **B&B/INN** | **FAMILY** | The spectacular setting is the main draw at the rustic Pisgah Inn, perched on a mountaintop at 5,000 feet. **Pros:** incredible views from its mile-high perch; unique location on the Blue Ridge Parkway; quality on-site restaurant. **Cons:** motel-like rooms; remote setting; often fully booked. $ *Rooms from: $275* ✉ *Blue Ridge Pkwy., MM 408.6, Waynesville* ☎ *828/235–8228* 🌐 *www.pisgahinn.com* ⏲ *Closed Nov.–Mar.* 🛏 *51 rooms* 🍽 *Free Breakfast.*

Brevard

40 miles southwest of Asheville.

This idyllic small town bordering Pisgah National Forest has a friendly, highly walkable downtown. It's far enough from Asheville to have its own vibe, but close enough to steadily grow, adding new breweries and restaurants nearly every year. Brevard is known throughout the southern Appalachians for its mountain biking, fly fishing and the 250 waterfalls in surrounding Transylvania County. In the summer, the Brevard Music Festival features some 80 classical music concerts, some with such noted visiting artists as cellist Yo-Yo Ma, violinists Joshua Bell and Midori, and pianists André Watts and Emanuel Ax.

Brevard residents go nuts over the white squirrels, which dart around the town's parks and the campus of Brevard College. These aren't albinos, but a variation of the eastern gray squirrel. Brevard capitalizes on their popularity by holding a White Squirrel Festival in late May.

GETTING HERE AND AROUND

You can reach Brevard via U.S. Route 64 from Hendersonville, or from the U.S. Route 276 exit off of the Blue Ridge Parkway. North Broad Street and Main Street are the two primary thoroughfares through Brevard.

Sights

Cradle of Forestry in America

HISTORIC SIGHT | FAMILY | The home of the first forestry school in the United States is on 6,500 acres in the Pisgah National Forest. Started in 1898 by Carl Schenck, who came here to work for the Biltmore Estate, the school trained some 300 foresters. Today you can visit the school's original log buildings, a restored 1915 steam locomotive, three miles of interpretive trails, and a visitor center with many hands-on exhibits. It sits on a scenic byway that connects with the Blue Ridge Parkway near Mt. Pisgah. ✉ *11250 Pisgah Hwy., Pisgah Forest* ✣ *Off U.S. 276* ☎ *828/877–3130* 🌐 *gofindoutdoors.org/sites/cradle-of-forestry* 🎫 *$6* ⏲ *Closed mid-Nov.–early Apr.*

DuPont State Forest

FOREST | FAMILY | Between Hendersonville and Brevard you'll find this 10,400-acre state forest with four major waterfalls, five lakes, and 80 miles of dirt roads to explore. It's ideal for biking, hiking, or horseback riding. Fishing and hunting are permitted in season. ✉ *U.S. 64 and Little River Rd., Cedar Mountain* ☎ *828/877–6527* 🌐 *www.dupontstaterecreationalforest.com* 🎫 *Free.*

Looking Glass Falls

WATERFALL | FAMILY | Getting to this waterfall is easy, as it's right beside the road in Pisgah National Forest, though parking is limited. Water cascades 60 feet into a clear pool, where you can wade or take a swim. There's a parking area and a sometimes slippery walkway down to the falls. ✉ *U.S. 276, Brevard* ☎ *828/877–3265* 🌐 *www.fs.usda.gov* 🎫 *Free.*

Sliding Rock Recreation Area

WATERFALL | FAMILY | This natural rock waterslide, fueled by 11,000 gallons of mountain water every minute, deposits you into a clear cold pool. Wear tennis shoes and bring a towel. Lifeguards are on duty daily 10 to 6 from Memorial Day to Labor Day (and usually on the weekends in September and October). On warm summer days the parking area is often very crowded. No picnicking is allowed, but there are grounds nearby. ✉ *U.S. 276, Brevard* ☎ *828/885–7625* 🌐 *www.fs.usda.gov* 🎟 *$5.*

Restaurants

The Falls Landing Eatery

$$$ | SEAFOOD | FAMILY | The hands-on owner has made this downtown mainstay one of the most recommended dining spots in Brevard. The menu skews to seafood, with standouts including fish-and-chips, mountain trout, and haddock, but the pork chops and filet mignon are excellent, too. **Known for:** dog-friendly sidewalk dining; local favorite; friendly service. $ *Average main: $24* ✉ *18 E. Main St., Brevard* ☎ *828/884–2835* 🌐 *www.thefallslanding.com* ⏲ *Closed Sun. and Mon.*

Rocky's Grill and Soda Shop

$ | SANDWICHES | FAMILY | This kitschy but fun version of an old-fashioned soda shop—an institution in Brevard since 1941—has burgers, hot dogs, and a wide range of ice cream creations. The tuna salad sandwich is a local favorite. **Known for:** the Elvis sandwich (grilled peanut butter and banana); delicious milkshakes, floats, and sundaes; perfect place to take the kids. $ *Average main: $8* ✉ *50 S. Broad St., Brevard* ☎ *828/877–5375* 🌐 *rockysnc.com* ⏲ *Closed Sun. and Mon.*

The Square Root

$$ | CONTEMPORARY | Chef-owned and globally inspired, this approachable mainstay serves creative regional entrées like local trout with grits and lobster sauce alongside rabbit-and-crawfish gumbo and chicken curry. Sit on the covered patio fronting a quiet alley or inside the soaring brick-walled dining room. **Known for:** lively bar crowd; locally adored cedar plank salmon; house-made limoncello martinis. $ *Average main: $25* ✉ *33 Times Arcade Alley, Brevard* ☎ *828/884–6171* 🌐 *www.squarerootrestaurant.com* ⏲ *Closed Sun. and Mon.*

★ **Vescovo**

$$$ | ITALIAN | Homemade gnocchi, divine seared scallops, and a brief but excellent wine list are among the highlights at this chef-owned Italian trattoria in Brevard's tidy Lumberyard Arts District. Live edge and sleek wood tables and chairs set a rustic homey tone. **Known for:** barrel-aged Madeira wine; inspired craft cocktails; addictive focaccia bread. $ *Average main: $33* ✉ *175 King St., Brevard* ☎ *828/885–7630* 🌐 *www.vescovobrevard.com* ⏲ *Closed Sun. and Mon.*

Coffee and Quick Bites

Cup & Saucer

$ | **VEGETARIAN** | Coffee shop in the front, grab-and-go sandwich-and-salad counter in the back, this downtown staple serves vegetarian-friendly grub and is a popular community hub. **Known for:** smoothies and specialty coffee drinks; mercantile shop with local gifts; stone-ground grits. *Average main: $12 ✉ 36 E. Main St. A, Brevard ☎ 828/884–2877 ⊕ www.cupandsaucernc.com ⏲ Closed Sun.*

Hotels

The Bromfield Inn

$$$ | **B&B/INN** | The two-acre grounds at this B&B feel like a private estate within walking distance of downtown. **Pros:** tubs and king-size beds in most rooms; tranquil escape; three-course breakfast. **Cons:** no kids under 14; no pets; no pool or gym. *Rooms from: $285 ✉ 60 Woodside Dr., Brevard ☎ 828/577–0916 ⊕ thebromfieldinn.com 6 rooms Free Breakfast.*

★ **Pilot Cove**

$$ | **HOUSE** | **FAMILY** | Spacious decks and wall-to-wall windows maximize the view at these mountainside luxury cabins. **Pros:** room to spread out; full kitchens; on-site hiking and biking trails. **Cons:** an 8-minute drive from downtown; not all cabins have views during summer; washer/dryer in each unit, but no daily housekeeping. *Rooms from: $195 ✉ 319 Gateway Junction Dr., Brevard ☎ 828/758–2683 ⊕ www.pilotcove.com 15 cabins No Meals.*

Nightlife

★ **185 King Street**

LIVE MUSIC | Part music venue, part burger joint, part nano-brewery, this Lumberyard Arts District destination serves as a hub of local culture. Bluegrass, blues, and soul bands play the intimate stage most nights. The pilsners, lagers, and barleywines at in-house Noblebräu Brewing are among the state's best. *✉ 185 King St., Brevard ☎ 828/877–1850 ⊕ www.185kingst.com ⏲ Closed Mon.*

Activities

Davidson River Outfitters

FISHING | Catch rainbow, brown, or brook trout on the Davidson River, named one of the top 100 trout streams in the United

States by Trout Unlimited. Davidson River Outfitters and its 15 guides arrange trips in the Pisgah and Nantahala National Forests and elsewhere, including on their private leases along the Davidson. It also has a fly-fishing school and a fly shop. ✉ *49 Pisgah Hwy., Brevard* ☎ *828/877–4181* 🌐 *www.davidsonflyfishing.com* 🎫 *One-person trout-fishing trips from $250.*

Waynesville

31 miles southwest of Asheville.

This is where the Blue Ridge Parkway meets the Great Smokies. Waynesville is the seat of Haywood County, and about 40% of the countryside is occupied by Great Smoky Mountains National Park, Pisgah National Forest, and the Harmon Den Wildlife Management Area. The town of Waynesville is a rival of Blowing Rock and Highlands as a summer retreat for the well-to-do, though the atmosphere here is a bit more countrified. The idyllic downtown area is charming and walkable. South Main Street is the main thoroughfare, lined for several blocks with small shops, craft breweries, and art galleries.

Folkmoot USA, an international festival, brings music and dancing groups from around the world to Waynesville in late July.

GETTING HERE AND AROUND

Waynesville is about 30 miles southwest of Asheville. From Asheville, take Interstate 40 West to U.S. Route 74 before the last few miles on U.S. Route 276 to Waynesville. If you're coming from Cherokee, about 19 miles west of Waynesville, you can take U.S. Route 74 East to U.S. Route 23, although the longer and much more scenic route is via the Blue Ridge Parkway.

Sights

Cold Mountain

MOUNTAIN | FAMILY | About 15 miles from Waynesville in the Shining Rock Wilderness Area of the Pisgah National Forest, this 6,030-foot rise had long stood in relative anonymity. But with the success of Charles Frazier's bestselling novel *Cold Mountain*, people want to see the region that Inman and Ada, the book's Civil War–era protagonists, called home. For a view of the splendid mass, stop at any of a number of overlooks off the Blue Ridge Parkway. Try the Cold Mountain Overlook, just past mile marker 411.9, or the Wagon Road Gap parking area, at mile marker 412.2. You can climb the mountain, but be prepared—the 10-mile hike to

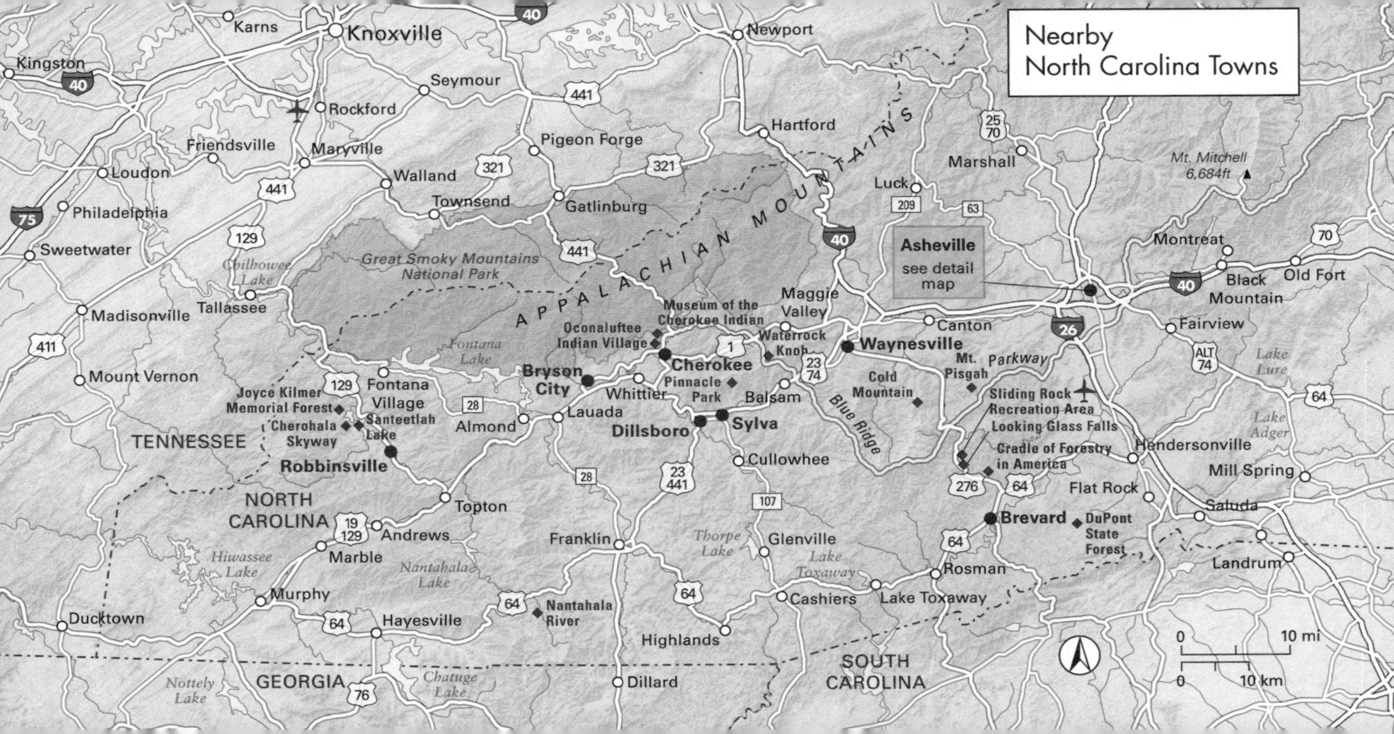
Nearby North Carolina Towns
Knoxville
Karns
Kingston
Newport
Seymour
Rockford
Hartford
Friendsville
Maryville
Pigeon Forge
Loudon
Walland
Philadelphia
Townsend
Gatlinburg
Sweetwater
Chilhowee Lake
Tallassee
Madisonville
Mount Vernon
Great Smoky Mountains National Park
APPALACHIAN MOUNTAINS
Fontana Lake
Fontana Village
Joyce Kilmer Memorial Forest
Cherohala Skyway
Santeetlah Lake
TENNESSEE
Robbinsville
NORTH CAROLINA
Topton
Andrews
Marble
Hiwassee Lake
Nantahala Lake
Murphy
Ducktown
Hayesville
Nantahala River
GEORGIA
Nottely Lake
Chatuge Lake
Almond
Bryson City
Lauada
Whittier
Oconaluftee Indian Village
Museum of the Cherokee Indian
Cherokee
Pinnacle Park
Waterrock Knob
Maggie Valley
Balsam
Dillsboro
Sylva
Cullowhee
Franklin
Thorpe Lake
Glenville
Lake Toxaway
Cashiers
Highlands
Dillard
SOUTH CAROLINA
Waynesville
Canton
Cold Mountain
Blue Ridge
Mt. Pisgah
Parkway
Sliding Rock Recreation Area
Looking Glass Falls
Cradle of Forestry in America
Brevard
DuPont State Forest
Rosman
Luck
Marshall
Asheville see detail map
Mt. Mitchell 6,684ft
Montreat
Black Mountain
Old Fort
Fairview
Lake Lure
Lake Adger
Hendersonville
Mill Spring
Flat Rock
Saluda
Landrum
0 10 mi
0 10 km
40
75
441
321
129
411
1
23 74
25 70
209
63
26
ALT 74
70
64
276
28
107
23 441
19 129
76

As the Blue Ridge Parkway winds its way through the mountains, stunning Mt. Pisgah comes into view.

the summit is strenuous as you ascend nearly 3,000 feet in elevation. *Blue Ridge Pkwy., MM 411.9, Waynesville* *828/298–0398 parkway information line* *www.nps.gov/blri.*

Shelton House and the Museum of North Carolina Handicrafts

HISTORIC SIGHT | The 1875 Shelton House is home to the Museum of North Carolina Handicrafts, featuring pottery, carvings, textiles and tinwork from 19th-century settlers and modern artisans. Exhibits include Cherokee items and a medical display from the post–Civil War era. The grounds include a barn used for events, an impressive community theater, and a two-bedroom rental apartment. Each June, the museum hosts the Blue Ridge Heritage Weekend Arts & Crafts Fair, drawing 80+ artists to Waynesville. *49 Shelton St., Waynesville* *828/452–1551* *www.shelton-house.org* *$10* *Closed Sun.–Wed. and Nov.–Mar.*

Restaurants

The Chef's Table

$$$ | **MODERN AMERICAN** | At the region's most celebrated restaurant, chef-owner Josh Monroe uses ingredients from his own farm and local purveyors to prepare dishes in an open kitchen. The award-winning menu includes dishes like lamb shank, trout, and deconstructed lasagna that are created with wine pairings in mind. **Known for:** hands-on chef who uses local ingredients; the best wine selection in town; classy date night experience.

$ *Average main: $28 ✉ 30 Church St., Waynesville ☎ 828/452–6210 🌐 www.thechefstableofwaynesville.com ⏱ Closed Sun. and Mon.*

Frogs Leap Public House

$$$ | **SOUTHERN** | This popular eatery partners with more than a dozen natural and organic producers to find the ingredients needed to create its rigorous "farm-to-fork" modern Southern menu, which changes frequently. The atmosphere is charming, with high pressed-tin ceilings and reclaimed barn wood accents, and the service is friendly. **Known for:** charmingly rustic atmosphere; informed servers and sophisticated meals; five-course chef's menu on weekends. $ *Average main: $29 ✉ 44 Church St., Waynesville ☎ 828/456–1930 🌐 frogsleappublichouse.com ⏱ Closed Sun., Mon., and periodically during winter. No lunch.*

★ **Singletree Heritage Kitchen**

$$$ | **SOUTHERN** | Singletree boldly proclaims their guiding principles, from integrity in sourcing to sustainability, and those values are conveyed in beautifully presented plates and, most importantly, in flavor. Seared duck breast and Parisian gnocchi with collards shine at dinner, but it's sandwiches like the Brasstown Melt—sliced steak on ciabatta with horseradish, provolone, arugula, and caramelized onions—that keep the midday shift bustling. **Known for:** light-filled digs; photo-worthy sandwiches; thoughtful wine and cocktail lists. $ *Average main: $27 ✉ 136 Depot St., #101, Waynesville ☎ 828/246–9760 🌐 singletreekitchen.com ⏱ Closed Sun. and Mon.*

The Sweet Onion

$$ | **SOUTHERN** | This casual restaurant serves delicious Southern comfort food like country fried steak, shrimp and grits, and blackberry barbecue short ribs. Business bustles at lunchtime for favorites like the pimento cheese fried chicken club. **Known for:** Southern comfort food; cheerful friendly staff; beer and wine only. $ *Average main: $18 ✉ 39 Miller St., Waynesville ☎ 828/456–5559 🌐 www.sweetonionrestaurant.com ⏱ Closed Sun. and Mon.*

Hotels

Andon-Reid Bed and Breakfast Inn

$$ | **B&B/INN** | The interior of this 1902 Victorian showplace is spacious and filled with sunlight, but it's the big grassy lawn overlooking the mountains and river that let you know you've arrived somewhere special. **Pros:** hospitable owners; cozy rooms and suites with fireplaces; delicious breakfasts served on the

patio. **Cons:** a bit of a walk to downtown; steps to climb; often booked up. *Rooms from: $195 92 Daisy Ave., Waynesville 828/452–3089 www.andonreidinn.com 7 rooms Free Breakfast.*

★ The Swag

$$$$ | **B&B/INN** | Sitting high atop the Cataloochee Divide on 250 wooded acres bordering the national park, the Swag is a luxurious escape that's truly away-from-it-all. **Pros:** sauna, hot tub, and racquetball court; fabulous mountaintop location; delicious meals included. **Cons:** two-night minimum stay; very expensive rates; books up fast. *Rooms from: $875 2300 Swag Rd., Waynesville 828/926–0430 www.theswag.com Closed late Nov.–mid-Apr. 14 rooms All-Inclusive.*

The Yellow House on Plott Creek Road

$$ | **B&B/INN** | Just outside town, this lovely two-story Victorian, painted a cheerful sunflower yellow, sits on 5 acres with gorgeous gardens, a fish pond, and shady trees. **Pros:** incredibly kind owners; great place to get away from it all; romantic atmosphere. **Cons:** very couples-oriented; not walking distance to restaurants and shops; some rooms are due for an update. *Rooms from: $199 89 Oakview Dr., Waynesville At Plott Creek Rd., 1 mile west of Waynesville 828/452–0991 www.theyellowhouse.com 10 rooms Free Breakfast.*

Nightlife

Boojum Brewery Taproom

BREWPUBS | Six-packs of Boojum are ubiquitous in beer aisles across the region for good reason—they brew some of the state's most creative and flavorful ales. Their downtown taproom serves next-level pub grub, including vegetarian options like Korean BBQ maple-soy tempeh tacos. Downstairs, The Gem bar has pool tables and foosball, plus a weekly schedule of karaoke, trivia, and live music. *50 N. Main St., Waynesville 828/246–0350 www.boojumbrewing.com Closed Tues.*

Frog Level Brewing Company

BEER GARDENS | The large comfortable tasting room at Waynesville's original brewery shows off with exposed brick and natural wood accents. In warm weather, the outdoor seating by the creek draws a crowd. There's a busy schedule of live music and yoga classes. *56 Commerce St., Waynesville 828/454–5664 www.froglevelbrewing.com.*

The Museum of the Cherokee Indian is one of the best places in the country for people of all ages to learn about Native American history.

Cherokee

51 miles west of Asheville; 3 miles from the Ocanuluftee entrance to Great Smoky Mountains National Park.

The Cherokee Qualla Boundary consists of almost 57,000 acres, and the town of Cherokee is its capital. The town is a window into the rich heritage of the tribe's Eastern Band. Although now relatively small in number—only about 14,000—these Cherokee and their ancestors have been responsible for keeping alive the Cherokee culture. They are the descendants of those who hid in the Great Smoky Mountains to avoid the Trail of Tears, the forced removal of the Cherokee Nation to Oklahoma in the 19th century. They are survivors, extremely attached to the hiking, swimming, trout fishing, and natural beauty of their ancestral homeland. You'll note that due to tribal efforts, all official signs in the Qualla Boundary, as well as many private commercial ones, are in the Cherokee language as well as in English.

GETTING HERE AND AROUND

The Blue Ridge Parkway's southern terminus is at Cherokee, and it's by far the most beautiful route to Cherokee and to Great Smoky Mountains National Park. A faster option is U.S. Route 23 and U.S. Route 74/441, connecting Cherokee with Interstate 40 from Asheville or from Franklin in the south. U.S. Route 19 reaches Cherokee from Bryson City to the west and I-40 to the east. Finally, if you're arriving from Tennessee or inside the park, you'll abruptly arrive in town a mile after passing the Oconaluftee Visitor Center on Newfound Gap Road (U.S. 441).

VISITOR INFORMATION

Cherokee Welcome Center. ✉ *498 Tsali Blvd., Cherokee* ☎ *800/438–1601* 🌐 *visitcherokeenc.com.*

★ **Museum of the Cherokee Indian**

HISTORY MUSEUM | FAMILY | Covering 12,000 years of history, the Museum of the Cherokee Indian is one of the country's best Native American museums. Computer-generated images, video projections, and sound effects help bring to life events in the history of the Cherokee. For example, you'll see children stop to play a butter-bean game while adults shiver along the snowy Trail of Tears. The museum has an art gallery, a gift shop, and an outdoor living exhibit of Cherokee life in the 15th century. ✉ *589 Tsali Blvd., Cherokee* ☎ *828/497–3481* 🌐 *visitcherokeenc.com* 🎫 *$12.*

Oconaluftee Indian Village

INDIGENOUS SIGHT | FAMILY | At the historically accurate Oconaluftee Indian Village, guides in traditional dress lead you through a 1760-era Cherokee village, while others demonstrate traditional skills such as weaving, pottery, canoe construction, and hunting techniques. ✉ *288 Drama Rd., Cherokee* ☎ *828/497–2111* 🌐 *www.visitcherokeenc.com/play/attractions/oconaluftee-indian-village* 🎫 *$25* 🕒 *Closed Nov.–mid-Apr.*

Native Brews Tap & Grill

$$ | STEAKHOUSE | FAMILY | This newcomer to Cherokee's dining options was an immediate hit, with entrées like roasted blackberry chicken and peanut-crusted trout with shrimp Florentine sauce that go beyond much of the basic fare available in town. They outsource their Native Brews label, but it's the place to find a craft IPA or stout in a place that only legalized alcohol sales in 2021. **Known for:** lively local bar scene; outdoor hangout space with games; hearty steak entrées. [$] *Average main: $19* ✉ *1897 Tsali Blvd., Cherokee* ☎ *828/497–2739.*

Peter's Pancakes and Waffles

$ | AMERICAN | FAMILY | Pancake houses are big in Cherokee, and Peter's is at the top of the stack. Many locals are regulars here, and you'll see why when you try the blueberry pancakes with country ham in the dining room with wide windows overlooking

Traditional crafts like weaving are preserved at the Oconaluftee Indian Village.

the Oconaluftee River. **Known for:** breakfast served until the afternoon; old-fashioned diner feel; perky service. $ *Average main: $11* ✉ *1384 Tsali Blvd., Cherokee* ☎ *828/497–5116* ⏲ *No dinner.*

Hotels

Harrah's Cherokee Casino Resort

$$$$ | **HOTEL** | The Harrah's complex now includes two hotels, doubling down on its status as North Carolina's largest lodging. **Pros:** spa, fitness center, and indoor and outdoor pools; rooms are much nicer than most alternatives in Cherokee; everything you need on the premises. **Cons:** heavily booked year-round with high-rollers; state's no-smoking laws don't apply here; huge casino environment not for everyone. $ *Rooms from: $376* ✉ *777 Casino Dr., Cherokee* ✥ *U.S. 19* ☎ *828/497–7777* ⊕ *www.harrahscherokee.com* *1,800 rooms* *No Meals.*

Performing Arts

Unto These Hills

THEATER | **FAMILY** | More than 6 million people have seen this colorful historical drama, which tells the story of the Cherokee people from 1780 to the present day. First presented in 1950, the outdoor spectacle has been updated over the years with new scripts and costumes. The show runs from early June to mid-August. Contemporary plays are also presented in the 2,100-seat

Mountainside Theater. ✉ *688 Drama Rd., Cherokee* ☎ *828/497–2111* 🌐 *cherokeesmokies.com/unto_these_hills.html* 🎟 *From $35.*

FISHING

Cherokee Qualla Boundary

FISHING | FAMILY | There are 30 miles of regularly stocked trout streams on the Cherokee Indian Reservation, called the Qualla Boundary. The public can fish on most of the Raven Fork, Oconaluftee River, and Soco watersheds. To fish in these tribal waters you need a catch-and-keep fishing permit, available at many reservation businesses or online for $10. Fishing is permitted year-round, from dawn to one hour before dusk. Only artificial lures are permitted. A North Carolina fishing license is not required. ✉ *Cherokee* ☎ *828/359–6110* 🌐 *fishcherokee.com.*

GOLF

Sequoyah National Golf Club

GOLF | This challenging course in a valley surrounded by green mountains was designed by Robert Trent Jones II and renovated in 2020. It has groomed bent-grass greens with bluegrass fairways. Pricing varies significantly by day, time, and season. ✉ *79 Cahons Rd., Cherokee* ☎ *828/497–3000* 🌐 *www.sequoyahnational.com* ⛳ *$110, 18 holes, 6600 yds, par 72.*

HIKING

Oconaluftee Islands Park and Trail

HIKING & WALKING | FAMILY | In downtown Cherokee you can cross the Oconaluftee River via a footbridge to this well-kept public park with picnic facilities and walking trails. During summer you can wade, tube, and swim in the river. On Thursday, Friday, and Saturday evenings in summer, there is often a bonfire and a Cherokee storyteller. ✉ *Tsali Blvd., Cherokee* 🌐 *visitcherokeenc.com/play/outdoor-adventure/oconaluftee-islands-park* 🎟 *Free.*

BIKING

★ Fire Mountain Trails

BIKING | FAMILY | The 11 miles of trails at this world-class mountain biking park are color-coded by difficulty and include jumps, banked berms, and elevated features. The climb is a challenge, but the descents are as flowy as they come. E-bike rentals are available in Cherokee from Bryson City Outdoors at ✉ *516 Tsali Blvd.* ✉ *State Rd. 1361, Cherokee* 🌐 *visitcherokeenc.com/play/outdoor-adventure/oconaluftee-islands-park* 🎟 *Free.*

Shopping

★ **Qualla Arts and Crafts Mutual**
CRAFTS | FAMILY | This is the nation's oldest Native American co-op. It displays and sells items created by more than 250 Cherokee craftspeople. The store has a large selection of museum-quality baskets, masks, and wood carvings, some of which can cost hundreds of dollars. ✉ *645 Tsali Blvd., Cherokee* ☎ *828/497–3103* 🌐 *www.quallaartsandcrafts.com.*

Bryson City

65 miles east of Asheville; 2 miles south of the Deep Creek entrance to Great Smoky Mountains National Park.

One of the lesser-known gateways to the Great Smokies, Bryson City is an idyllic little mountain town on the Tuckasegee River. The town's most striking feature is the former city hall with a four-sided clock. The depot of the Great Smoky Mountains Railroad is in the heart of downtown, and gift shops, restaurants, craft breweries, and ice cream stands are all within easy walking distance.

GETTING HERE AND AROUND

Bryson City is a 15-minute drive from Cherokee on U.S. Route 19. Near Bryson City are two entrances to the national park, Deep Creek and Lake View Road, often called the Road to Nowhere.

Sights

★ **Great Smoky Mountains Railroad**
TRAIN/TRAIN STATION | FAMILY | Bryson City's historic train station is the departure point for the Great Smoky Mountains Railroad. Diesel or steam locomotives take you on a 32-mile journey along the Tuckasegee River or a 44-mile trip passing through the Nantahala Gorge. Open-sided cars or standard coaches are ideal for picture-taking as the mountain scenery glides by. Trips are offered year-round, but with very limited schedules January to March. There's a café on board serving basic fare like pizza and hot dogs. Your ticket gives you free admission to the nearby Smoky Mountain Trains Museum and its room-size functional model train dioramas. **TIP→ During the holiday season, the town booms as pajama-clad families arrive for Polar Express–themed rides.** ✉ *45 Mitchell St., Bryson City* ☎ *800/872–4681 toll-free reservations line* 🌐 *www.gsmr.com* 🎫 *From $58.*

Swain County Heritage Museum

HISTORY MUSEUM | FAMILY | Located in the gold-domed Swain County Courthouse dating from 1908, this charming museum has displays on the history of settlers of this mountain area, including a one-room schoolhouse and a log cabin. It also serves as a visitor information center for both Bryson City, Swain County, and Great Smoky Mountains National Park. ✉ *2 Everett St., Bryson City* ☎ *828/488–7857* 🌐 *www.swainheritagemuseum.com* 🎫 *Free.*

Tsali Recreation Area

TRAIL | Regarded as one of the top mountain biking trail systems in the eastern United States, the four loop trails at Tsali offer ride opportunities from 4 to 14 miles. There's a campground and restrooms. Bike rentals are available from Tsali Cycles in Bryson City (🌐 *www.tsalicycles.com*). ✉ *Bryson City* ☎ *828/479–6431* 🌐 *www.fs.usda.gov* 🎫 *Free.*

Restaurants

★ The Bistro at the Everett Hotel

$$ | MODERN AMERICAN | The best place to eat in Bryson City, this wood-paneled bistro serves hearty dinner entrées like mountain trout with quinoa and brown rice or meatloaf made from four different locally sourced specialty meats. The dining room is a rustic yet elegant space in a 1908 building that formerly housed Bryson City Bank. **Known for:** a favorite for any type of celebration; local twists on classic dishes; craft cocktails and craft beers. $ *Average main: $25* ✉ *16 Everett St., Bryson City* ☎ *828/488–1934* 🌐 *www.theeveretthotel.com/bistro.html* ⏲ *Closed Mon. and Tues.*

The High Test Deli and Sweet Shop

$ | FAST FOOD | FAMILY | This little sandwich shop is known for pressed Cubans, roast beef hoagies, and corned beef on rye, or you can opt for a bowl of chili. While you're waiting, explore the old service station memorabilia. **Known for:** local favorite Cuban sandwich; ice-cream sandwich cookies; friendly, upbeat owners. $ *Average main: $9* ✉ *145 Everett St., Bryson City* ☎ *828/488–1919* 🌐 *www.thefillingstationdeli.com* ⏲ *Closed Sun. and Mon.*

Hotels

★ Aloft in the Smokies

$$ | APARTMENT | FAMILY | These six spacious lofts in downtown Bryson City are comfortable for an extended stay or a large family, with two bedrooms in each unit. **Pros:** tasteful attractive design; full kitchens and laundry within units; plenty of room. **Cons:** upstairs bathrooms slightly smaller; no hotel amenities; no gym.

Powered by diesel or steam locomotives, the Great Smoky Mountains Railroad is one of the best ways to take in the region's stunning scenery.

Rooms from: $175 *115 Everett St., Bryson City* *828/538–0480* *www.aloftinthesmokies.com* *6 lofts.*

★ The Everett Hotel

$$$ | **B&B/INN** | A handsome downtown bank building from 1905 is now a charming boutique hotel with rooms that have wide-plank paneling and soaring ceilings, creating a rustic atmosphere. **Pros:** surprisingly sophisticated rooms; good bistro on first floor; rooftop terrace with a firepit. **Cons:** priced a little higher than nearby lodgings; steps to climb; books up fast. *Rooms from: $239* *16 Everett St., Bryson City* *828/488–1976* *www.theeveretthotel.com* *10 rooms* *Free Breakfast.*

Gorgeous Stays

$ | **RESORT** | **FAMILY** | The 10 off-the-wall accommodations at this "glampground" range from a renovated double-decker English bus to a super hero–themed tiny house. **Pros:** memorable creative accommodations; amenities like a pool table and firepits; friendly convivial atmosphere. **Cons:** not everyone will love the hostel atmosphere; shared bathhouse for showers; no Wi-Fi in units. *Rooms from: $120* *11044 US-19, Bryson City* *828/421–2282* *gorgeousstays.com* *11 units* *No Meals.*

Hemlock Inn

$$$ | **B&B/INN** | **FAMILY** | This folksy friendly mountain inn on 55 acres on a hilltop near Bryson City, operated by the same family since 1969, is the kind of place where you can relax in a rocking chair, catch up on reading, or play a game of Scrabble. **Pros:**

unpretentious vibe; delicious Southern-style food; peaceful surroundings. **Cons:** no Wi-Fi, TVs, or in-room phones; family-style dining not for everyone; alcohol only allowed in rooms. *Rooms from: $248* *911 Galbraith Creek Rd., Bryson City* *828/488–2885* *www.hemlockinn.com* *23 rooms* *Free Breakfast.*

Nightlife

★ Mountain Layers Brewing Company

BREWPUBS | Mountain Layers has a cozy bar on the first floor and a larger space on the second floor, plus a rooftop deck with nice views of the mountains. It serves its own ales, porters, and stouts, and there's often a food truck parked out back. *90 Everett St., Bryson City* *828/538–0115* *www.mountainlayers-brewingcompany.com.*

Activities

WHITEWATER RAFTING

★ Nantahala Outdoor Center

WHITE-WATER RAFTING | **FAMILY** | NOC claims to be America's largest outdoor recreation company, with more than one million visitors a year arriving to raft on the mighty Nantahala and other nearby rivers like the Chattooga, French Broad, and Pigeon Rivers. Their 500-acre outpost on the Nantahala feels like its own town, with three restaurants, a hotel, an outfitter, a bike shop, a ropes course, and a stop for the Great Smoky Mountains Railroad. Choose between guided and unguided floats through the 1,600-foot-deep Nantahala Gorge's manageable Class III rapids. If you choose to go on your own, you'll watch a short safety video before NOC shuttles you upriver with an inflatable "duckie" to paddle at your own pace. *13077 U.S. 19 W, Bryson City* *828/785–4834 local reservations* *noc.com* *Guided raft trips from $59; duckie rentals from $35* *Rafting closed Nov.–Feb.*

Wildwater

WHITE-WATER RAFTING | **FAMILY** | This company offers whitewater rafting and kayaking on the Nantahala River, as well as zip-lining for kids and adults. The operator also offers four-wheel-drive tours and glamping in yurts. *10345 U.S. 19 S/U.S. 74 W, Bryson City* *866/319–8870 toll-free reservations, 828/488–2384 Nantahala rafting* *wildwaterrafting.com* *Guided rafting on Nantahala River $55, duckie rentals from from $35* *Closed Nov.–early Apr.*

Robbinsville

98 miles southwest of Asheville.

If you truly want to get away from it all, head to Graham County in the far southwestern corner of North Carolina. Robbinsville, the county seat, is a gateway to the Snowbird Mountains, Santeetlah Lake, Fontana Lake, and the Joyce Kilmer Memorial Forest, known for its giant virgin poplars and sycamores. You can access the national park via the Twentymile entrance, Fontana Dam, and Parson Branch Road in this area, and you're likely to have hiking trails all to yourself.

GETTING HERE AND AROUND

Robbinsville is 40 minutes southwest of Bryson City on U.S. 74. You can access the "Tail of the Dragon" scenic drive (U.S. 129) and the Cherohala Skyway, a National Scenic Byway to Tennessee, via Robbinsville.

Sights

★ Cherohala Skyway

SCENIC DRIVE | Many motorists swear that this 43-mile National Scenic Byway rivals the beauty of any comparable stretch on the Blue Ridge Parkway. You're unlikely to encounter traffic, and the solitude found on short hikes to peaks like Huckleberry Knob, a bald with 360-degree views, may be the highlight of your trip. ✉ *Robbinsville* ✣ *N.C. 143/T.N. 165, between Robbinsville and Tellico Plains, TN.*

Joyce Kilmer Memorial Forest

FOREST | **FAMILY** | One of the last remaining sections of old-growth forests in Appalachia has incredible 400-year-old yellow poplars that measure as large as 20 feet in circumference, along with huge hemlocks, oaks, and sycamores. Don't expect sequoias, but you're still likely to turn a corner on the trail and gasp with amazement at the scale of these behemoths. If you haven't seen a true virgin forest, you can only imagine what America must have looked like in the early days of settlement. A two-mile trail, moderately strenuous, takes you through wildflower- and moss-carpeted areas. During June, the parking lot is an excellent spot to see the light shows of the synchronous fireflies, which blink off and on in unison. ✉ *5410 Joyce Kilmer Rd., Robbinsville* ☎ *828/479–6431* 🌐 *www.fs.usda.gov* 🎫 *Free.*

Santeetlah Lake

BODY OF WATER | FAMILY | Dammed in 1928, this lake's name means "blue waters" in the Cherokee language. Cheoah Point Beach, in a cove on the north shore, is an attractive popular place to swim. Santeetlah has 76 miles of shoreline, with good fishing for crappie, bream, and lake trout, and is part of the Nantahala National Forest. ✉ *Cheoah Point Recreation Area, NC 1145, Robbinsville* ☎ *828/479–6431* 🌐 *www.fs.usda.gov* 🎫 *Free.*

Stecoah Valley Cultural Arts Center

HISTORIC SIGHT | Mountain crafts and artwork are displayed—and much of them are for sale—at this cultural hub that promotes and pays tribute to the people and traditions of Graham County, including the native Cherokee. During summer, the Appalachian Evening Concert Series brings the region's best folk and bluegrass musicians to perform in the center's restored historic theater. ✉ *121 Schoolhouse Rd., Robbinsville* ☎ *828/479–3364* 🌐 *stecoahvalleycenter.com* 🎫 *Free* 🕒 *Closed Sun.*

Restaurants

Willow Tree

$$ | SOUTHERN | Robbinsville's best restaurant is a chef-owned gem serving specialties like local mountain trout with lemon-caper butter sauce and a grilled ribeye. Seating is inside and on the porch of a historic home. **Known for:** smoked trout dip; BYO wine or beer (it's a dry county); rich desserts like chocolate cobbler. [$] *Average main: $22* ✉ *302 Ford St., Robbinsville* ☎ *828/260–8158* 🕒 *Closed Sun. and Mon. Lunch only Tues.–Thurs.*

Hotels

Fontana Village Resort

$ | HOTEL | FAMILY | Fontana Village bustles during summertime with vacationing families here for activities like hiking, mountain biking, mini golf, disc golf, a small water park, and, of course, Fontana Dam. The resort's lodge is comfortable but shows its age. **Pros:** several on-site restaurants and bars; fun amenities; hiking trails and swimming pools. **Cons:** limited dining options; carpet and tile are dated; some room balconies overlook the parking lot. [$] *Rooms from: $129* ✉ *300 Woods Rd., Robbinsville* ☎ *800/849–2258* 🌐 *fontanavillage.com* 🛏 *93 rooms* 🍽 *No Meals.*

★ Huffman Creek Retreat

$$ | HOUSE | FAMILY | The mountain hollow that's home to these seven cabins perfectly captures both sunrise and sunset over the creek. **Pros:** some cabins have amenities like a movie theater room; fresh trout can be delivered for dinner; 5 miles of hiking trails (and hammocks) throughout the property. **Cons:** limited phone service and no in-cabin WiFi; long drive to restaurants; some cars may struggle to reach some cabins. *Rooms from: $199 ✉ 1633 Huffman Creek Rd., Robbinsville ☎ 828/475–4497 huffmancreekretreat.com 7 cabins No Meals.*

River's Edge Treehouse Resort

$$ | **HOUSE** | These six treehouses, with the Cheoah River running below, are the best place to stay in Robbinsville proper. **Pros:** wide porches overlooking the river; fun amenities like a horseshoe pit; friendly family-run atmosphere. **Cons:** road noise from across the river; too far to walk to restaurants; three back treehouses have views impeded by the front three. *Rooms from: $215 ✉ 195 Old U.S. 129, Robbinsville ☎ 828/735–2228 www.riversedgetreehouses.com 6 treehouses No Meals.*

★ **Snowbird Mountain Lodge**

$$$$ | **B&B/INN** | Listed in the National Register of Historic Places, Snowbird Mountain Lodge is everything you expect from a rustic inn, with two massive stone fireplaces, solid chestnut beams across the ceiling, and beautiful views across the valley. **Pros:** private hot tubs in some rooms; 100 acres of grounds to explore; private lake access with complimentary paddleboards. **Cons:** remote location; books up fast; no kids under 12. *Rooms from: $409 ✉ 4633 Santeetlah Rd., Robbinsville ☎ 828/479–3433 snowbirdlodge.com 23 rooms Free Breakfast.*

Tapoco Lodge

$$ | **HOTEL** | **FAMILY** | Like an oasis after miles of driving remote roads, Tapoco Lodge offers large stylish rooms in a lodge that's on the National Register of Historic Places. **Pros:** two on-site restaurants alongside the Cheoah River; hike from the lodge to Bear Creek Falls; close to the "Tail of the Dragon" scenic drive. **Cons:** no TVs in rooms; no cell service; not all rooms have a river view. *Rooms from: $199 ✉ 14981 Tapoco Rd., Robbinsville ☎ 828/498–2800 tapoco.com 27 rooms No Meals.*

Sylva and Dillsboro

47 miles southwest of Asheville.

Sylva, a town of 2,500 people, is home to four breweries, an underground medicinal herb shop, two first-class bookstores, and an open-container law that allows you to mingle in the street and peruse galleries and shops with a glass of wine. If that alone doesn't make it the coolest town in western North Carolina, its proximity to Dillsboro—just three miles away—makes it an undeniable gem. Dillsboro carries its own appeal as a jumping-off point for the Great Smoky Mountains Railroad, with dining options like the ingredient-obsessed Foragers Canteen, perched between the tracks and the Tuckasegee River.

Dillsboro is 14 miles south of the Oconaluftee entrance to the national park via U.S. 441, making it an excellent alternative to Cherokee for exploring the park. Sylva is 3 miles to the east.

Sights

Pinnacle Park

NATURE PRESERVE | In this 1,500-acre public park, you can tackle a grueling climb to the top of the namesake Pinnacle or take a short walk on the state's only certified Nature Forest Therapy Trail. Brochures at the parking area include a map and guided prompts to help you clear your mind as you experience the forest. *2110 Fisher Creek Rd. pinnacleforesttherapy.com Free.*

Restaurants

★ **Ilda**

$$ | **ITALIAN** | Don't tell anyone else, but Ilda may be North Carolina's best restaurant west of Asheville. Owners Santiago and Crystal defected from New York to Crystal's hometown during the COVID-19 pandemic, leaving behind Michelin stars to chase their dream of a community-driven Italian restaurant without pretension. **Known for:** pancetta with a slow-poached egg; addictive pastas like squid ink spaghettoni; cocktails built with care. *Average main: $24 462 W. Main St. 828/307–2036 www.ildainsylva.com Closed Mon. and Tues.*

Lulu's on Main

$$ | **SOUTHERN** | **FAMILY** | Lulu's feels old-school—there are old-timey quilts hanging from the walls—but the food is decidedly forward-thinking, from the Thai chicken soup to the savory meatloaf Manhattan. Vegetarians also feel right at home, thanks to options like a marinated tempeh sandwich with kimchi and Szechuan sauce at lunchtime. **Known for:** friendly Southern service; community gathering place; healthy options that don't skimp on flavor. *Average main: $19 678 W. Main St., Sylva 828/586–8989 lulusonmain.com Closed Sun.*

Coffee and Quick Bites

White Moon

$ | **CONTEMPORARY** | This bustling bistro transforms from a coffee shop into a cocktail bar after hours. Stop in for a to-go cappuccino, or stay awhile amidst the calming greenery for smashed avocado toast topped with a farm egg. **Known for:** delicious smoothies; coffee alternatives like matcha and golden lattes; trendy hangout. *Average main: $9 545 Mill St., Dillsboro 828/331–0111 www.whitemoonnc.com.*

Hotels

★ **Outland Great Smoky Mountains**

$$ | **APARTMENT** | Each suite at this tucked-away chalet has a steam shower and a soaking tub, making it a perfect place to recuperate after a long day of hiking or exploring. **Pros:** high ceilings in the upstairs units; shared clubhouse with stylish furniture; gas fireplace in each room. **Cons:** some rooms are smaller; 10-minute drive to restaurants; not all furnishings are luxury-level. *Rooms from: $159 285 Lone Oak Dr. 6 suites No Meals.*

Whistle Stop Inn

$ | **B&B/INN** | This welcoming B&B occupies an 1878 home whose age is an advantage rather than a deterrent. **Pros:** wonderful hosts; delicious breakfast; walkable to restaurants. **Cons:** noise travels; steep driveway; not all rooms have a king-size bed. *Rooms from: $139 364 Haywood Rd., Dillsboro 828/354–0470 thewhistlestopinn.net 4 rooms Free Breakfast.*

Nightlife

Innovation Station

BREWPUBS | Name your brewery Innovation and you'd better hold yourself to high standards. This Jackson County staple exceeds expectations with seasonal delights like a beet and basil saison. There are three locations—Innovation Station in Dillsboro, the original brewery in Sylva, and an outpost in Cullowhee. In Dillsboro, the Tuckasegee River runs directly under the porch, so sipping comes with a view. There's usually a food truck in the parking lot. *40 Depot St., Dillsboro 828/226–0262 www.innovation-brewing.com.*

Index

Photo Credits

Front Cover: Name: Ali Majdfar [Description: Tom Branch waterfall, North Carolina]. **Back cover, from left to right:** Bob Pool /Shutterstock. Jadimages/Shutterstock. Digidreamgrafix/Shutterstock. **Spine:** Jason Elridge/Shutterstock. **Interior, from left to right:** Sean Board/iStockphoto (1). Warren Bielenberg/NPS (2-3). **Chapter 1: Experience Great Smoky Mountains National Park:** Sean Pavone/Shutterstock (6-7). Alisa Kessler/Tennessee Tourism (8-9). Alisa Kessler/Tennessee Tourism (9). Steven Bridges/Dollywood (9). Kellie Sharpe/One Lane Road Photography (10). Anthonyheflin/Dreamstime (10). Tim Mainiero/ Shutterstock (10). Sean Pavone/Shutterstock (10). Steven McBride Photography, Inc. (11). Nicholas Lamontanaro/Shutterstock (11). Eric Brinley/Shutterstock (12). Quasargal/Dreamstime (12), Dawn Majors/Tennessee Department of Tourist Development (13). Warren Bielenberg (16). NPS Photo (16). Friends of the WNC Nature Center (16). NPS Photo (16). NPS Photo (17). NPS Photo (17). Ken Wilson (17). Mircea Costina/Shutterstock (17). Flickr/Courtesy of Great Smoky Mountains National Park (18). Photodigitaal.nl/Shutterstock (18). Flickr/Courtesy of Great Smoky Mountains National Park (18). Jinning Li/Shutterstock (18). Hbak/Dreamstime (19). Michaelmeijer/Dreamstime (19). JayL/Shutterstock (19). Flickr/Courtesy of Great Smoky Mountains National Park (19). William Silver/Shutterstock (20). William Silver/Shutterstock (21). **Chapter 3: Great Smoky Mountains, TN:** Cynthia Kidwell/Shutterstock (43). Dean Fikar/Shutterstock (52). Anton Foltin/Shutterstock (54). Theron Stripling III/Shutterstock (58). Theron Stripling III/Shutterstock (59). Kelly VanDellen/Shutterstock (61). **Chapter 4: Great Smoky Mountains, NC:** Jo Crebbin/Shutterstock (71). Aclyn Novak/Shutterstock (79). Susan Montgomery/Shutterstock (80). Zack Frank/Shutterstock (84-85). Mark Van Dyke Photography/Shutterstock (90). Jill Lang/Shutterstock (92). **Chapter 5: The Tennessee Gateways:** Kevin Ruck/Shutterstock (97). Matthew L Niemiller/Shutterstock (103). Sean Pavone/Shutterstock (107). Digidreamgrafix/iStockphoto (114). Jon Kraft/Shutterstock (118). Journal Communications Inc./Nathan Lambrecht (124). **Chapter 6: The North Carolina Gateways:** Frederik Flagstad/iStockphoto (131). Derek Olson Photography/Shutterstock (136). Nolichuckyjake/Shutterstock (144). Konstantin L/Shutterstock (153). Craig Zerbe/iStockphoto (162-163). Joshua Moore/iStockphoto (170). Courtesy of the Museum of the Cherokee Indian, Cherokee, NC. (173). Carrie Hanrahan/Dreamstime (175). Bob Pool/Shutterstock (179). **About Our Writers:** All photos are courtesy of the writers except for the following. Stratton Lawrence Courtesy of Claire van der Lee.

*Every effort has been made to trace the copyright holders, and we apologize in advance for any accidental errors. We would be happy to apply the corrections in the following edition of this publication.

Fodor's InFocus GREAT SMOKY MOUNTAINS NATIONAL PARK

Publisher: Stephen Horowitz, *General Manager*

Editorial: Douglas Stallings, *Editorial Director;* Jill Fergus, Amanda Sadlowski, *Senior Editors;* Brian Eschrich, Alexis Kelly, *Editors;* Angelique Kennedy-Chavannes, *Assistant Editor;* Yoojin Shin, *Associate Editor*

Design: Tina Malaney, *Director of Design and Production;* Jessica Gonzalez, *Senior Designer;* Jaimee Shaye, *Graphic Design Associate*

Production: Jennifer DePrima, *Editorial Production Manager;* Elyse Rozelle, *Senior Production Editor;* Monica White, *Production Editor*

Maps: Rebecca Baer, *Senior Map Editor;* Mark Stroud (Moon Street Cartography), *Cartographer*

Photography: Viviane Teles, *Director of Photography;* Namrata Aggarwal, Neha Gupta, Payal Gupta, Ashok Kumar, *Photo Editors;* Jade Rodgers, *Photo Production Intern*

Business and Operations: Chuck Hoover, *Chief Marketing Officer;* Robert Ames, *Group General Manager*

Public Relations and Marketing: Joe Ewaskiw, *Senior Director of Communications and Public Relations*

Fodors.com: Jeremy Tarr, *Editorial Director;* Rachael Levitt, *Managing Editor*

Technology: Jon Atkinson, *Executive Director of Technology;* Rudresh Teotia, *Associate Director of Technology;* Alison Lieu, *Project Manager*

Writer: Stratton Lawrence
Editor: Brian Eschrich
Production Editor: Jennifer DePrima

3rd Edition

ISBN 978-1-64097-648-1

ISSN 1943-0108

PRINTED IN CANADA

10 9 8 7 6 5 4 3 2 1

About Our Writer

Stratton Lawrence lives by the sea in Charleston with his wife and two globetrotting children, who have logged many miles hiking and biking through southern Appalachia. Stratton frequently contributes to Fodor's, *Travel + Leisure*, and *AFAR*.